24b1

E. M. FORSTER: PASSION AND PROSE

Arthur Martland

E. M. Forster:
Passion and Prose

THE GAY MEN'S PRESS

First published 1999 by GMP Publishers Ltd,
P O Box 247, Swaffham PE37 8PA, England

World Copyright © 1999 Arthur Martland

Arthur Martland has asserted his right to be identified as the author of this work
in accordance with the Copyright, Designs and Patents Act 1988

A CIP catalogue record for this book is available
from the British Library

ISBN 0 85449 268 2

Distributed in Europe by Central Books,
99 Wallis Rd, London E9 5LN

Distributed in North America by InBook/LPC Group,
1436 West Randolph, Chicago, IL 60607

Distributed in Australia by Bulldog Books,
P O Box 300, Beaconsfield, NSW 2014

Printed and bound in the EU by WSOY, Juva, Finland

CONTENTS

For S C and all the Krishnas

NOTE

1) The following abbreviations are used to refer to the works of E. M. Forster:

AH	*Abinger Harvest* (1942).
AN	*Aspects of the Novel and Related Writings* (1974).
AS	*Arctic Summer and Other Fiction* (1980).
CB	*Commonplace Book* (1988).
CS	*Collected Stories of E. M. Forster* (1947).
GLD	*Goldsworthy Lowes Dickinson* (1938).
HE	*Howards End* (1973).
HE-MS	*The Manuscripts of Howards End* (1973).
HD	*The Hill of Devi and Other Indian Writings* (1983).
LJ	*The Longest Journey* (1984)
LTC	*The Life to Come and Other Stories* (1972).
Lucy	*The Lucy Novels* (1977).
M	*Maurice* (1971)
PTI	*A Passage to India* (1978).
PTI-MS	*The Manuscripts of A Passage to India* (1978).
RWV	*A Room With A View* (1977).
TCFD	*Two Cheers For Democracy* (1972).
WAFT	*Where Angels Fear to Tread* (1975).

2) In the extracts quoted in this work from the manuscript drafts of Forster's novels, the symbols used in the Abinger Edition of the manuscripts have been preserved. These symbols were devised to show the various deletions and insertions made in the manuscripts by the writer, and are primarily intended to reveal the chronological order in which the changes to the text occurred.

The use made in this book of those drafts does not depend upon demonstrating exactly when Forster employed a particular phrase or idea, simply that he used it prior to producing the final published text. A particular knowledge of such details would neither add to, nor detract from, the arguments advanced in this work. For a more detailed discussion of individual manuscript drafts the interested reader is directed to the appropriate Abinger Edition, details of which are to be found in the Bibliography.

3) All the texts of the poems of Walt Whitman quoted in this work have been taken from modern editions based on the "Deathbed edition", the green hard-bound issue of 1891–92.

INTRODUCTION

During the 1980s, interest in Forster's novels increased primarily as a result of a highly successful series of films based upon his work. David Lean's 1984 film of *A Passage to India* tapped into the nostalgia market, which Granada Television had successfully exploited at about the same time with their mammoth version of Paul Scott's *The Jewel in the Crown* (though neither work presented a glowing endorsement of British imperialism). Likewise the Merchant/Ivory depiction of *A Room with a View* the following year had an instant appeal with its sumptuous views of Florence and its art — its equally nostalgic and rose-tinted look at Edwardian country life offering an idyllic mis-statement of the past which relieved many from a strife-torn present. With their success, other films of the works soon followed.

What Forster would have made of this is open to speculation; no doubt, he would have hoped that viewers would become readers of his work. But I suspect he would bemoan what seems the inevitable, if unintended, effect of trivialisation which a celluloid transcription seems to have upon the written word. Textual nuances, sometimes difficult to apprehend upon a first reading, are lost in the move from word to picture, however skilled and sensitive the film-maker. By tracing back the word beyond the well-crafted screenplay to Forster's own pen, the reader will discover much that he, or she, had hardly suspected. Open a book of Forster criticism and many diverse aspects of his work may be covered, but of the impact of sexuality on his writing, little will be said. It is now well-known that Forster was homosexual; the Merchant/Ivory film version of *Maurice*, as much as his posthumously published writings, have made that clear. But until comparatively recently there has been no attempt to look at the overall influence upon Forster's fictional writings that his being homosexual had. When I began my research for this book in 1989, little had been written upon the subject, and in the years thereafter only a moderate amount of relevant criticism appeared in print. That situation changed in 1997 with the publication of *Queer Forster*, a collection of essays by various writers, edited by Robert K. Martin and George Piggford. This book attempted a difficult task, trying to examine the influence of Forster's sexuality in his work from the perspective of 'queer theory', whilst at the same time acknowledging that the definition of a 'queer perspective' is far from settled (1-2). This work to is intended to augment what has already been written on the writer by a concentrated examination of Forster's work in relation to his sexuality and as such will complement earlier studies, acting as a counter-balance to that trend in the Forster critical establishment which seems always to downgrade the influence of sex, subtly attempting to deny it had anything other than a peripheral influence on his writings.

One might ask why, with so many contemporary gay literary scholars, comparatively little seems hitherto to have been written in the field of Gay Studies on such a major writer. Perhaps this lack is explained by Forster having been such a closeted man; an out-gay writer might command more interest. Oscar Wilde's martyrdom has fired imaginations and earned him a place in the Gay Hall of Fame, but Wilde never wanted to be outed, and if he could have kept his homosexuality as secret as Forster did, he would have been quite happy to do so. For those subterfuges of survival, in which Forster and many others were so well-versed, and which many in a less remote past have personally known, seem often to attract censure, rather than understanding, from some parts of the gay community. Gay men in particular have often liked their heroes also to be martyrs, from St Sebastian via Judy Garland to Derek Jarman, which may explain why Forster, erroneously regarded in his later years as somewhat of a wrinkled old Establishment prude, has not received the attention of gay critics which his stature as a writer deserves.

After his death in 1970 Forster's work came under attack from homophobic critics, some of whom used his sexuality as a stick with which to beat him. One might have thought that gay critics would have mounted a defence of the writer. Unfortunately not so, for some gay critics seemed almost to be in an unholy alliance with the homophobes, and both Forster and his writings were condemned for their reticences over homosexuality.

The trend in gay critics openly denigrating Forster and his writings can be traced back to the novelist Angus Wilson's sustained attack on him which began as early as 1954. The criticism, initially voiced in private, was continued in public for many years after Forster's death. According to Margaret Drabble, Wilson's biographer, his disparagement of Forster's reputation found new impetus in 1957 following a disastrous interview Wilson (and his partner, Tony Garrett) had conducted with Forster. Wilson, having drunk 'too much of Forster's Dubonnet', harangued the writer, and Forster was caustic in reply (Drabble 1995, 222). It was left to Garrett to record the interview which Wilson subsequently wrote up for the magazine *Encounter*. That article did not relate the nub of his argument with Forster, but Drabble sees the interview as a moment when Wilson's private criticism became more strident. Although the two writers remained on visiting terms, Wilson expressed 'a lack of respect for what he saw as Forster's lack of moral courage', asking why Forster could not come out and declare himself as a homosexual. He criticised him further for avoiding the issue of homosexuality when invited by the BBC in 1958 to make a radio programme with Lord Wolfenden on any topic of his choice — soon after the Wolfenden Report on homosexual law reform had been published. Wilson felt Forster should have used the moral authority he had built up in the previous decades, as a spokesman for humanist and liberal values, to speak out againt the oppression of homosexuals, thereby striking a blow for reform and hastening the slow process which had limped along for many years (Drabble 1995, 223).

Wilson's attack on Forster continued throughout the 1960s, and in the seventies even made it into a book review he wrote for *Gay News* (October

1976). This denigration however was not shared by Garrett. A few months before Wilson's article appeared, the *Gay News* editor Denis Lemon visited the couple at their home. Wilson launched into his familiar attack on Forster (and on Somerset Maugham) for not giving evidence to the Wolfenden Committee; Lemon added that Noel Coward had also failed to speak up. Garrett, however, would not join the attack, and defended the choice of Forster and the others to remain silent, arguing that it 'would have been very foolish for a highly successful public figure to come out alone from a whole generation' and that they should not have been expected to do so (Drabble 1995, 481).

Both Forster and Garrett would have been aware of the very real dangers of coming out in the 1950s, even if Wilson thought the risks negligible. In 1954 there had been the sensational trial on charges of homosexual conduct of Lord Edward Montagu, Michael Pitt-Rivers and Peter Wildeblood, which had resulted in the imprisonment of the defendants. Wildeblood's book on the trial and its aftermath, *Against The Law*, published in 1955, details the abuse they suffered, and the Establishment ploys used against Montagu in particular. Might not Forster have risked a similar fate had he acceded to Wilson's proposal that he accept the martyr's crown? In his book Wildeblood argues that he was drawn into the prosecution case as part of a political conspiracy to get at Montagu. Being a friend of Montagu's, he was simply used and discarded once his value to Montagu's enemies had ended. Forster would have been especially keen to protect his own close friends from any similar abuse. Coming out might have won him initial support from Wilson, but, being of differing temperaments, it would only be a matter of time before further differences of opinion between them would be voiced.

Garrett himself was forced to resign from his job with the Probation Service in Suffolk in 1960, because of the rumours circulating locally about Wilson and himself. A police prosecution of both Garrett and Wilson for homosexual offences seemed so likely at the time that the lawyers for Wilson's publisher asked the couple if their passports were in order (Drabble 1995, 260-1). Faced with the possibility of prosecution himself, Wilson did not come out and face the worst that the authorities could do to him: the highly risky course which he had formerly been so eager to urge on Forster. The crisis was resolved by Garrett's resignation, thereby silencing the concern over his fitness to work in the criminal justice field.

The most damaging and persisting attack on Forster, however, came in 1974 with the publication of the pamphlet *With Downcast Gays*. The authors of the work, Andrew Hodges and David Hutter, launched a bitter, ideologically blinkered assault on the writer. Forster was condemned in the kind of language Christian demagogues reserve for the Antichrist. Their attack was very similar to that of Wilson: according to the authors, Forster could be singled out for special condemnation, as unlike fellow closet writers like Somerset Maugham, Henry James and Hugh Walpole, he had supposedly 'claimed a larger reputation as a moralist and social commentator'. Hodges and Hutter acknowledge that he 'gently chipped away at conservative institutions and religious beliefs, propounding instead the value of freedom, individual commitment and above all personal honesty', but far from giving him credit for this significant achievement, because the writer's honesty did not extend to coming out he is accused of having guarded his reputation at the expense of 'gay people whom he betrayed' (Hodges and Hutter, 18). They blame Forster for not taking centre stage in the drama of homosexual law reform and go on to award him the title of 'Closet Queen of the Century'. Should any of their readers not suffiently despise him after that, they characterise any praise of the writer by gays themselves as 'apologetic and self-oppressive', asking 'What other minority is so sunk in shame and self-oppression as to be proud of... [such a] traitor?' (21).

Anthony Grey, secretary of the Homosexual Law Reform Society during the period of the Wolfenden reforms and, as such, more involved in the struggle for gay rights at that time than Wilson was, spoke out in defence of Forster in his book on that period *Quest for Justice*. Grey commended Forster's small role in homosexual law reform, noting that Hodges and Hutter's 'vitriolic attack' on the writer was entirely unwarranted. He argued that if 'being of his generation and class, Forster felt obliged to stay in the closet and do good works behind the scenes, that surely does not of itself constitute treachery' (Grey, 78). Grey also noted that on a visit to Forster in the mid-1960s he had been questioned at length about the work of the Society and that the writer made a generous donation of a few thousand pounds towards its upkeep. Forster, who regularly supported his impecunious friends, dismissed Grey's gratitude saying, 'I am the only bugger of us all who has any money.' Grey adds that 'Most "buggers with money" lacked Forster's generosity' (Grey, 77).

It is these individual acts of generosity which are the key to Forster's motivation. In *The Longest Journey* he sets out his belief that the 'earth is full of tiny societies', that is, full of small groups of friends and related individuals who represent society to each individual in that group. He sees these small groups as more relevant than the 'great world' which is largely a fiction. True society to Forster means a group of mutually supportive friends. It is easy to see why he felt this; it could hardly be otherwise for a homosexual man in a wider homophobic society. If Forster had contemplated coming out he would have taken into account the effects it would have had on his friends, noting how Lord Montagu's friends had been used to bring about his downfall. Forster could have sacrificed himself but he also knew that he alone would not have been enough for the authorities, all of his friends would have been investigated and some would never have survived that onslaught. To a man who would rather have betrayed his country than his friend the decision to come out would not have been so simple as his critics supposed.

Despite all the bitter criticism of him, it is wholly wrong to assert that Forster said nothing in public about homosexual law reform. One early article he wrote, championing, in his rather reticent way, the cause of reform, 'Society and the Homosexual: A magistrate's figures' was published by *The New Statesman and Nation* on 31 October 1953. Forster's starting point in the article was the recent assertion by a police court magistrate that approximately 600 cases of 'importuning male persons' passed through his court in one year.* Forster thought the figure exaggerated, and subtly criticised the police by raising questions about the methods employed to gain convictions. He surveyed the dangers homosexuals faced in a hostile society, from imprisonment and blackmail to 'medical treatment', 'the methods of which are still controversial', and on dismissing society's usual remedies for the problem of its homosexual citizenry, he proposed a new departure:

> More satisfactory [a remedy] (if it could be achieved) would be an immediate change in the law. If homosexuality between men ceased to be per se criminal — it is not criminal between women — and if homosexual crimes were equated with heterosexual crimes and punished with equal but not with additional severity, much confusion and misery would be averted; there would be less public importuning and less blackmail.

Forster declared his pessimism that anti-homosexual laws would be repealed for some years to come, believing that hostile constituents would prevent even the most liberal Members of Parliament from voting in favour of reform. To help to change negative public opinion against homosexuals and to foster a positive atmosphere for change, he called for 'less social stigma under the existing law', hoping that 'more discussion, less emotion, fewer preconceptions' would become widespread. Forster felt that the movement for change had begun, noting that the 'stigma attaching to the homosexual is becoming more proportioned to the particular facts of each case' and that 'Some courts make increasing use of probation'.** Despite his caution, Forster ends the article by asserting that there was 'certainly ground for hope'.

Forster's hesitant style, his old-fashioned pleas for tolerance and understanding on behalf of the homosexual, would not be acceptable to most gays today. After almost thirty years of gay liberation, they strike us now as timid and unchallenging. But the atmosphere in which Forster wrote was very different, and political lobbying was conducted differently. Forster's tactic was not to scare the oppressor away, but to bring him to an understanding of his ignorance. Forster sought to persuade, believing that confrontation could provoke the very opposite of what one wanted to achieve. It was a political stance which was severely criticised in the 1960s, but one which few of Forster's contemporaries thought of as unproductive.

---

* Peter Wildeblood identified the magistrate as Mr E. R. Guest. The magistrate's 'grotesque misstatement was much quoted as a sign of the decadence of the age and the prevalence of homosexuality; Mr Guest's subsequent explanation that he had in fact said sixty cases a year went almost unnoticed.' (Wildeblood, 175).

** Some probationers may well have been fortunate enough to have been supervised by Bob Buckingham, Forster's close friend, or Tony Garrett, Angus Wilson's lover. Both Buckingham and Garrett were probation officers in the 1950s. The scientist Alan Turing's experience of probation however was devastating.

By 1958, when Wolfenden was front-page news, Forster again entered the public arena with two letters in favour of reform. The first appeared in *The Spectator* on 17 January 1958. Forster wrote to condemn publicly the police harassment of homosexual men in Wells. He noted that 'Evidently the scientific conclusions and humane recommendations of the Wolfenden Report cut no ice in that city. Nor is Wells unique'. He strongly denigrated the police use of agents provocateurs (in this instance a homosexual man was used by the police to entrap others), noting that the Report itself had catalogued the widespread iniquity of such practices, and finished by attacking the then Conservative government which had 'chosen to ignore' the Report (73).

His second letter was sent to *The Times* where it was published on 9 May 1958. Forster wrote to criticise a working party of the Church of Scotland which had recommended that the Church should not support the Wolfenden reforms 'partly on the ground that the conduct with which it deals is "an offence to all right thinking people"'. Forster pointed out a previous pro-Wolfenden letter published in *The Times* on 19 April, signed by a group of 'married women of position and distinction' headed by Lady Hester A. Adrian (and including several noted women such as Enid Bagnold, Iris Murdoch and Myfanwy Piper), which would demonstrate that a large number of right thinking people did in fact favour reform. Was the Church 'proposing to dismiss the signatories to that letter as ethically negligible?'

In fact the letter from the 'married women' was itself written in support of a previous letter which had urged the cause of reform and had appeared in *The Times* on 7 March. That letter was signed by '33 distinguished signatories', who included Angus Wilson. Quite why Forster wrote to support the letter from the 'married women of position and distinction', rather than the earlier one with 33 distinguished signatories, is not clear. Perhaps aware of Wilson's personal distaste for him, he chose not to provoke his sarcasm by writing, somewhat belatedly, in their support. Possibly he felt that his earlier letter to *The Spectator*, in January of the same year, had already made his own views on the matter quite clear enough — Forster being goaded into his second letter by his anger against those opponents of reform who persisted in pretending that Wolfenden was 'supported by no one of integrity or repute'.

Social theorists could explain Forster's stance in relation to his alienation as a homosexual, even if within a wider world he enjoyed considerable prestige as a man of letters. For most of his adult life his public role was that of the defender of individual rights and promoter of the ideal of individual responsibilities. This view perhaps blinded him to the value which could be derived from collective action. But how can he be castigated for this? His pessimism about seeing the decriminalisation of male homosexual activity dominated much of his life, and weakened his effectiveness as a campaigner for homosexual rights. Perhaps he could have done more: he could have come out, whatever the consequences for his friends, had he not been the person he was, yet what he did was not quite so insignificant, and in marked contrast to others who, for whatever reason, did nothing to advance the cause of reform.

With such attacks on him from the gay side we can hardly be suprised that Forster's work has had a varied reception amongst ostensibly non-gay critics. The elevation of his writings into what was formerly regarded as the literary canon can really be said to have begun with the publication in 1944 of Lionel Trilling's study *E. M. Forster*. Trilling later expressed the view in his Preface to the 1967 edition that Forster's work, which had formerly been read as 'a private experience to be kindly but cautiously shared with a few others of like mind', had subsequently become 'a general possession, securely established in the literary tradition of our time' (Trilling, 5). As a critic Trilling noted Forster's comic manner (9), his textual playfulness (which irritated) (10), and his 'moral realism' (12). The epithet which characterised Forster for a generation however was 'liberal', for Trilling observed that he was a writer who was not only firmly committed to the doctrines of liberalism but also, paradoxically perhaps, 'at war with the liberal imagination' itself (14). Trilling's study firmly and persuasively placed the discussion of Forster within the debate about liberalism and its values and set the agenda for much of the critical work on the writer which was to follow.

One significant aspect of Forster's output, however, namely the influence which his sexuality had on his creative life, was to remain unexplored, in print at least, until after the writer's death in 1970. And just as homosexuality was excluded from, yet visible within, Forster's work (the subject of the present book), so was this aspect excluded from any prime consideration in the critical work on the writer undertaken prior to his death. Nevertheless, in the more notable critical work on him, the importance of biographical detail of homosexuality in any assessment of Forster's work was acknowledged — particularly later by Wilfred Stone. Like Forster himself, though, neither critic could spell out exactly what they had thought significant. Trilling it seems did not know in 1944 nor even until much later that Forster was a homosexual; Stone clearly knew, but could not openly say what he knew in print.*

Trilling notes that to some academic theorists biographical facts concerning a writer are intrusive elements in any attempt at 'pure' literary criticism, but in discussing Forster he nonetheless acknowledges, at least obliquely, their importance in any analysis of this particular author's work:

> Biography intrudes itself into literary judgement and keeps it from being 'pure'. As we form our opinion of a particular work, certainly the sole object of our thought should be the work itself. But it seldom is — and although we call extraneous the facts that thrust themselves upon us, they inevitably enter into our judgement. We are always conscious of an author, and this consciousness does not rise only from elements in the

---

* According to Gore Vidal, after Trilling's book came out, the writer Truman Capote told the critic that Forster was 'queer'. Trilling was said to have been 'astounded; had never suspected; had not, plainly, a clue to what the books that he had praised were about'. (Vidal 1996, 191)

work; the extraneous personal facts that reach us are never wholly
ignored.

Literary facts are as intrusive as personal facts, though no doubt
they are more 'legitimate'. The author's whole career presents itself to
us not improperly as an architectonic whole of which each particular
work is a part; and the shape of that career, the nature and pace of its
development, the past failures and successes or those which we know
are to come, the very size of the structure, the place of any single unit
in the logic of the whole — all bear upon our feelings about any
particular work. (Trilling, 98)

Having asserted the importance of biographical detail Trilling goes on to
highlight his own inability to account for the progression of Forster's work.
Nevertheless he flags the importance of such detail and because he did not
know nor guess the writer's homosexuality, he notes that there is something of
considerable importance which is unavoidably absent from his discussion; and
he hopes in particular that a 'future biographer' will be able to explain the
apparent creative gap between '1910, the year of *Howards End*, and 1924, the
year of *A Passage to India*, and the second and possibly permanent retirement
after the great success of this last novel'. Trilling was in no doubt however that
'even unexplained, the facts suggest an unusual relation of a man to his craft'
(98), but of that 'unusual relation' he is as silent as the object of his study.

This critical commentary characterised most, if not all, of the published
criticism of Forster's work which appeared prior to his death, though like Trilling, the most astute critics managed to find a place where, if they knew more,
they could suggest what they knew and its importance to their subject. In *The
Mountain and the Cave*, Wilfred Stone drops appropriate hints for the as yet
uninformed reader. An example of this is his handling of the discussion of a
review which Forster had written in 1938 of Frank Harris's book on Oscar
Wilde. Forster had observed in the article that public attitudes to homosexuality had improved since Wilde's day, and Stone in his discussion notes Forster's
contribution to the public debate over the recommendations of the Wolfenden
Report. In his subsequent comment on Forster's attitude to this issue, Stone
revealed himself to have been totally aware of Forster's own homosexuality:

The issue of homosexuality is, of course, far more important to Forster
than these judicious words would suggest. If Forster has generally been
on the side of the underdog, it is at least partly because he has always
sympathized with this alienated minority. And if the cause of art and
sensitivity has seemed to him beleaguered, it is partly because society has
forced some of its ablest practitioners to live half-secret lives. His
liberalism is inseparable from these facts. (Stone, 354)

Stone neatly links Forster's 'liberalism' to the sufferings of an 'alienated
minority', to 'the cause of art' and to those of 'its ablest practitioners', whom

society had forced into 'half-secret lives'. He could not then take his analysis much further, at least in print, but he had said enough for astute readers to comprehend. Stone also littered his study of Forster with other give-away clues. He noted the influence on Forster of Goldsworthy Lowes Dickinson (72-98) and of Edward Carpenter (87-8), mentioned in passing that Rickie in *The Longest Journey* is a latent homosexual (193) and commented that for Forster the fact that the writers André Gide and Stefan George were homosexual was 'a fact of special interest' (377), although he did not say why this was so. Stone could not deal wholeheartedly with the issue however, for his subject was still alive when *The Mountain and the Cave* was being written in 1956–57 and Forster had clearly not wanted to allow any revealing biographical material to be included in his book. When Stone wrote asking for Forster's assistance, the writer replied defensively, stating that he believed Stone did not want to write a critical study of his books but a biography of him and that he felt that the biographies of living authors were not worth the effort (Lago and Furbank 2, 261). Following the intervention of Basil Willey, then the Edward VII Professor of English Literature at Cambridge, Forster changed his mind and agreed to help Stone but on his own terms, declaring: 'I cannot favour either a biography or a literary study with biographical emphasis'; he suggested that like 'Professor Trilling', Stone undertake 'a purely literary study'. Stone, wishing to obtain Forster's cooperation, had no real option but to accede to these terms; he wrote to Forster to accept, noting that 'The real inappropriateness, ... would have been my proceeding in a "biographical emphasis" against your wishes', and accepting that Forster had a strong 'desire for privacy (in and out of books)' (Lago and Furbank 2, 262). Despite Forster's precautions, the fact of his homosexuality was revealed in the book to those who could read the signs, just as this fact was evident in his own fictions to those who could decode his sub-texts.

Only after Forster's death in 1970 could Stone openly deal with the issue of homosexuality and the writer's work. The publication of *Maurice* and of the 'unpublishable' short stories in the 1970s provided critics with an opportunity to home in on this aspect of Forster's creative life, and discussion in some of the reviews of these works led to sporadic comments on similar aspects noted in Forster's 'publishable' fiction (see, for example, the articles collected by Gardner in his *E. M. Forster: The Critical Heritage*). Later publication of other private works (for example, 'Kanaya', the 'Locked Diary', Forster's *Commonplace Book*, his letters), and the frank biographical detail provided in 1977–78 by P. N. Furbank in *E. M. Forster: A Life*, meant that work could begin on examining the relationship between Forster's writings and his sexual orientation. Some early critics in this new phase of criticism, though, could still not appreciate what exactly they had been reading. Joseph Epstein, reviewing *Maurice* for *The New York Times Book Review* of 10 October 1971, declared:

> Now that Forster is known to have been a homosexual, others, homosexual and heterosexual alike, will no doubt wish to return to his other

works to rake them over for homosexual strains and illusions... The homosexual influence in Forster's other novels, if it exists at all, is so negligible as scarcely to be worthy of notice. [quoted in Pinchin, 86-7]

Such ignorance could perhaps be excused were it not for the critic's dogmatism, though once he realised the stupidity of his error, Epstein's criticism of Forster became vitriolic, declaring that Forster's deception had robbed his work of any semblance of greatness (Epstein, 1985).

Another critic, David Lodge, writing a review in *The Tablet* of 23 October 1971, was deprecatory towards *Maurice*, and argued that the fault lay in Forster writing the book for

himself and his own coterie, losing the sense of that ideal audience — austere, discriminating, yet catholic — for whom, like all good writers, he wrote his other books. *Maurice* is one more proof that in literary matters artistry is more important than sincerity. (Gardner, 474)

What Lodge fails to acknowledge is that it was such a supposedly 'austere, discriminating, yet catholic', and no doubt he means also, heterosexual, audience, who had proved to Forster the need for a retreat into a world of private unpublishable fiction. The friends who formed the first audience for *Maurice* consisted of a highly intelligent and not ill-informed group, and proved to be a critical audience also. Had the novel been published shortly after it was written, critical analysis of it might have proved less dismissive. And despite Lodge's final comment, it should perhaps be noted that 'artistry' devoid of 'sincerity' is not a concept Forster would have approved of, and the reason why ultimately he could only express certain aspects of his artistic sincerity in private works.

The critics however were predominately heterosexual, or seemed to be so, and adopted an orientational distance between themselves and their subject. If authorial sexual differences can register in fictional writing, so too can the sexual preferences of critics in their critical writings. In his essay 'What I Believe', Forster asserted that 'bodies are the instruments through which we register and enjoy the world' (TCFD, 70-1), implying that what we apprehend and the frame of reference within which we apprehend an object, is mediated and conditioned through that which the body desires, or chooses to desire. In this analysis, sexual orientation, which signals the objects of desire, is of prime importance. If the body is repressed then the marks of that repression could be made visible in examining what such a subject registers. For many decades after the publication of his novels and short stories, the homoerotic coding of his fiction still remained undiscussed in print. Repression not only controlled the way in which literature was conceived and written but also the way in which it was criticised. This critical bias was well known to Forster, as his diary entry of 25 October 1910 shows. The entry relates to Forster's idea for an unfinished essay, 'On Pornography and Sentimentality', and in it he proposes an examination of the relationship between literature, its criticism and sexual orientation; and he speaks of his need:

> To work out: — The sexual bias in literary criticism, and perhaps
> literature. Look for such a bias in its ideal and carnal form. Not in
> experience which refines. What sort of person would the critic prefer to
> sleep with, in fact. (AS, xvi)

Critical blindness to his homoerotic sub-texts, however, also allowed Forster,
on occasion, to reveal more about his characters and about himself, giving just
enough information to those who could read the signs while not saying sufficient
to alert the homophobic. Trilling's naive characterisation of reading Forster as
'a private experience to be kindly but cautiously shared with a few others of like
mind' (5) takes on a subtler meaning here.

In the late 1970s critics began to make use of the private Forster material
which had become available. Jeffrey Meyers in *Homosexuality and Literature
1890–1930* devoted a short chapter to Forster in which he discussed mainly
the 'unpublishable' works but also considered *A Room with a View* in the light
of its creator's homosexuality. Both Oliver Stallybrass and Elizabeth Heine who
edited the Abinger edition of Forster's works make reference to the writer's
sexuality in their Introductions to individual works; however their comments
were mainly incidental and were not followed through into any extended critical consideration. Except where they dealt with the 'unpublishable' works, the
issue of sexuality seemed isolated from other issues in their introductory pieces,
almost as if to neutralise the topic and head off any possible controversy which
might follow on from a concentration on this aspect of Forster's creative life.
After the publication of *Maurice*, no critic pretending to assess the writer's
works could omit a reference to his homosexuality. What appears to characterise the great majority of criticism published since Forster's death however is the
fact that references to Forster's homosexuality are invariably peripheral; rarely
is his sexual orientation presented as a major issue. The idea also seemed to
prevail that somehow Forster's sexuality was too trivial or, perhaps, too partisan
a topic to provide a basis upon which his output could be critically assessed.
Homosexuality as a specific topic in Forster criticism of this period seems lost
in a sea of articles and books which continued to discuss Forster the humanist,
Forster the liberal, Forster and Bloomsbury; rarely did one read of Forster the
homosexual man in a homophobic society. One notable exception to this,
however was Norman Page's monograph, *E. M. Forster's Posthumous Fiction*,
where the critic began to grapple with the influence of the author's sexuality on
his writing as a whole.

The fact that Forster's posthumously published fiction had revealed his
homosexuality to the world seemed almost regrettable to the Forsterian critical
establishment, who clearly seemed to view his homosexuality as a demerit to be
downplayed, if not excused. In his Introduction, in 1979, to *E. M. Forster: A
Human Exploration*, a collection of essays on Forster, John Beer expressed his
concerns about the wealth of information that had recently appeared concerning

the author's sexuality:

> This large new array of knowledge has, indeed, given a sharp turn to
> his literary reputation, encouraging commentators to treat much of his
> fiction as displaced accounts of homosexual relationships. The latter
> inference seems to be misguided, however. It would be truer to say that
> Forster was drawn to those aspects of love which were common to all
> human relationships, heterosexual or homosexual. (Das and Beer, 3)

Beer's attempt to present Forster's homosexuality within the framework of
a heterosexist critical stance seems designed to guard Forster's reputation from
any possible accusation that his work might not have the 'universal' value which
had been claimed for it by critics from Trilling onwards. The publication of
Maurice in 1971, had not, in general, been greeted by enthusiastic critical
reviews, and had led some to re-evaluate Forster's oeuvre somewhat negatively.
One such critic, George Steiner, wrote: 'Inevitably, *Maurice* will strengthen one's
feeling that Forster is a minor master who produced one major novel, and that
his gifts are less representative of modern English literature than some critics
have argued' (Gardner, 482). Whilst the impulse to guard Forster's work from
the ill-informed critical prejudices of a critic like Steiner can be commended,
Beer's defence of the writer is likewise flawed. The statement that 'Forster was
drawn to those aspects of love which were common to all human relationships'
misrepresents the author. Forster's real knowledge of love was inextricably linked
to his homosexual orientation. When he deals with the love between a man and
a woman, he does so in a practical ignorance of the subject, and after *A Room
with a View* with increasing reluctance. Forster made a clear distinction between his public and his private writings which was entirely based on the
degree to which he felt able to express his own sexuality. An argument which
seeks to imply there is no distinction between the experiences of a homosexual
and that of a heterosexual, claiming as Beer does that 'When he [Forster] writes
positively about human love... his remarks remain valid for all kinds of relationships' (3), denies a central fact of the writer's life and his work, and of human
sexualities more generally.

Beer attaches importance to Forster's sexuality primarily in the degree to
which it 'gave him an "outsider's" view of things, making him look at the world
from a point of view which did not regard marriage and the procreation of
children as central' (3). The evidence provided below in the analysis of *The
Longest Journey*, however, will show that it is debatable whether or not Forster
believed that such things as marriage and procreation were central. Certainly
he discounted marriage for himself, but procreation, if only by a proxy Stephen
Wonham, was an important issue to him. And of course, one need not be non-
heterosexual, nor an outsider, to provide a non-conventional attitude towards
marriage and procreation.

Beer's attempt to protect Forster's reputation from the denigration of homophobes
seemed to give weight to the idea that to approach Forster from the vantage point

of his sexuality would inevitably imperil the author's standing. Frederick P. W. McDowall in his 1982 review of Forster criticism since 1975, reiterated the supposed dangers in viewing Forster's work in relation to his sexuality:

> The impact, for better or for worse, of Furbank's biography and of the posthumously published homosexual works has been to make us see Forster plain, and indeed, in a different light. His eminence as a novelist remains unassailed, it seems to me, whereas the new revelations about him and his newly published fiction have sometimes seemed to strengthen, and then to diminish, our conception of him as public presence, humanist sage and dedicated artist. Forster will undoubtedly occupy a place somewhat less august in the annals of contemporary literature than he did in the years 1945 to 1970 [i.e. before the publication of *Maurice*], but it is safe to say that he will never sink to the obscurity that overtook him, in the period 1930 to 1943, as an important novelist. (Herz and Martin, 311)

McDowall goes on to praise and then attack Furbank's biography of Forster, stating that 'The emphasis upon the personal life tends to stress that aspect out of all due proportion' (313). Again the inference is clear: McDowall, like Beer, argues that the fact that Forster was a homosexual ought not to be seen as the major influence of his work. That, for Forster himself, his sexuality was the most important factor of his life, and that it clearly influences his work throughout his public and private writings, is downgraded in critical terms. For the gay critic who recognises the centrality of the writer's homosexuality, the effect is rather similar to that experienced by Forster himself, for it appears to create the development of two spheres of critical discourse. Firstly, a public sphere where Forster's homosexuality can be mentioned (for to deny it is now impossible), but in which its influence is downplayed, ostensibly to protect Forster's reputation, and secondly, a private sphere in which it seems the subject can be addressed but by a select critical audience.

Perhaps chastened by the criticism of McDowall and others, when Furbank together with Mary Lago, in 1983, produced the first volume of *The Selected Letters of E. M. Forster*, Furbank's Introduction to the collection began with a warning against using biographical material in an examination of a writer's work. Furbank argued that Forster would have agreed with Proust's assertion, in *Contre Sainte-Beuve*, that biography is irrelevant to a writer's output, arguing that 'a book is the product of an other me than the one we display in our habits, in society, and in our vices'. Furbank's assertion is that according to Forster's experience ' the person or personality who sat writing his own novels was a quite distinct one', that he 'ceased to exist the moment someone entered the room', and that there was little to be gained by questioning 'the person who replaced him' about the sources of his art. To back up his assertion about Forster, he referred to an earlier interview with the writer:

He [Forster] once remarked to some interviewers: 'What was it Mahler said? 'Anyone will sufficiently understand me who will trace my development through my nine symphonies'? This seems odd to me; I couldn't imagine myself making such a remark.' He added: 'It seems too uncasual'.

We must not expect, then, when reading Forster's letters, any more than from reading his biography, to trace the creator to his lair, or to find 'explanations' of his novels. (Lago and Furbank 1, vii)

The comment that the biographies of writers are 'irrelevant to their works' is plainly a ridiculous assertion, and Furbank's quotation of Proust's remark seems primarily an attempt to protect himself from the further wrath of those critics who would prefer even a dead Forster to remain closet-bound. His assertion that there is 'an other me than the one we display in our habits' etc. is far from convincing. In *Contre Sainte-Beuve*, Proust is said to have defined the artist's task as 'the releasing of the creative energies of past experience from the hidden store of the unconscious, an aesthetic which found its most developed literary expression in *À la recherche [du temps perdu]*' (Drabble 1993, 794). Forster made no such elaborate claims to create his work in a similar way, rather what he did say seems to confirm the importance of having some biographical knowledge at hand when considering his works critically. Furbank's unfortunate, perhaps, choice of Proust to compare the writer with is certainly intriguing, for as with Forster, Proust's work can hardly be viewed without relation to author's homosexuality, as Jeffrey Meyers has already shown.

Furbank's quote from Forster regarding Mahler is taken from an interview he himself, together with F. J. H. Haskell, conducted in 1952 (Dick, 7-16). His comment was in answer to a question on Trilling, who had written that Forster had asserted 'that the older... [he] got the less it seemed to... [him] to matter that an artist should "develop"' (Dick, 16). Trilling had opined that the author's career had presented itself as an 'architectonic whole', the question posed by the interviewers relating therefore to his development as a writer. Forster's answer here was not related to biography, as Furbank wrongly implies, but to the idea that an artist should show a clear progression in his or her work. His reply referring to Mahler could be viewed as an attempt to forestall what would seem to be logically the next question, that is, 'Why did your fictional work seem not to develop after *A Passage to India*?', which would raise the issue of why he gave up fictional writing for a public audience. To answer truthfully would have meant revealing his homosexuality.

Furbank and Haskell's interview also provides evidence to contradict Furbank's assertion that 'We must not expect... when reading Forster's letters, any more than reading his biography, to trace the creator to his lair, or to "find" explanations for his novels.' The interviewers asked him how much he would admit to modelling his fictional characters on real people; Forster replied: 'We all like to pretend we don't use real people, but one does actually' (Dick, 13). Their next question was whether or not all of his characters had real-life models. Forster replied:

> In no book have I got down more than the people I like, the person I think I am, and the people who irritate me. This puts me among the large body of authors who are not really novelists, and have to get on as best they can with these three categories. We have not the power of observing the variety of life and describing it dispassionately. (Dick, 14)

He was then asked about how he went about the process of turning a real person into a fictional one:

> A really useful trick is to look back upon such a person with half-closed eyes, fully describing certain characteristics. I am left with about two-thirds of a human being and can get to work. A likeness isn't aimed at and couldn't be obtained, because a man's only himself amidst the peculiar circumstances of his life and not amid other circumstances.... When all goes well, the original material soon disappears, and a character who belongs to the book and nowhere else emerges. (Dick, 14)

Forster's description of his creative processes reveals the importance of his biographical details as a starting point for the analysis of his work. He clearly reveals that many characters started out as 'about two-thirds of a human being'. It is true that he adds 'a likeness isn't aimed at' and 'When all goes well, the original material disappears', but two-thirds is a significant percentage, and it is debatable that 'the original material soon disappears' in all his writings. His clear assertion however that 'In no book have I got down more than the people I like, the person I think I am, and the people who irritate me', and that he does not write 'dispassionately', certainly flags the importance of biography to his work. This is not to infer that his books are really romans-à-clef, but to affirm that his passion, his homosexuality, is not separate from his art.

Despite the caveats of Beer, McDowall and Furbank, some critics proceeded to look at Forster's writing in relation to his sexuality. In the late 1970s Judith S. Herz had noted the operation of a 'double plot' in much of Forster's fiction whereby a 'surface heterosexual romance' obscured an 'interior homosexual romance':

> For in many of his stories and novels... two story lines, a surface heterosexual romance and an interior homosexual romance, are held in tension, much of the energy of the narrative deriving from the conflict between what the plot claims as its main business and what the suppressed inner narrative insists on in the plot's despite. (Herz, 18)

Ira Bruce Nadel's essay, 'Moments in the Greenwood: Maurice in Context' (1982), presented the novel within the context of the homophobic society in which it was created (Herz and Martin, 177-90), the article appearing in the

same collection of essays that contained McDowall's criticism. Perhaps because
this article dealt with *Maurice*, such an approach was acceptable — one could
hardly ignore homosexuality in discussing it — but would the same degree of
acceptability have applied if the essay had looked at, say, *Where Angels Fear to
Tread* in the same way? During the 1980s, Tariq Rahman wrote a series of
articles dealing with the 'double plot' in a number of Forster's works and examining the relationship between those works and the writer's sexuality. And a
more recent contribution to the field, in 1994, was provided by Parminder
Bakshi in her examination of homosexuality and *A Passage to India* (Davies and
Wood, 23-64). Bakshi discusses the novel seeing it within 'the Orientalist
tradition of English literature' [but] noting that 'the Orientalism is constantly
redefined by homo-erotic desire' (62).

Returning to Forster's literary output, a major restriction on his creativity was
censorship. Historically, writings other than ecclesiastical, legal or medical ones
which deal openly with the subject of sexuality, especially with deviant sexuality,
have tended to be published privately and for a carefully considered, limited and
select readership. Censorship laws have traditionally prevented the appearance
of some books and self-censorship has endeavoured to bypass such confrontation with authority. However the application of censorship laws, in England as
well as in most other Western countries, has historically proved erratic, producing a situation where, whilst it is known that the graphic details of sexual
activity were normally deemed unpublishable, the exposition of sexual feeling
itself has at various times been allowed and at other times condemned, and
even, in certain periods, both allowed and condemned.

The dangers of state censorship was well known to Forster, as was a need for
self-censorship. In a lecture delivered at the Congrès International des Ecrivains
in Paris on 21 June 1935 (and published in *Abinger Harvest* as 'Liberty in England') he noted the effect that British censorship laws had had on both writers
and publishers in recent decades. In particular he cited the problems which had
attended the initial publications of D. H. Lawrence's *The Rainbow* (1915), Radclyffe
Hall's *The Well of Loneliness* (1928) and James Joyce's *Ulysses* (1922). He reserved
his severest censures however for the authorities who had recently suppressed
James Hanley's novel, *Boy.* This book deals with homosexuality on merchant
ships, in particular the sexual exploitation of one particular ship's boy. The
novel had been published in 1931 by a small publishing company, Boriswood
Limited. The book had been circulated without incident for three years before
the Lancashire Police in 1934 decided to summon the publishers for having
'published an obscene libel'; on being advised by their counsel to plead guilty,
they were subsequently fined £400 at the Manchester Assizes.

The dangers of state censorship was well known to Forster, as was a need for
These events impressed upon Forster the fact that publication of even a
mildly contentious work could prove to be a time-bomb set to explode whenever any particular police authority in Britain chose to set it off. To publish a
work like *Maurice* therefore would have seemed fraught with never-ending
dangers, let alone the problems which would personally have attended its re-

lease. Writing to Christopher Isherwood in 1938, he cited the effect publication would have on a close working-class friend, the policeman Bob Buckingham,
as a reason why it could not yet be effected (Lago and Furbank 2,159). And as
he lived with his mother until her death in 1945, there was always her reaction
to consider. The realities of censorship, and the penalties which could be imposed for ignoring it, were concerns which dogged Forster for practically all his
life, and those, like Hodges and Hutter, who criticise him for not publishing
Maurice in the 1930s or 1940s (Hodges and Hutter, 19) do so in complete
disregard of the facts of his situation.

When it came to writing fiction for the general public, Forster knew he
was expected to produce novels where only heterosexual passions were deemed
to have any ultimate validity. In all of his works for public consumption Forster
consciously suppressed any overt textual references to homosexuality, but as the
feminist critic Hélène Cixous points out, homosexual desire is not so easily
dismissed, for 'at the same time that you repress a certain homosexuality, symbolically, substitutively, it comes through various signs — traits, comportments,
manners, gestures — and it is seen still more clearly in writing' (Lodge, 292-3).
And homosexuality does assert itself in Forster's writings time and time again
both with and without his permission. As Freud disclosed, repression does not
silence, it merely displaces, relocates or reshapes that which is silenced into
something which can be spoken of, or be written about, albeit ambiguously.

It is this very quality of ambiguity which Jeffrey Meyers sees as a direct
result of homophobic repression and notes how it can be said to characterise
most of the public writings by closet homosexual novelists, sometimes even
acting as the stimulus to greater achievement:

> The clandestine predilections of homosexual novelists are both an
> obstacle and a stimulus to art, and lead to a creative tension between
> repression and expression. The novels become a raid on inarticulate
> feelings, and force authors to find a language of reticence and evasion,
> obliqueness and indirection, to convey their theme.... If a specifically
> homosexual tone, sensibility, vision or mode of apprehension exists, then
> it would be characterized by these cautious and covert qualities, and by
> the use of art to conceal rather than to reveal the actual theme of the
> novel... (Myers, 1-2)

Judith S. Herz's observation on the operation of a double plot, a creative
strategy which thrives on the presence of ambiguity, seems relevant here also.
This element, referred to by Herz as the tension between what the plot claims to
be doing and 'the suppressed inner narrative', seems, according to the critic
Robert Glück, to be a common feature of the work of many gay writers. Glück
states that gay writers have not generally tried to create their own mythology
independent of the heterosexual world, rather 'in the last three hundred years,
they have sought to modify the sexual terms they have received, inscribing less a
"reverse discourse" of homosexuality, than a subdominant one, a transcription

of the original into a distant, unrelated key' (quoted in Bergman, 26). In discussing Glück's views, David Bergman notes Foucault's observation that there is not on one side a discourse of power and on the opposite side a discourse that runs counter to it, but that discourses are tactical elements or blocks operating in a field of force relations. Bergman applies this to homosexual writers, asserting that 'Since homosexuals have fashioned their sense of themselves out of and in response to the heterosexual discourse about them, homosexuality — even as conceived by homosexuals — cannot be viewed outside of the contructs of heterosexuality' (Bergman, 26).

Given the silence of earlier published critics on the origins of Forster's textual ambiguities, the majority of his reading public seemingly remained in ignorance of any 'interior homosexual romance', though assuredly some could detect this hidden aspect of a work. An example of this may be seen in Charles Sayle's analysis of 'The Story of a Panic' conveyed privately to John Maynard Keynes and others in 1904. Sayle had suggested that a sexual relationship had existed between the two male characters in the story, the boy Eustace and the Italian waiter Gennaro. Forster at first denied this, for it had not apparently been his conscious intention to present such a relationship, but later he realised that he had unwittingly done so. He acknowledged that he had deceived himself over the work's subtle resonances, and admitted that the story had excited him as he wrote it, just as the violence in a scene between Philip and Gino in *Where Angels Fear to Tread* had aroused him, in ways he did not quite understand, whilst writing it (LJ, 302-3; Furbank 1, 113-4).

Paradoxically, perhaps it is also possible to see how public blindness to textual homosexual inferences enabled Forster not only to hide but also to reveal more than he would have been able to do so with today's more knowing readership. Paul Webb, in his Introduction to a collection of poems by the Uranian poet* Rev. E. E. Bradford, notes that Bradford 'churned out openly and cheerfully gay verse from 1908 to 1930' and spoke, in public, in favour of male love, considering it 'to be better and more moral' than heterosexual love (Bradford, 11). Webb puts forward reasons why Bradford was not attacked by the public for his views. First, he says, 'is the old saying about there being none so blind as those who will not see', people in general accepting his poetry as representing platonic, that is, non-sexual, love, and second, that it was 'in public at least, a more sexually "innocent" age than our own' (14). Due to the general lack of

---

* This is a term now applied to a varied group of British poets who, towards the end of the nineteenth and in the early part of the twentieth century, wrote works which dealt favorably with the subject of male love. The term 'Uranian' derives from the speech given by Pausanias in Plato's *Symposium*. 'The Uranian, or Heavenly, Aphrodite... is sprung from a mother in whose birth the female has no part, but she is from the male only; this is that love which is of youths only, and the goddess being older has nothing of wantonness. Those who are inspired by this love turn to the male, and delight in him who is the more valiant and intelligent nature; any one may recognize the pure enthusiasts in the very character of their attachments. For they love not boys, but intelligent beings whose reason is beginning to be developed, much about the time at which their beards begin to grow. And in choosing them as their companions, they mean to be faithful to them, and to pass their whole life with them...' (Plato, trans. B. Jowett).

public knowledge regarding sexual behaviour and identities, Forster was able in one sense to write more openly than one might have supposed possible in an ostensibly homophobic society. Many of his early critics and readers clearly did not grasp all that Forster had placed in a work, for his literary stratagems of deception had worked, some even on himself. Much remained a secret to all but those informed readers who could read between the ideological lines, for as the critic Thomas E. Yingling observes, 'gay writers... have found literature less a matter of self-expression and more a matter of coding: from Byron through John Ashbery, the consistent locus of parody in gay texts suggests a self-consciousness about what texts may or may not do' (quoted in Bergman, 105).

By examining some of the earlier drafts of Forster's novels it can be seen that he was careful to excise any overt references to homosexuality in those works he intended for publication. This did not mean however that all such references were removed for, as was noted in the case of 'The Story of a Panic', Forster admitted that he was not always aware of the full import of what he had actually written. Certainly the drafts of his earlier works show that he had not been able to excise all references to homoerotic feeling, but by the writing of *Howards End* in 1910, when his creative crisis was just beginning, he was endeavouring to exclude almost every manifestation of dubious desire, though he did not succeed in this. It is worth remembering however, that although homosexuality may not be mentioned in that novel, cross-class heterosexuality is, though such a subject had, of course, been permissible in English literature for centuries; still, the mention of it caused concern to Forster's publisher and to some of his readers.

Forster's fear of the public disclosure of his homosexuality, and a sly hint that he was hiding this fact in his writing, do find strong echoes in his short story 'The Curate's Friend'. The 'friend' referred to here is a 'Faun', who perhaps 'came over to England with the Roman legionaries to live with his friends in camp' (CS, 90). The Curate's relationship with the Faun prevents his marriage to Emily, still he is happy (97), and wisely realises the need to keep the joy of his new friendship a secret, for if he 'breathed one word' of it, his 'present life, so agreeable and profitable, would come to an end'. And so instead of speaking openly of his new friendship in a 'lyrical and rhetorical treatment, so suitable to the subject', and 'so congenial' to his profession, he was constrained to use 'the unworthy medium of a narrative', and 'to delude' his readers by declaring the tale to be simply 'a short story, suitable for reading in the train' (CS, 98-9).

Forster himself, however, had friends with whom he could share his secret life, and if at times he attempts 'to delude' both his readers and himself, it is only because a wider society had demanded it. The author's tale relied on fantasy to provide a superficially deceptive gloss on those issues raised, which the writer felt his public might not accept. Norman Page, in his discussion of 'Albergo Empedocle', analyses Forster's use of fantasy. In that story, there are clear references to homosexuality in the text, yet in 1903 it was printed in the popular magazine *Temple Bar*. Page suggests that these aspects of the plot had escaped 'the literary watchdogs' because the writer had used fantasy, and that

'Forster may have resorted to fantasy, as he so often did in his shorter fiction, in part because it permitted statements and situations to be presented or hinted at which could hardly otherwise have found their way into print' (Page, 32).

One further aspect of Forster's work, which he seems to share with other similarly placed writers, is the use he makes of irony. An unnamed reviewer* of Forster's work in 'A Chalice for Youth', which appeared in the *Times Literary Supplement* of October 1971, noted that Forster's homosexuality was central to his work and that it 'informs the essential properties of his novels, the voyeuristic distancing of the narration, the ironic tone, the self-deprecating humour...' The same reviewer also noted that Forster often seemed to express a bleak tone:

> but he expressed this bleak vision with a self-deprecating irony that
> refuses to be altogether serious, and never reached toward tragedy. If one
> says that tragedy and homosexuality do not sit well together, but irony
> and homosexuality do, this is not to be taken as a judgement of a sexual
> state, but as an observation of social attitudes. Forster was a sensitive
> judge of such attitudes, and he wrote, one might say defensively, to
> preserve his place in the society which would ostracize him if it knew.
> But cunning defensiveness suited his talent, and he made out of self-
> deprecation, transference, and evasion a personal and functioning style.
> (P. Gardner, 487)

When we examine the theoretical definition of verbal irony provided by M. H. Abrams, it can be seen why this mode of writing should be of interest to a writer who wished to hide aspects of his personality whilst simultaneously allowing in fiction for the occasional slip of the narrational mask. Abrams notes that in 'most of the critical uses of the term "irony" there remains the root sense of dissembling or hiding what is actually the case; not, however, in order to deceive...' (Abrams, 91). Abrams subsequent definition of 'verbal irony' elucidates Forster's use of it in his fictional writings:

> Verbal irony... is a statement in which the speaker's implicit meaning
> differs sharply from the meaning that is ostensibly expressed.... Some-
> times... the meaning and evaluations may be subtly qualified rather than
> simply reversed, and the clues to the ironic counter-meaning under the
> surface statement may be indirect and unobtrusive. That is why recourse
> to irony by an author carries an implicit compliment to the intelligence
> of readers, who are invited to associate themselves with the author and
> the knowing minority who are not taken in by the ostensible meaning.
> (Abrams, 91-2)

Forster's use of irony could also be looked at in the context of what we now know as 'camp humour', that is 'a network of puns, innuendoes, and allusions

---

* Later identified as Samuel Hynes (Das and Beer 281).

arrayed with bawdy abandon' (Bergman, 112). Joseph Bristow's definition of 'camp' explains its action as 'a discourse which thrives on a principle of ironically turning accepted values on their heads' (Bristow 1991, 84). Examples of its use in *A Room with a View* are Mr Beebe's comment on Mr Emerson and his son that they get people's backs up 'not unnaturally' (RWV, 7-8) and Lucy Honeychurch's observation, whilst fingering a model of the leaning tower of Pisa, 'How wonderfully people rise in these days!' (RWV, 53). It is the Rev. Eager's subsequent hypocritical attack on the Emersons which prompts her to buy the 'tower' and what it represents. A similar camp approach to humour can be seen in *A Passage to India*, where in the climactic scenes at the Krishna Temple at Mau, a degree of intentional bathos is provided by the narrator pointing out 'the small European-ised band' who, during the seemingly most sacred rituals, are playing 'Nights of Gladness' (PTI, 276). In his private life, Forster was also not afraid to camp it up, as he showed when he signed one of his letters 'Charlotte Bartlett' (Lago and Furbank 1, 91), another 'Tosca' (Lago and Furbank 2, 245), and Lago and Furbank note that 'those [letters] to W. J. H. Sprott are, almost invariably, in a vein of guileless "camp" frivolity' (Lago and Furbank 1, xii).

Social disapprobation of homosexuality ultimately led to Forster's inability to write fiction for public consumption. The development of the creative crisis which followed the success of *Howards End* was profoundly influenced by his sexual orientation. He became weary of the sort of work he felt his predomi-nantly heterosexual readership had expected him to produce. In his diary entry for 16 June 1912, he explains his difficulties in writing fiction:

> Having sat for an hour in vain trying to write a play, will analyse the causes of my sterility... 2. Weariness of the only subject that I both can and may treat — the love of men for women & vice versa. (LTC, xiv)

And a later letter to Forrest Reid in February 1913 throws further light on Forster's dilemma:

> You ask about about my work... I am dried up. Not in my emotions, but in their expression... I see beauty going by but have nothing to catch it in. (Lago and Furbank 1, 187)

These two extracts reveal that part of Forster's crisis involved his feeling that he was cramped by the conventions of his public writing rather than with writ-ing itself; he felt his choice of subject-matter was restricted by his readers' preferences, and that whilst he had 'emotions', 'their expression' could not be effected in writing meant for the public. His outpouring of essays, articles and reviews during this period, together with *Maurice* and the 'unpublishable' stories, show that he still could produce completed work of considerable merit, although it was the creation of publishable fiction which seemed to elude him.

As Forster acquired a greater knowledge of his own sexual orientation, initially from Goldsworthy Lowes Dickinson and Edward Carpenter, though later from other writers, and as he acquired more practical sexual experience of his own during the First World War in Alexandria, he became more acutely aware of the need to suppress the knowledge of his sexuality from the general public. During this period he completed *Maurice* and several short stories which dealt with homosexual themes and which were seen only by a select and sympathetic readership known personally to the writer. In a later letter to Forrest Reid in January 1915, Forster told him about *Maurice*, hoping that he would read and enjoy it, adding 'you will be glad to know I have written something, and am not as sterile as I am obliged to pretend to the world' (Lago and Furbank 1, 217). It is significant to note Forster's assertion that he felt he had to 'pretend' to be creatively sterile, that is, be publicly silent about the nature of his creativity, and that what works he had produced were officially at least invisible. This pretence of sterility however did foreshadow very real difficulties with his writing of fiction for publication as the tortuous histories of *A Passage to India* and of the uncompleted 'Arctic Summer' show.

One further piece of evidence which supports the theory that Forster's difficulties in writing were primarily linked to his sexuality comes from a letter he wrote to Siegfried Sassoon in July 1923 in which he records his delight in writing the homoerotic story 'The Life to Come'. 'Why can't I always be writing like this — it is the only freedom,' he tells Sassoon (Lago and Furbank 2, 43). But throughout his life Forster knew, when it came to his work, of his own 'capacity for being wounded in his most private parts', and that for him it was 'natural that a writer should act the mystery man' (LJ, 303).

In a letter to G. L. Dickinson of 8 May 1922, Forster reiterated his writing malaise, linking it not only to his weariness with contemporary fictional forms, but also to his experience of grieving (or rather his initial lack of it) for his dying lover Mohammed el Adl and to the inability of publishable fiction to express the true measure of his loss and his desire (Lago and Furbank 2, 26).

He was to write later, in 1964, that he would have been a more famous writer if he had written, or rather published more, adding that 'sex has prevented the latter' (LTC, xiv).

Whilst Forster's fictional works which were published during his lifetime rely on the use of ambiguity to give at least some expression to their creator's repressed passion, the same cannot be said of his journalism, nor of his critical work on other writers and thinkers. It would appear that because the reading of fiction is in a way a less public activity — most often there is only the lone reader and the text, rarely by comparison a public reading — Forster felt he could relax his guard a little, for his prime aim in fiction is to address the reader in his or her own 'private' world. In his works of journalism however and in his critical work he addresses a more 'public' world (either through the medium of a newspaper or in speaking to an academic world). This would account for the fact that whilst his public fictional works show aspects of ambiguity, his other public works do not show this to the same degree. In his essays and articles it is clearly Forster himself who speaks and who must himself account for every word; in fiction he can hide behind the mask of the narrator. This is why in his articles on Edward Carpenter, his essays on Proust, on Stefan George, on Cavafy and on other homosexual writers (including T. E. Lawrence, Forrest Reid and Ronald Firbank), Forster does not reveal, let alone address, the fact that they were all homosexual and that this aspect of their personalities had profound effects upon their lives and works. If Forster had displayed a knowledge of this he might have found his views on the matter openly solicited and the basis of his knowledge publicly examined.

In his first essay on André Gide, 'Gide and George', in 1943, Forster made no mention of the writer's sexuality. When Gide died in 1951, however, Forster wrote a further article, 'Gide's Death', and noted that 'He [Gide] was what *The Times* obituary notice of him sagely termed "heterodox" (i.e. homosexual)' (TCFD, 235). Forster is very careful to distance himself from this aspect of Gide, however, by prefacing this observation with the remark that 'His equipment contained much that was unusual and bewildering', implying Gide's sexual orientation was part of that 'unusual and bewildering' aspect of the writer. And nowhere in his panegyric of the author does Forster relate Gide's sexuality to his work.

Perhaps not surprisingly, one further exception to my general observation regarding Forster's non-fictional works is his biography of Goldsworthy Lowes Dickinson, written, like the second article on Gide, after the subject's death. Because of its length, however, it would seem to be aimed at the same kind of private readership as his fictional works, and hence in the biography Forster does fleetingly infer that Dickinson was homosexual,* though he does not take the bull by the horns and say so openly, nor does he analyse how this affected the life and works of his subject.

The clearest evidence that Forster had censored his non-fiction work is provided by an examination of his discussion of the work of Herman Melville in *Aspects of the Novel*. The notes that Forster made in 1926 for his Clark Lectures on Literature, given at Cambridge in 1927, are to be found at the beginning of his *Commonplace Book*. In his notes on Herman Melville and *Billy Budd*, Forster notes 'Billy Budd has goodness — faint besides Alyosha's and rather alloyed by H M's suppressed homosex:!' (CB, 17). A similar reference is made later to Henry James and that 'H J in The Turn of the Screw is merely declining to think about homosex, and the knowledge that he is declining throws him into the necessary fluster' (18). In Forster's lecture, however, and in its public printed form, these observations, first made in private, are not repeated, nor even hinted at (AN, 97-9).

---

* Those references which reveal something, but by no means all, about Dickinson's sexuality are carefully couched in muted language (see Oliver Stallybrass's Introduction to the Abinger Edition of Goldsworthy Lowes Dickinson, xiv).

Useful insight into Forster's experience of his sexuality can be gained by examining some contemporary prevailing social attitudes towards same-sex male
love. Whilst sexual contact between males has in Western societies been officially condemned for centuries, emotional attachments between men have not;
in the nineteenth century in particular the concept of 'manly love' was in
general accepted.

According to the social historian Jeffrey Richards in his essay on the subject in *Manliness and Morality*, during the nineteenth century and into the early
part of the twentieth what was then referred to as 'manly love', defined as a
strong emotional bond between two males which did not involve shared sexual
activity, was generally met with social approbation. For the English elites, all-
male groups in public schools, the professions and government were the norm;
and in general the open, faithful and close bonding between males was actively
commended. Such friendships could draw on the historical antecedents of
similar bonds in ancient Greece and in medieval Europe, of knights, squires
and chivalric brotherhoods, and could even find a scriptural model in the love
of David for Jonathan which was 'passing the love of women'. In *Where Angels
Fear to Tread* and *The Longest Journey* as well as in *Maurice*, Forster alludes to
the love of David and Jonathan, and in his uncompleted novel 'Arctic Summer'
he attempted to look at contemporary masculinity and femininity by a discussion of the meaning of chivalric brotherhood in his contemporary society. An
echo of the theme of chivalry is also to be found in the bathing scene at the
'Sacred Lake' in *A Room with a View*. The pool is referred to as 'a call to the
blood and to the relaxed will, a passing benediction whose influence did not
pass, a holiness, a spell, a momentary chalice for youth' (RV, 133). The 'call to
the blood' indicates a blood-brotherhood, just as the 'chalice for youth' recalls
the quest of the Arthurian knights for the Holy Grail. The homoeroticism of
that bathing scene however is, in the novel, in marked contrast to the sterile,
destructive 'medievalism' of Cecil Vyse; and the title of the last chapter of the
work looks forward to 'The End of the Middle Ages' (RV, 205).*

In the latter part of the nineteenth century such apparently non-sexual
male friendships began to be called into question. Widespread sensational public interest had been provoked in 1871 by the trial of Boulton and Park, two
male homosexual transvestites, who were charged with indecent behaviour (cross-
dressing in public) and with 'conspiring to commit sodomite acts'. Various
would-be moral reformers spoke out against the alleged vices of Sodom and
debilitating self-abuse which they saw as endemic in the English public schools

---

* In his Introduction to *Sexual Heretics: An Anthology of Male Homosexuality in English Literature from
1850 to 1900*, Brian Reade identifies Edward Fitzgerald's essay *Euphranor, A Dialogue on Youth*,
published anonymously in 1851, as the book which 'gave perhaps currency to the romantic notion of
bringing chivalrous values to male friendships' (5). Reade briefly traces the links between notions of
chivalry and male love through J. A. Symonds's poem in honour of Walt Whitman, 'The Song of Love
and Death' (c. 1875), to the Uranian writers C. P. C. K. Jackson and the Rev. E. E. Bradford. Jackson's
article on 'The New Chivalry' appeared in 1894, and Bradford made *The New Chivalry* the title of one
of his books of homosexual poems in 1918. (Reade, 4-6)

of the period (Mangan and Walvin, 111-2). Legal, medical and social discourses began to be more precisely formulated (the word 'homosexual' itself
only came into general usage in the latter part of the nineteenth century) and
gradually public awareness of the subject increased.

What really brought the subject to public attention though were a series
of prosecutions which followed the general criminalisation of male homosexuality by the 'Labouchère amendment' to the Criminal Law Amendment Act of
1885. Prior to this only sodomy (the legal definition of which had varied over
time) had been illegal, not only between men but also between men and women
and between men and beasts. Under the new law, sensational trials were inevitable, the two most notorious being those surrounding the Cleveland Street
scandal of 1889–90 (when a male brothel staffed in part by telegraph messenger boys was discovered in London's Cleveland Street) and the trials of Oscar
Wilde in 1895. The law against male homosexuality was further extended by
the Vagrancy Act of 1898 which made it an offence to importune for immoral
purposes — a law which was, and is, almost exclusively applied against homosexual men.

Despite the violence wielded by the law it would not be accurate to say
that sexual love between men could not be dealt with by writers, for John
Addington Symonds, Henry Havelock Ellis and Edward Carpenter, amongst
others in England, managed to do this even after the trials of Oscar Wilde,
though much of their earlier work was published privately, and the positive
outlooks and apologetics of these writers do find expression in Forster's own
work. Likewise, manly love could be discussed and presented so long as sexuality was not obviously linked to it, though assuredly for some readers it had a
sexual resonance in their own lives.

Jeffrey Richards observes that the theme of manly love survived in fiction
well into the twentieth century, apparently unhindered by the homophobic atmosphere generated after the fall of Wilde. The main characteristic of such
fiction seems to be that the bond between the two male protagonists was forged
in their shared schooldays. Richards notes that 'Even though the schools began
to frown on emotional male friendships after the 1880s, they continued to be
sanctioned and promoted in popular fiction' (Mangan and Walvin, 114). In
support of this he quotes the examples of *Gerald Eversley's Friendship* (1895) by
J. E. C. Welldon, *The Hill: A Romance of Friendship* (1905) by Horace Annesley
Vachell, and *Tell England* (1922) by Ernest Raymond. All three novels celebrate
the growth and maintenance over time of male love, and none sees marriage as
a bar to the continuance of such bonds; similarly all 'share a deeply emotional
fervent Romantic perspective' (Mangan and Walvin, 116). Another novel, similar
to the three mentioned above, is *Tim* (1891) by Howard Overing Sturgis. In
this novel, however the friendship between the young man, Carol, and 'a delicate, skinny little boy' (AH, 121), Tim, is shattered by Carol's fiancée who
refuses to marry a man with an intimate friend. Unlike those other novels, here
— as in Forster's own works — women are often shown as interfering in male
friendships. Forster had met Sturgis and included an article he had written on

him after his death in *Abinger Harvest* (AH, 119-26). Whilst he did not mention Sturgis's homosexuality, Forster noted that the author 'wrote and he lived for his personal friends' (AH, 126).

Returning to Ernest Raymond and his novel *Tell England*, it can be seen how innocent a subject 'manly love' could seem to both a writer and his or her audience. Many years after the novel's publication, in a book of autobiographical reminiscences *The Story of My Days*, Raymond recorded how completely ignorant he had been about the subject of homosexuality when he wrote the novel:

> [A]... thing that is a cause of wonder to me as I re-read the book [*Tell England*] is the indubitable but wholly unconscious homosexuality in it. The earlier part was written when I was eighteen or nineteen; the latter part in my twenties, and in those far-off days 'homosexuality' was a word which — absurd as it may seem now — I had never heard.... I did not know that homosexuality could exist in embryo without even knowing itself for what it was, or desiring the least physical satisfaction...
> (Raymond 1968, 180)

If authors had such little notion of any link between manly love and manly sex, then it would seem safe to assume that their ignorance was reflected in the sexual naivety of many of their readers.

Widespread public acceptability of the theme of manly love would explain why, for example, Forster could freely express Rickie's admiration of Gerald's virility and athleticism in *The Longest Journey*; the two men had met at their public school, so it seemed not unnatural that Gerald should be praised by the crippled Rickie for embodying some of the physical prowess extolled by the school authorities, and to express such praise would not necessarily lay the writer, or the character, open to any imputation of homosexuality.

Stories which dealt with adult male love generally had to rely on childhood bonding as an acceptable starting point, which invariably meant that the protagonists came from similar social strata (hence perhaps Rickie's problems in *The Longest Journey* in expressing his love for Stephen Wonham, believed at first to be his social inferior). Of male love outside of this context there seems to have been little available in fiction except that printed privately for a covert readership; a notable example of this genre being the pornographic novel, *Teleny or the Reverse of the Medal: A Psychological Romance of Today*, published in London in 1893 (Bartlett, 241).

As well as being a suitable topic for lawgivers, discussion of homosexuality at this period was also seen as an appropriate subject for scientific and ethical discourses. Medical writers such as Richard von Krafft-Ebing in his *Psychopathia Sexualis* (1886) and Iwan Bloch in *The Sexual Life of Our Time* (1908) provided a scientific perspective on homosexuality, and the German sexologists, Karl Heinrich Ulrichs and Magnus Hirschfeld a social and political one. In England, the field was led by John Addington Symonds in *A Problem in*

Greek Ethics (1883), by H. Havelock Ellis in his study *Sexual Inversion* (1897), and by Edward Carpenter in *The Intermediate Sex* (1906). Forster himself in the early part of his life seems to have been drawn to the idea, promoted first by Ulrichs and later by Krafft-Ebing, that homosexuality was congenitally acquired, and in *The Longest Journey* we can see his consideration of this theory. One further, private consideration also for Forster was his belief that his father and other family members had also been homosexual (Beaumont 1993, 16), and not suprisingly this seemed to him evidence of a sort in support of the notion of hereditary acquisition. Further links to the ideas of Krafft-Ebing can be seen in *Maurice* when the protagonist undergoes hypnotherapy similar to that described in *Psychopathia Sexualis*. The utopian homoerotic views of Carpenter and of the homosexual American writers Henry David Thoreau and Walt Whitman similarly find their way into Forster's work, most notably in *A Room with a View*. The later dissemination throughout Western society of the ideas of Sigmund Freud however, led to a general suspicion of close male friendships and this meant that they could no longer be innocently viewed as free of a sexual element both in life and in literature. In his study of the Uranian Poets, Timothy d'Arch Smith notes that the movement was dying by 1930 (d'Arch Smith, 154), perhaps as a consequence of the inability of writers to sustain the theme of male love, for either man or boy, without arousing an irresistible degree of public curiosity or outright hostility.

To many homosexuals the culture of ancient Greece provided a source of comfort, for in its literature homosexual love was praised, but the approbation seemed primarily confined to relationships between older and younger men and within strict social rules and taboos, sexual love between men of similar ages seemingly not so readily commended (Dover, 16);* moreover for some Greek philosophers, notably Plato, the highest expression of homosexual love was essentially non-physical.

Despite the qualifications some of the the ancient Greeks writers may have placed on homosexuality, or rather paederasty as it should perhaps more correctly be called, these did not stop its civilisation from being a source of strength and affirmation to homosexual men since the Renaissance through to the present-day. And in *Where Angels Fear to Tread, The Longest Journey, A Passage to India* and *Maurice*, Forster writes of love between adult males using references drawn from his classical studies. With Forster ancient Greece was a personal touchstone for feeling; the praise of athletic attainments, the adoration of the male form, the democracy of Eros and the Theban Band all find expression in his work. In this however he was not unusual, for the public schools in general inculcated a respect for ancient Greek civilization in its

---

* The historian John Boswell suggests however that writers have wrongly inferred from the literary stereotypes of fourth-century Athens that all homosexual relationships in ancient Greece were age-related, whereas the actual evidence suggests that 'this picture is exaggerated even for Athens, and homosexual relationships in the rest of ancient Europe were certainly far more varied and flexible than this, probably not much different from their heterosexual counterparts' (Boswell, 71).

teaching of the Classics, and the works of contemporary writers like Walter Pater and A. E. Housman popularised these and other selected aspects of ancient Greek culture. Like many of the Uranian poets, Forster utilised references to ancient myths in his work, frequently using them as an encoded language, as pointers to homoerotic associations; an example of this, from *The Longest Journey*, being Stephen Wonham's link with the bisexual shepherds described in the *Idylls* of the ancient Greek writer Theocritus (LJ, 88, 111-4).

Homosexuality and male love were not therefore taboo subjects but ones in which the public discourse was controlled by science, the Church, social attitudes generally and the laws of censorship. Knowledge of a more practical, less sentimental kind was restricted to what would be viewed perhaps by us today as an ill-informed few; many of course were profoundly misinformed. And until the debate about homosexuality is settled, then no doubt new perspectives will continue to shift the debate surrounding the subject in general, and in particular the creative practices of those who happen to be homosexual — gay, queer, or whatever.

Other, more personal aspects of his life as a homosexual intruded into Forster's work, namely the influence of friends such as Hugh Owen Meredith, in *Maurice* and *The Longest Journey*, and of Mohammed el Adl and Sayed Ross Masood in *A Passage to India*, as well as the need Forster felt to keep his mother, Alice Clara Forster, *née* Whichelo (known as 'Lily') in ignorance of her son's preferences.

One further feature of the writings by homosexual men of the late nineteenth and early twentieth century which Forster shared was an interest in travel and ethnographical writing. According to David Bergman, 'no literary form was more congenial to gay writers of the nineteenth and early twentieth centuries than the ethnographic study, and it was in ethnographic discourse that homosexual writers often found the terms for their attack on heterosexuality'. Bergman notes that this type of study provides the gay writer with 'the opportunity to subvert several types of otherness', for 'The foreign, attacked by xenophobic heterosexual discourse, is elevated, and the pagan (non-Christian) is extolled for its honesty, vision, and humanity' (Bergman, 35).

At first glance it may not be apparent how Forster's writing could be described as ethnographic (apart obviously from his essays on India and Alexandria), however in his fiction we can see ethnographical modes of discourse co-opted into his work. His Italian novels praise certain aspects of that country, and compare them unfavorably with the coldness and emotional repression found in the English character in general — in *Where Angels Fear to Tread* Sawston has nothing to compare favourably to Monteriano. Whilst the southern races of Europe fare badly in imperialist discourse, being, within its terms, allegedly the degenerate people of past great empires, still to Forster they possess qualities unknown to the average blinkered chauvinist. J. A. Symonds praised Italy in his writings and the country was associated generally with a relaxed attitude to sexuality in general and homosexuality in particular. Similarly, in *A Room with a View*, Forster presents the pagan world with its acceptance of human sensuality on a higher moral plane than the debased medieval body-hating Christianity of northern Europe; and in the 'unpublishable' story 'The Life to Come' the Indian ruler represents an 'honesty, vision, and humanity' which is completely alien to the Christian missionary Pinmay. Likewise, it was in India, not in England, that Forster in *A Passage to India* found a setting and a myth, in the story of Krishna and his milkmaids, whereby he could express his fantasy of formerly separated pairs of lovers joined together by their love to the divine. Forster however never recommended a total retreat to more favorable climes; he was aware that every society has its own peculiar drawbacks and he preferred to remain in England where he did, intermittently, find a love to sustain him.

So it can be seen that Forster, being homosexual, was effectively silenced in his public writings during both the conventional processes of creation and of publication. He was placed in a position, which according to Thomas E. Yingling is a not uncommon one for gay writers, in which he had to work through the basic 'contradiction of being empowered to speak but unable to say' (quoted in Bergman, 11). Yet despite this his writings do bear the imprint of his sexuality, whether consciously as in the camp verbal irony of *A Room with a View*, or unconsciously as in 'The Story of a Panic'. And whilst showing a resistance towards literary convention, which he privately condemned as for him creatively destructive, nevertheless he was aware of how he could 'bend' socially acceptable conventions to his own ends — such as his praise of the values of ancient Greece, of athletic prowess and of 'manly love' — using them thematically in his works and exploiting the constrained potential they gave him for limited self-expression.

Lastly, throughout this work reference is made to Forster as 'homosexual'. Robert K. Martin in *Queer Forster* described the writer as 'an author who is so clearly gay' (1). I would dispute his use of 'clearly', but as a settled definition of 'gay' seems as elusive as that for 'queer', would not wish in this work to be drawn into semantics. A conscious decision was made to use 'homosexual' rather than 'gay', believing that readers are sophisticated enough to comprehend any negative connotations that word might convey, without an intrusive, authorial nannying on my part, though I believe some preliminary discussion of the pitfalls attendant upon the use of 'homosexual' would help to set the word in context.

To describe Forster as 'gay' seems inappropriate, for the cultural connotations presently attached to the word (basically linked to the lifestyle choices available to the present-day gay man and unknown to Forster himself) appear alien to the world in which the writer was at his most productive. In his Introduction to *Sexual Sameness: Textual Differences in Lesbian and Gay Writing*, Joseph Bristow warns of the dangers posed to gay and lesbian critics (and to their works) by an unthinking use of the word 'homosexual':

---

* According to Jeffrey Weeks the word 'homosexual' was first used in 1869 'coined by the Swiss doctor Karoly Maria Benkert... it did not enter English currency until the 1890s' (Weeks 1977, 3).

Homosexuality is the word we are still too often made to share, even though it is clearly one we have jointly learned to subvert and resist. This unhelpful and misleading sexual, legal, medical, and ultimately moral classification has for many decades compounded our differences, and in its exceptionally inflexible implementation it has served to mask a great many confusions about sex, gender, and sexuality that saturate western culture. (Bristow 1992, 3)

Bristow notes the appearance of the word in the late Victorian period when 'the category of the homosexual became a clinical definition* that recognised for the first time, as Michel Foucault put it, a type of person, rather than a sexual activity'. Bristow's main objection to the term is that 'homosexuality denies the gendered difference between men and women who desire their own sex' (3). As this critique deals entirely with male homosexuality, the profound differences between male and female homosexuality are not to the fore in the discussion of the issues presented, though Bristow's observation ought to be borne in mind by the reader. Similarly, 'homoeroticism' when used in this work will only refer to eroticism between men, though clearly it could also be a term applied equally to eroticism between women. Where the word 'gay' has been used it is applied sparingly to denote a particular late twentieth-century position and primarily in situations where critics have chosen to use the term in their own discussions to refer to male homosexuality.

WHERE ANGELS FEAR TO TREAD

Although the first of Forster's novels to appear in print, in 1905, *Where Angels Fear to Tread* was not his first attempt at writing a novel; that distinction belongs to the unfinished 'Nottingham Lace'. Forster's second attempt was his 'Lucy' novel, which after much re-writing eventually became *A Room with a View*, though only after the author had completed and published, in 1907, yet another novel, *The Longest Journey*.

The development of Forster's creative life between 'Nottingham Lace' and *A Room with a View* will be considered later in this study. Particular aspects of Forster's work and its relationship to his homosexuality however are apparent in his first two published novels. *Where Angels Fear to Tread* demonstrates the importance of Italy as a land in which homosexual romance may prosper. The character of Gino acts as a human embodiment of the easy masculine power, brutality and sensuality which enlightens and excites the sexually repressed Philip Herriton (and which seemed to delight Forster also). England, or rather the narrow England which Sawston society represents in the novel, can offer no comparable experience. The romance of Italy for Forster is derived in part from its past links to ancient Greece, and this aspect of his work is further developed in *The Longest Journey*. In that novel, however, England does prove to be the setting of homoerotic romance and the character Stephen Wonham occupies a similar position to that of Gino, whereby he becomes the object of desire for Rickie Elliot, a character who, like the sexually inexperienced Philip Herriton, is in part based upon Forster himself.

The problems associated with English life, mainly of sexual and emotional repression, and the eulogising of certain aspects of Italian social life, continue as themes in Forster's later work. The young lovers in *A Room with a View* find their salvation in Florence, though the philosophy which informs their new freedom derives mainly from Anglo-Saxon sources — primarily Walt Whitman and Edward Carpenter. The openly homosexual upper-class socialist Carpenter, who lived in a country retreat with George Merrill, his working-class lover, supplied Forster with a framework of ideas which enabled him to come to a positive understanding of his own sexuality; and a subsequent visit to Carpenter's home also provided Forster with the impetus to write *Maurice*, his private 'unpublishable' novel dealing with sexual love between men.

For Trilling, and for many readers since, the story of *Where Angels Fear to Tread* 'begins in a comedy of manners, goes on to fierceness and melodrama and ends in an enlightened despair' (Trilling, 52). For Tariq Rahman, however, who bases his analysis of the novel in part on the work of Judith S. Herz, the comedy of manners provides the surface heterosexual plot which obscures the homosexual under-plot that deals primarily with the relationship between Gino and Philip, yet also covers male relationships in Italy in general, and Philip's acceptance of what, outside of its artistic heritage, Italy offers to him. Rahman's analysis, of course, is supported by the wealth of material now available on Forster's private life and works; he, unlike Trilling, had the sure knowledge of Forster's sexual orientation upon which to construct his analyses of the texts.

The ambiguity of words, the fact that they may mislead, intentionally as well as unintentionally, is a theme found in *Where Angels Fear to Tread*, and Forster's narrator soon alerts readers to the possibility that there is a another, less socially respectable, story secreted beneath the apparently straightforward 'surface' one of a doomed Anglo-Italian heterosexual romance. The fact that with new knowledge comes a new reading of a text, and that much may lie hidden in but a few simple words, is disclosed in the novel after only a few opening pages. Once previously suppressed material comes to light then a re-evaluation of what had been written under its influence is inevitable; ignorance had formerly led seemingly innocent and apparently uncomplicated statements to be accepted unquestioningly, but with additional knowledge any continuance of naivety becomes untenable. Just as the information concerning Forster's homosexuality has led to a re-examination of his work, so too does the knowledge of Lilia's real desires prompt Mrs Herriton to re-read her daughter-in-law's letter and to discover new meanings within it. The ambiguity of Lilia's words is revealed ironically, and the humour of it may at first distract the reader from the seriousness of the narrator's disclosure. When Mrs Herriton first received Lilia's letters, she accepted their content at face value; once she hears however that Lilia has become romantically attached to a young Italian, she re-interprets her most recent letter and the entry in Baedecker concerning Monteriano, the town in which Lilia is staying:

> She would not allow herself to be frightened by the unknown. Indeed she knew a little now.... She recalled phrases of this morning's letter: 'We love this place — Caroline is sweeter than ever, and busy sketching — Italians full of simplicity and charm'. And the remark of Baedeker, 'the inhabitants are still noted for their agreeable manners', had a baleful meaning now. (WAFT, 13)

The casual reader could easily pay little attention to this passage, believing perhaps that it reflects merely the imagined fears of an over-protective old woman. The narrator, however, intrudes to observe that Mrs Herriton had no imagination but 'she had intuition, a more useful quality, and the picture she made to herself of Lilia's fiancé did not prove altogether wrong' (WAFT, 13). The implied lesson is clear: the writer knows how to write what superficially may seem acceptable, indeed uncomplicated, both to himself and to his readers; intuitive and informed readers, though, may correctly infer more. In the case of the letter it is Lilia who hides facts from her mother-in-law, just as in this novel Forster refrains from spelling out too overtly for his readers the precise nature of the relationship between Philip and Gino.

One of the themes of the book is that for many people (in Edwardian England at least), much of life's passion lies hidden beneath staid convention. An original reviewer of the novel for the *Manchester Guardian* noted that the work dealt with 'the revelation of suppressed qualities beneath conventional exteriors, as in Philip Herriton, the passion for Italy beneath the cold, critical English nature' (reprinted in P. Gardner, 49); yet another critic, C. F. G. Masterman in the *Daily News*, wrote that the 'triumph of the ordered conventional world over the revolt of the incongruous, queer, and passionate desires is one of the motifs of the tale' (P. Gardner, 53). The characters who fight most against convention are of course Philip Herriton and Caroline Abbot, but the novel's main concern is with Philip whose 'incongruous, queer, and passionate desires' seem to mirror Forster's own.

In a letter he wrote to R. C. Trevelyan on 28 October 1905, Forster made it clear that Philip Herriton is the central character of the novel and that the object of the book is the 'improvement' of Philip. Forster declared that he wanted Philip's 'improvement' to be a surprise, hoping to achieve 'the sentimental, but the sentimental reached by no easy beaten track' (Lago and Furbank 1, 83). What exactly Forster meant by 'sentimental' is not clear from this letter on its own. However, in his biography of Forster, P. N. Furbank provides a definition of what Forster meant when he used the word, for at this time Greece had become Forster's private 'stronghold for sentiment' (Furbank 1, 110). 'Greece' in this context meant not the modern state of Greece but ancient Greece and what, more precisely, Forster, under the tutelage of his friend Goldsworthy Lowes Dickinson, a famous Cambridge classicist, saw as its ever relevant values and ethos — this embodied the 'sentimental' that Philip was meant to achieve. Forster's understanding of certain ancient Greek values delineates the goals towards which Philip, and to a lesser extent Caroline, must move; these values are also the prime yardsticks by which all the characters in the novel are judged by their creator. This can be seen most clearly at the close of the novel, when the three main protagonists, Philip, Gino and Caroline, are reconciled. Forster's narrator describes the triumph of their fleeting union by reference to the ancient Greek legend of the goddess Selene's love for the beautiful youth Endymion. Despite Caroline's inclusion here with the male protagonists, the relationships which are praised in the book are those between men who meet on a supposed democratic, equal footing and often, as Lilia in particular finds out, such relationships are conducted, as in ancient Greece, to the exclusion of women.

Whilst Greece's past provided much inspiration and material for Forster to use in his fiction, so too did his own life experiences and those of his friends. According to Forster in a manuscript memoir (quoted WAFT, x), 'two-thirds' of the character of Philip Herriton was based on that of the musicologist Edward Joseph Dent, a friend of Forster at Cambridge; indeed it was Dent who later suggested the title of the novel which was acceptable to Blackwood, the book's publisher. Dent had earlier spent all of his university vacation periods in Italy, researching into the history of music, in particular the work of Alessandro Scarlatti. Whilst recounting his journeys to Italy, he had encouraged Forster to visit the country, providing him with information regarding suitable accommodation, when and where to visit, and advice on modes of travel.

Dent was also sympathetic to Forster's sexual leanings. He was one of the first people permitted to read *Maurice* and he frequently discussed with Forster the homosexual element in both literature and music (Lago and Furbank 1, 222-3). He undoubtedly would have disclosed to his friend the charms of Italian youth and have told him where they might be obtained. As a result of such promptings Forster set off to visit Italy and Austria on 3 October 1901 — with his mother, Lily, unavoidably in tow. This first visit, and a subsequent one in 1903, were to provide much of the background material Forster used in both *Where Angels Fear To Tread* and *A Room with a View*.

Other titles originally suggested for the novel were 'From a Sense of Duty', by Dent, and 'Monteriano', 'Rescue' and 'Gino' by Forster. Significantly Forster's putative titles emphasise the location in Italy, the fact of rescue, and ambiguously this could refer to the failed 'rescue' of Lilia or to Gino's 'rescue' of Philip and, perhaps, of Caroline also from the crippling conventions of Sawston society; 'Gino' as a title would serve to impress upon the reader his, rather than Philip's, status as the central concern of the novel. And to one early reviewer, Gino was the outstanding character in the novel for, unlike the 'hen-pecked de-sexed husband of England', Gino is one of those 'blatantly masculine specimens that unspoiled Italy can still boast of' (P. Gardner, 46).

Whatever changes of emphasis these former titles may reveal, what is clear is that at the time of composition Forster was concentrating mainly on the male characters involved, that is, Philip and Gino. Of the other titles proposed for the novel, 'Monteriano' draws attention to the importance of place, consequently some discussion would appear necessary on what Italy as a setting appeared to mean to Forster.

Philip's first real knowledge concerning Gino comes from Caroline Abbott, though at the opening of the novel he has already acquired a good knowledge of Italy itself. In one of the earliest discussions between him and Miss Abbott regarding Lilia's proposed marriage, Philip asks her sarcastically about Gino, 'And is he good-looking?' Miss Abbott affirms: 'Very good-looking. All his features are good, and he is well built' (WAFT, 18). She then continues to provide further biographical information about him which falls into a recognised formula, frequently used by Forster in his fiction to describe those males who are, or are about to become, the objects of homoerotic interest to others. Like Fielding and Aziz in *A Passage to India*, Gino has served in the army, and like other attractive young males in Forster's work (for example, George Emerson in *A Room with a View*, Stephen Wonham in *The Longest Journey*), his social position, being the son of a dentist, is seen as somewhat inferior to that of his ultimate admirers. Similarly Gino, like Aziz, and Gerald in *The Longest Journey*, is a good sportsman, here in his chosen field of pallone in which he was a proficient player; and Philip, it is noted, 'loved to watch pallone' (WAFT, 24). Prowess in sport, an emphasised virility, and youth are common aspects of the male love objects represented in Forster's work.

Despite his initial sarcasm and hostility, when Philip actually meets his supposed adversary (for he was sent out to protect Lilia from the brutish Italian), his interest in Gino soon takes on a different aspect. Philip muses as he watches Gino eating 'slippery worms' of spaghetti that he 'had seen that face before in Italy a hundred times — seen it and loved it, for it was not merely beautiful, but had the charm which is the rightful heritage of all who are born on that soil'. Philip however did not want to see that face opposite him at dinner for it was 'not the face of a gentleman' (WAFT, 23). To what extent Philip as a character is aware of the implications of his observations is unclear, for it was part of Forster's declared method during the course of this novel gradually to 'exhibit new pieces of him — pieces that he did not know of, or at all events had never used' (WAFT, 149). Nevertheless Philip clearly associates Italy with beautiful male faces, and with the love of them and their heritage. Given Forster's own homosexual orientation and Philip's homoerotic relationship with the Italian, it is revealing to note exactly what Italy signified, during Forster's early life, in relation to male love.

The critic Tariq Rahman recalls, as many others have also recognised, that in the late nineteenth and early twentieth centuries Italy had a reputation as a land favourable to homosexual romance: 'Italy was notorious since the Renaissance as the land where homosexual pleasures could be procured' (Rahman 1988, 54). Evidence of this reputation abounds in the writings of the period and in the activities of those homosexual artists who found refuge in Italian resorts. Writing in the 1880s, the orientalist and commentator on sexual customs Sir Richard Burton noted that, 'For many years... England sent her pederasts to Italy, and especially to Naples whence originated the term "Il vizio Inglese"' (Burton, 209). And Rahman cites as evidence for the continuance, in this period, of Italy as a place of homosexual pilgrimage, writers such as Frederick William Rolfe, known also as 'Baron Corvo' ,* the Uranian poet Horatio Robert Forbes Brown and John Addington Symonds, amongst others, who 'had either written about erotic liaison with Italian youths or settled down in Italy' (Rahman 1988, 54). In his own writings on that country Forster certainly conceives of it as a place where men could associate with other men, especially with men of the lower classes, more freely than was possible in England.

To what extent Forster was familiar with the work of the writers named by Rahman is uncertain, but there is clear evidence in his letters and diaries of his acquaintance with some of Symonds's public writings on Italy. Writing to

---

* Rolfe's *Stories Toto Told Me*, consisting of tales 'told to him by a simple, illiterate [Italian] peasant boy', and some of his poems in praise of young men, apeared in various British periodicals at the turn of the century (Rolfe, *Collected Poems*, 1974). *The Venice Letters*, written to Charles Masson Fox and describing Rolfe's sexual exploits with certain young gondolieri of that city in 1909–10, were not fully published until 1974, although versions of them had been in circulation before that. A. J. A. Symons, Rolfe's biographer, and the poet A. E. Housman, had both read and commented on the letters before their publication (*The Venice Letters*, 12-13).

Goldsworthy Lowes Dickinson on 15 December 1901, Forster refers to Symonds's essay on Perugia in his *Sketches in Italy and Greece*. In 1892 Symonds published *In the Key of Blue*, a collection of essays on art and literature, the central essay of which describes the gondolier Augusto, Symonds's nineteen-year-old lover, against the background of Venice, the young man's place of birth; and, as will be discussed later in relation to *Maurice*, Forster seems to have been aware of this book. Symonds wrote widely on Italian art and on the debt it owed to ancient Greece, a subject of special interest to Forster, and it is more than likely that so sensitive and acute a reader as he was would have been receptive to Symonds's observations both on Italian art and on Italian society.

Many other closeted British homosexuals found Italy congenial and welcoming. The sexologist Havelock Ellis in his *Sexual Inversion*, originally written the 1880s in partnership with Symonds, noted the attraction Italy had for homosexual men (Ellis 1, 39 and 58). In 1900 the poet and classicist A. E. Housman discovered Venice, and a gondolier named Andrea, and subsequently made a number of return visits there in succeeding years, for 'his foreign visits meant, above all, freedom — a temporary escape from the conventional sexual morality by which... he felt imprisoned' (R. P. Graves, 150 & 163). Likewise, the novelist E. F. Benson, creator of *Mapp and Lucia*, whilst ostensibly celibate and inhibited in England, is thought to 'have disported himself [on the Isle of Capri]... with that abandon which accompanies the certain knowledge that one will never be found out.' His biographer, Brian Masters, observes that by the time of Benson's first visit to the island in the summer of 1896 it already had a reputation for its 'population of beautiful, obliging men and women' (Masters, 185). The trials of Oscar Wilde in the preceding year had led many of those homosexuals who could afford it to leave Britain. One of Benson's friends, John Ellingham Brooks, was just such 'a refugee from an England bound by post-Wildean moral rigidity, and there were on the island a number of other single men who were enjoying the sensation of being left alone' (Masters, 117).

It was not only British homosexuals who found a more liberal climate in Italy; their European counterparts flocked there also — two notable foreign residents being Friedrich Krupp and Wilhelm von Gloeden, further pointing to its popularity with homosexual men of the period. Friedrich Krupp, the German arms magnate, lived apart from his wife for many years in a 'pleasure palace on Capri. When local complaints were investigated in 1902, a story appeared in the Italian newspapers, photographs proved that he had seduced boys and he was forced to leave the country' (Meyers, 8; see also Ellis 1, 39). Whether he had to leave the country because of local feeling, once his activities had become publicly known, or to avoid further scandal from leaking out, is not clear. Harry Oosterhuis suggests the accusations were part of a political plot to discredit the kaiser's armament policy. A similar scandal, also politically motivated, erupted four years later when two of the kaiser's advisors were accused of homosexuality (Oosterhuis and Kennedy, 5).*

---

* cf. Forster's 'unpublishable' story, 'What Does It Matter? A Morality', where accusations of homosexuality are made, and exploited, for political ends.

Wilhelm von Gloeden was a Prussian nobleman and artist who specialised in classicist photographs of beautiful youths in Arcadian settings taken
near Taormina in Sicily around the turn of the century (Weiermair, 5). His
pictures of (frequently naked) young males delicately posed, were produced
without attracting the attentions of the censor, and without expressions of
concern from the Church or the families of the youths involved (Weiermair,
11). Tourists regularly bought his photographs as souvenirs of their visits to
Sicily, and many apparently were quite oblivious to the sexuality expressed in
them.

Von Gloeden and his imitators helped to spread the fame of Italian male
beauty far beyond that country's borders, for even in England itself, at the end
of the nineteenth century, Italian youths were in vogue in Uranian art circles.
Some observers however patriotically argued that Italy certainly did not possess
the finest examples of masculine beauty. Writing in 1897, in an article on 'Pho-
tographic Studies' in the magazine *Photogram*, Robert H. Hobart Cust
contended that 'the much belauded Italian model is not that vision of physical
beauty that might be expected... [for] the average English lad is quite the
equal, if not the superior of the Italian.' And his words were echoed the following year by James Rooth who confidently affirmed that better English models
of youthful male beauty 'were easy to find in bathing places' (d'Arch Smith,
64-5).

Despite the praise given to Italy by European artists, it would be wrong to
infer that the country was without constraints on its homosexual citizenry and
their suitors. Writing on 'Same-sex Love' in 1903, the German homosexual
Edwin Bab noted that in Italy, and in France, same-sex intercourse is exempt
from legal punishment, but added, 'in Italy, despite the lack of a penal clause,
they throw stones at a man if it is supposed of him that he has intercourse with
men or youths' (Oosterhuis and Kennedy, 60).

Given the ubiquity in artistic circles of the time of the association between
Italy and male intimacy, it is hardly suprising that the theme of male friendship
also occurs in a number of the essays Forster wrote, or initially prepared, during
his first two journeys in that country. When visiting Rome in 1902, he made
sketches for the essay 'Malconia Shops'. In it Forster discusses the antiquities
exhibited in the Kirchner Museum, and takes care to describe the scene depicted on a bronze toilet case which shows Jason and his argonauts taking
refreshment on land:

[o]ne is drinking water from a wine-cup as he leans on his spear beside
the splashing spring: others have drunk and are sitting in perfect
physical bliss, having reached the goal of their desire, and found its
happiness not illusory.... As the heroes are refreshed, their faculties
awake in their fullness, and strong and vivid is the love they bear and
have borne for each other. That love has never died, but has shared the
eclipse and the weakness of the body. (AH, 168-9)

That Forster saw direct links between this ancient ideal of unifying love between comrades and contemporary Italy can be seen in the following passages from another related essay of his, 'Gemistus Pletho', and from an early draft of what was later to become *A Room with a View*. In 'Gemistus Pletho', initially written on Forster's diversionary journey to Greece during his second Italian trip in 1903, he writes about the fifteenth-century Greek writer Pletho, who bemoaned the demise of ancient Greece. In the essay Forster agrees with Pletho that the values of ancient Greek civilisation had long since left the Hellenic Republic. Nonetheless those same values have blossomed in Italy, and may even do so in England:

> [the] revival of ancient Greece which he [Pletho] so ardently desired became even more impossible. He did not see that the revival had really taken place in Italy; that Greece is a spirit which can appear, not only at any time, but also in any land. (AH, 182)

In the Lucy novels, the collected early drafts of 'Old Lucy' and 'New Lucy' which were later to become *A Room with a View*, we can see how Forster began to draw together the themes of male love, ancient Greece and contemporary Italy. He applies the resultant mixture of ideas to the young men he encountered on his travels, presenting not only the possibility of the ideal, but also the apparent failure of its manifestation in those same young men, whose admirable and dubious traits of character recall Gino in *Where Angels Fear to Tread*, and which could so easily recall Symonds's Augusto, Housman's Andrea or any other manly specimen of the 'much belauded Italian model':

> The Italian boys are the cupbearers of the Gods and the Italian youths are the Gods themselves. Of course 'youth' is not the proper word, for in a land like England where they do not exist there is of course no name for them. But there was a name for them in ancient Greek, and in Latin, and there is a name for them in their own tongue. And having passed through all Olympus by the age of 25, and having pestered you «<with> for pennies» \with dead flowers & stale fruit & fresh antiquities/as Ganymede and «grossly overcharged you in <on> [sic] your cab » \having shaken you to a jelly in a cab & then grossly overcharged you/ as Apollo, and misdirected you or dropped your<boxes>\ trunks /in the mud as Mercury, they<become>suddenly become, if you have complied with their<demands>\ extortions /, very fat and corporeal and spend the rest of their days leaning against anything that will support them<, aimiable [sic] and unlovely>. But if you do not comply they suddenly become very thin and though \\ [—] for mortals govern the lives of the gods as much \now/ as they did in the days of Homer [—] //they have fallen from heaven it is <alway[s]>often in their mind, and when they are thinking of it, it does not make you happy to see them. (Lucy, 11-12)

The mention of Ganymede is, of course, a significant reference to the legendary cupbearer of the gods; a youth adored, abducted and subsequently possessed by the god Zeus in the form of an eagle, and whose name has been ubiquitously used as a euphemism for 'catamite' in ephebophilic literature throughout Western history. These Italian Ganymedes are all working-class youths employed in physical labour of one kind or another, and are the type of rough trade that excited Forster, Rolfe, Housman, Benson et al. They are also the types who dominate Forster's description of Florence at the opening of Chapter 2 of *A Room with a View*. There we read of river men at work with spades and sieves, boatmen, a tram conductor, little boys, one old man selling buttonhooks, and soldiers, 'good-looking, undersized men' with their officers 'looking foolish and fierce' (RV, 14).

Discussions about national character are an important feature of Forster's writings, and the traits of men who inhabit a country are deemed important by two of his characters in this novel, Philip and his mother. Mrs Herriton asserts that Italy may be full of beautiful pictures and churches, but that one 'cannot judge a country by anything but its men'; to which Philip ruefully rejoins: 'That is quite true' (WAFT, 57). Note that Forster specifies 'men', women being excluded from any summation of nationality. This observation in the novel ironically points the fact that the only English man we see in any depth in the work is Philip, the other main English characters being women; indeed only Gino perhaps could be described as particularly masculine, though he shares this attribute with his many friends and acquaintances.

Looking at an earlier draft of *Where Angels Fear To Tread* we can see the familiar Forsterian pattern whereby male love and the crossing of class boundaries are romantically linked; Philip's dilemmas are specifically connected to these issues. A passage which was subsequently removed by Forster from the final version of the novel clearly makes the point that male liaisons across the barrier of class were one of Italy's many attractions:

> Let us have the truth, though it is the saddest truth in all the world. O friends, dear friends of mine, whom I have made in Italy! — cabmen, waiters, sacristans, shop assistants, soldiers, friars, porters at wayside stations, lighthouse-keepers, boatmen at Syracuse, muleteers in the Sabines, stokers on Adriatic steamers! — we have been friends for years, I think, when we first met, for the stress went out of life and we understood each other's gestures, and talked or were silent as we chose. You told me everything, and I told you more than I shall ever tell my true and tried acquaintance here. Then we parted with warm handgrasp, wondering why we had been kept apart so long. And, thank goodness, I shall never see one of you again!
>
> So it was with Philip, my true and tried acquaintance, who on this occasion, as on so many others, feels and behaves as I do. (WAFT, 158)

As Forster was accompanied on both of his early journeys to Italy by his mother, it is unlikely that the narrator's account of his Italian experiences in the above extract corresponds exactly to that of the author; as Furbank affirms, Forster's first trip to Italy was a 'timid outing' and neither he nor his mother made any Italian friends. Nevertheless, in the author's imagination, there is no reason why 'Philip, my true and tried acquaintance' might not enjoy adventures that were denied his creator; Philip may well 'feel', if not quite behave, 'as I do'. Furbank goes on to point out however, quoting in part from an earlier draft of the 'Lucy' novel, that Italy had nonetheless 'warmed Forster and given him a vision, and ever afterwards he would think of it gratefully as "The beautiful country where they say 'yes'"', and the place "where things happen"' (Furbank 1, 96).

The physical and emotional relationships between men that Forster writes of invariably possess the ability to cross class and race boundaries. The essentially democratic nature of his ideal of male love is so often in his novels placed in direct opposition to the conventional heterosexual institution of marriage. Marriage is invariably presented as a prison, at least for the male partner, and often for the female. Also it usually involves people from similar class backgrounds, unlike male relationships in Forster which generally transcend differences of class and race.

Frequently Forster's ambivalent attitude towards women is to the fore. In *Where Angels Fear To Tread*, Lilia's demands for her husband's attentions and her sense of social superiority are shown to threaten her spouse's affability towards his fellows, especially those low-class males with whom Gino prefers to associate (WAFT, 35). Gino, we read, 'delighted in travel, and seemed to pick up friends all over the country', and 'Lilia often heard what a favourite he was' (WAFT, 43). When his friend Spiridione speaks of those who are *simpatico*, Gino declares that 'There are such men, I know', but has no idea where to find a woman with the same quality (WAFT, 39). Lilia does not have her husband's freedom of association and her imprisonment in marriage is presented sympathetically. Nonetheless the point is made: she, being a married woman, cannot meet Gino's friends without encountering the severe difficulties placed in her way by social convention and the tyranny of her husband. Deep down in Gino there was 'plenty of brutality' (WAFT, 45) and Lilia soon realises that he has married her for her money. Her marriage had caused her to be estranged from almost all of her family and friends; in Italy she was friendless and a prisoner in her own home. Philip, being a man, is not similarly constrained and can enjoy an easy association with Gino and his circle.

Lilia's justifiable complaint leads to the following observation from the narrator, which not only reflects her experience of Italian society, but also reveals Forster's grossly idealised and partisan view of Italian (male) social life, where women disrupt a 'brotherhood' which has been 'accomplished at the expense of sisterhood', for once a man introduces a woman into the scene 'immediately all your wonted [male] acquaintance there desert you' (WAFT,

36). After a frustrating talk with Gino, Lilia realises the restrictions placed on her as a woman by continental society:

> Italy is such a delightful place to live in if you happen to be a man. There one may enjoy that exquisite luxury of socialism — that true socialism which is based not on equality of income or character, but on the equality of manners. In the democracy of the *caffè* or the street the great question of our life has been solved, and the brotherhood of man is a reality. But it is accomplished at the expense of the sisterhood of women. Why should you not make friends with your neighbour at the theatre or in the train, when you know and he knows that feminine criticism and feminine insight and feminine prejudice will never come between you! Though you become as David and Jonathan, you need never enter his home, nor he yours. All your lives you will meet under the open air, the only roof-tree of the South, under which he will spit and swear, and you will drop your h's, and nobody will think the worse of either. (WAFT, 35-6)

Although Forster is a writer who frequently employs irony, and clearly there is irony in this extract, nevertheless it is difficult not to feel that the narrator, and his creator, share similar outlooks where not only positive, and potentially threatening, attributes such as 'insight', but also negative attributes such as 'criticism' and 'prejudice', can be assigned to the 'feminine'. On a more down-to-earth note, the narrator's tetchiness with regard to women may echo the effect that travelling with his mother to Italy may have had on Forster. With her almost constantly by his side, opportunities for him freely to socialise with attractive working-class males would be practically non-existent. His biblical reference to the friendship between David and Jonathan serves as a obvious signifier of manly love, and as we can see from Forster's essay 'Via Nomentana', to open, democratic, universal and civilised male love.

'Via Nomentana' describes an evening walk in the Campagna; Forster musing on the ideal of friendship writes of that affection which 'flashed forth for a moment in David and Jonathan but first shone as a heaven in ancient Greece, proclaiming to barbarians that human affection need not be confined to the home circle or extended to the harem' (Furbank 1, 90). It is this ideal of friendship which conventional (Sawston) heterosexuality appears to threaten, although as we can see later with Caroline Abbott and in Gino's apparent heterosexual promiscuity, relationships with women do not always threaten such male friendships, indeed Caroline is instrumental in the later reconciliation of Philip and Gino.

Given Forster's views it is perhaps easier to see why Lilia dies so suddenly in the novel. Christopher Gillie complains that Forster 'cheats the reader's expectations by removing Lilia' (Gillie, 97), but the novel is primarily concerned with Philip and Gino, and although Lilia had brought the two together, she was also somewhat in their way. Early in the novel, the narrator wastes no time in pointing out the negative effects upon Philip of Lilia and Gino's marriage:

> Lilia's marriage toppled contentment down forever. Italy, the land of
> beauty, was ruined for him.... It was on her soil and through her
> influence that a silly woman had married a cad. He hated Gino, the
> betrayer of his life's ideal and now that the sordid tragedy had come it
> filled him with pangs, not of sympathy, but of final disillusion. (WAFT,
> 55)

We notice not only Philip's fury at the marriage, but also that his anger is directed at Gino, whom he dubs 'the betrayer of his life's ideal' — which 'ideal' it is not quite clear. Has Gino betrayed him by failing to live up to Philip's ideal of friendship or that of the ancient Greeks, and how did this ruin 'Italy, the land of beauty'? Clearly it is bound up with the position which Gino holds for Philip of embodying both artistic and homoerotic desire. Italy had seemed to promise him a fulfilment he would never know in Sawston. The reality of Gino's character — heterosexual, moody, boorish and not particularly sensitive to Philip's adulation of Italian art — brings Philip's idealisation of him crashing down to earth, and so Lilia's marriage comes to imply a profound betrayal, bringing pangs of 'final disillusion'. Reversal of this state of affairs would appear to demand an alteration in Philip or the parting of Lilia and Gino, and both these events occur. By removing Lilia, Philip is presented with the rescue of her baby as a further reason to encounter Gino and subsequently to discover those new facets of his character which would entrance him. Once Lilia has gone, the female 'barrier' to male friendship is removed, though the erection of a new 'barrier' is threatened by the reappearance of another woman, Caroline Abbott.

Despite the negative and ironic references to Lilia, she is not solely blamed for the early difficulties of the marriage, as Gino's failings as a husband are also detailed. The end of their union was predicted by the narrator who warned that the institution of marriage, at least between members of differing national groups, seems to be inescapably doomed to failure (WAFT, 50-1).

In general in Forster's work heterosexual relationships between members of different nationalities suffer because of national prejudices and attitudes. Male friendships, however, such as that of Philip and Gino, and of Fielding and Aziz in *A Passage to India*, survive longer under such pressures because the ideal of friendship that guides them is that of ancient Greece. This, to Forster, is potentially far stronger than any nationalistic ideology; for 'Greece is a spirit which can appear, not only at any time, but also in any land' and, as such, although the ideal may flourish in some lands more than others, it is not any one land's perquisite. This is not to assert that male friendships wholly withstand nationalism, for clearly in *A Passage to India* they do not, though the narrator in that novel notes that an Anglo-Indian woman will come more quickly to hate a native than will an Anglo-Indian man.

This freedom to love without apparent discrimination, which had so vexed Lilia, is presented as one of Gino's virtues; 'he made friends with the people he liked, for he was that glorious invariable creature, a man' (WAFT, 46). It is, therefore, not surprising that as a character he becomes attractive to Philip Herriton and undoubtedly to Forster himself. Although the character of Philip was asserted by Forster to have been based primarily on Dent, he also acknowledged that Philip possessed elements of himself (Colmer, 58). There are obvious surface similarities between Philip Herriton's life story and that of his creator. Philip, like Forster, 'was a tall, weakly-built young man', and 'as a boy, he was keenly conscious of these defects'; the description of Philip proceeds:

> His face was plain rather than not, and there was a curious mixture in it of good and bad. He had a fine forehead and a good large nose, and both observation and sympathy were in his eyes. But below the nose and eyes all was confusion, and those people who believe that destiny resides in the mouth and the chin shook their heads when they looked at him (WAFT, 54).

A relative of Forster's had likewise expressed concern that the shape of the writer's chin had indicated he would be unlikely to prove successful in life. This likeness is taken up in the 1991 film version of the novel, where Rupert Graves, who plays Philip, is made to look rather like a young Forster. The biographical similarities continue for both Philip and his creator were bullied at school (WAFT, 54 and Furbank 1, 42-3). Philip 'had got a sense of beauty and a sense of humour' (WAFT, 54), surely qualities also possessed by Forster; he went to Italy for the first time at the age of twenty-two (WAFT, 54), as did Forster (Furbank 1, 80); and both were forced to travel there in the company of uncongenial female relatives. In other Forster works we find similar characters who share attributes with their creator, Rickie in *The Longest Journey* and Edgar in 'Nottingham Lace', for example; and just as Philip admires the masculinity of Gino, so does Rickie admire Gerald and Stephen, and Edgar admire Sidney. Clearly Forster described covertly some of his own sexual fantasies in bringing characters like himself into intimate proximity with virile young men.

Forster paid a second visit to Italy shortly after Easter 1903, again with his mother and on this occasion also with her friend Mrs Mawe. He accompanied them as far as Florence, leaving them there and taking a short trip to Greece, before returning to Italy to meet up again with his mother and his friend E. J. Dent. They later attended a performance in Florence of Donizetti's opera *Lucia di Lammermoor* which he used as the basis for the scene at the theatre in *Where Angels Fear to Tread*. He returned to England in August of the same year.

Between Forster's first journey to Italy and his second, a significant major personal event had occurred. Forster recorded that he had finally accepted his own homosexual orientation, in the winter of 1902, and that this, and his move to agnosticism, were reconstructing his life (Furbank 1, 121). On his second trip to Italy, as with Philip Herriton's third, a significant change of perception had occurred. In the description of Philip's first and second, hesitant and disturbing visits to Italy, we may find echoes of Forster's own initial visit. Similarly Philip's third experience of Italian society generally is to him more pleasing (and more 'physical', for he spends more time in the company of men he likes rather than in looking at Italian art), and he has had time to assimilate the disillusion and subsequent reorientation occasioned by his first encounter with Gino, who for Philip continued to embody all he had hoped to find in Italy. Likewise, when Forster went to Italy for a second time, he did so with a firmer understanding of his own sexuality, which correspondingly affected his perception of what he experienced there.

Philip's changed attitude to Gino and Italy appears superficially to have been triggered off by Miss Abbott telling him of the baby, and how Gino had apologised for their tussle eighteen months earlier, the narrator pointing out how 'This tiny piece of civility had changed his mood' (WAFT, 88), and adding:

> What did the baby matter when the world was suddenly right way up? Philip smiled, and was shocked at himself for smiling, and smiled again. For romance had come back to Italy; there were no cads in her; she was beautiful, courteous, lovable, as of old (WAFT, 88).

In his discussion of this scene, Trilling sees Philip's change of attitude purely in his relation to the country itself (Trilling, 60), failing to emphasise that the romance of Italy for Philip is inextricably related to his friendship with Gino. The homoerotic element in their relationship is simply not recognised, even though it is clear that it is the possibility of restoring this bond with Gino which brings back the idea of Italian 'romance' to Philip; by conventionally referring to Italy by the pronoun of 'she', Forster fudges what seem to be Philip's real feelings on the matter, namely that 'beautiful, courteous, lovable' are the adjectives he would readily apply to Gino and not merely to the place of his birth.

On Philip's return to Monteriano their relationship enters a new phase initiated by a night at the opera. That evening Caroline 'rejoiced in the existence of beauty', and Philip 'forgot himself as well as his mission. He was not even an enthusiastic visitor. For he had been in this place always. It was his home' (WAFT, 95). The phrase 'he had been in this place always' clearly refers to a spiritual place rather than the physical one, and recalls Forster's notion that the spirit of ancient Greece, in which Philip begins now to find 'his home', can appear at any time and in any land.

An ironically described incident, of a seemimgly misdirected love letter, heralds further revelation of the nature of the friendship between Philip and Gino and its ability, unlike heterosexual love, to encompass the friendship of others. By accident Philip finds himself at the theatre in Monteriano holding a billet-doux, supposedly intended for the leading soprano of the performance. Philip, appealing to the crowd for guidance in returning the letter to its originator, is informed by the audience that it was written by a young man and that his 'innamorato is to the left' (WAFT, 96). When he hands back to the young man the note and the bouquet it had been placed in, Philip becomes himself the object of affection, for 'his own hands were seized affectionately' and, Forster adds, it 'all seemed quite natural' (WAFT, 96). The friendly young man turns out to be Gino, and Philip is swiftly guided towards his box: 'Amiable youths bent out of the box and invited him to enter it' (WAFT, 97). Significantly Philip only joins Gino once the Englishwomen, Caroline and Philip's sister, have vacated the theatre. Philip has ostensibly received the love note from Gino by chance, but clearly for Forster he was its intended recipient, though the writer could not have mused openly on the good fortune of this happenstance. In a novel written for general publication in Britain during the Edwardian period, Gino could not have sent a billet-doux directly to Philip without revealing too much about their relationship, but under the cloak of a humorous misdirection, ironically narrated, both men can effectively exchange such letters and the sentiments they contain. And who but a select and knowing readership would see more.

In the opera box, surrounded by his new male friends, Philip is supremely happy, and it is not insignificant that these friends are young and working class, nor that similarly honoured along with him is a soldier, and again, significantly, a private not an officer:

Philip had whispered introductions to the pleasant people who had pulled him in — tradesmen's sons perhaps they were, or medical students, or solicitors' clerks, or sons of other dentists. There is no knowing who is who in Italy. The guest of the evening was a private soldier. He shared the honour now with Philip (WAFT, 97).

'There is no knowing who is who in Italy,' that is, male love there promises to be free of the class-consciousness which plagues English society. Here Philip can be unselfconsciously 'enchanted by the kind, cheerful voices, the laughter that was never vapid, and the light caress of the arm [of Gino or of the soldier?] across his back' (WAFT, 97). The young private soldier is one of a type which recurs in Forster's writings and it was a fact of special interest to Philip, when he first heard of Gino, that the Italian had just finished his military service as a private (WAFT, 19).

It falls to Caroline to register the guilt and unease that might well have attended this celebration were Philip (and thereby possibly Forster prior to accepting his homosexuality) not now at home in such male company. She was 'bathed in beauty within and without' and felt a happiness she had felt only once before, on the night Gino and Lilia had told her of their love. That night she now begins to see as evil; she feels shame and 'began to beat down her happiness, knowing it to be sinful', but the music, applause and laughter of Monteriano and its 'angry young men' haunt her dreams that night and triumph, leaving her on awakening to view her home in provincial England and not Monteriano as the cause of her distress (WAFT, 98-9). Her struggle mirrors that early period of disquiet with regard to Italy felt by Philip and it leads her into closer sympathy with him and his 'unconventionality' (WAFT, 101)

The love between Lilia and Gino had failed to transcend the national and cultural differences between them, as Mrs Herriton had predicted (WAFT, 50). But as for the love of Gino and Philip, 'the two men parted with a good deal of genuine affection. For the barrier of language is sometimes a blessed barrier, which only lets pass what is good' (WAFT 124). Though parting, 'genuine affection' remains and some aspects of the national and racial divide, that is 'language', appear to have aided rather than hindered the growth of their affection. Male friendships may possibly succeed because the social demands placed upon such relationships are small compared to those placed, in general, on heterosexual relationships within marriage. The union of Lilia and Gino brought into conflict differing national, gender and class expectations which could not be reconciled. Male love, because of its ambiguous position in most societies, appears to have transcended those divisions. Such attachments, being largely unseen, unregarded, misregarded or wholly condemned without consideration, can thereby contain a freedom of action unknown to a heterosexual relationship. Heterosexual relations, especially in marriage, have nearly always been 'public' relationships also; homosexuality nearly always a private relation. Whilst Lilia and Caroline are significant characters in the surface 'heterosexual' romantic plot, in the 'homosexual' under-plot they are purely conduits in the relationship between Philip and Gino.

The death of Lilia's and Gino's son is, of course, the time of greatest crisis in Gino's and Philip's friendship. In the violence that follows there is in Gino's torture of Philip a strong hint of sexual sado-masochism, which Forster himself belatedly acknowledged. Forster defended his initial ignorance of the implications of this passage of the novel by declaring that when he was younger he could write about beauty and lust without knowing which was which, for 'neither has nor needs to have a name' (LJ, 302-3).

Before writing *Where Angels Fear to Tread*, Forster had completed a short story, also set in Italy, in which he had similarly failed to realise until much later what exactly he had been writing about. In May 1902 on a visit to Ravello during his first trip to Italy, he had begun to write 'The Story of a Panic'. In his posthumously published essay, 'My Books and I', Forster reveals that one early reader of the story, Charles Sayle, had suggested to John Maynard Keynes, a Cambridge friend of Forster's, that the story dealt with bestiality and buggery.* This

---

* Sayle had suggested that Eustace, the fourteen-year-old English boy at the centre of the story, had been buggered by an Italian waiter at his hotel and that, finding the experience congenial, Eustace had gone out to bugger a goat (LJ, 302). The text of the story does not obviously seem to support Sayle's interpretation, though it may be noted in passing that Forster's description of the waiter, Gennaro, does recall that of Gino. And according to the narrator, Eustace was thought a rather delicate boy, but 'what he really needed was discipline' (CS, 2).

opinion subsequently reached Forster who reacted angrily, maintaining that he had written nothing about sex in the story. In later years however, Forster realised that 'in a stupid and unprofitable way', Sayle had been quite right and that this had triggered his angry denunciation. Forster, whilst denying Sayle's interpretation of his story, nonetheless admitted that he had been aroused as he wrote it, and that the passages which had excited him most were those of which Sayle had declared that 'something was up'. Forster went on to link this arousal to the excitement he experienced whilst writing of the violence between Gino and Philip, declaring that this too had stirred him though he neither knew nor wondered why, averring that even if he had heard of masochism he should have denied any connection (LJ, 302).

Later in the writer's career it was quite possible to see how Philip's humiliation by Gino could provide a vicarious release for Forster himself, when he stated that he too desired 'to love a strong young man of the lower classes and be loved by him and even hurt by him' (LTC, xiv).* Forster denied in 'Kanaya' (his private record of his stay at the home of the Maharajah of Dewas Senior) that he gained any satisfaction from adminstering pain, whilst recording an incident in which he did just that. Kanaya was a catamite provided for him by the heterosexual, but sympathetic, maharajah. He subsequently annoyed Forster by propositioning the maharajah himself. Fearing a scandal if he dismissed him, Forster continued to see Kanaya, but noted:

> I resumed sexual intercourse with him, but it was now mixed with the desire to inflict pain. It didn't hurt him to speak of, but it was bad for me, and new in me, my temperament not being that way. I've never had that desire with anyone else, before or after, and I wasn't trying to punish him — I knew his silly little soul was incurable. I just felt he was a slave, without rights, and I a despot whom no one could call to account (HD, 324).

Returning to *Where Angels Fear to Tread*, the critic John Colmer found the fight scene 'extraordinary' and 'comparable in its subterranean implications with the wrestling scene between Birkin and Gerald in Lawrence's *Women in Love*' (Colmer, 61), but he failed to follow through the implications of his observation. He argued that Philip and Gino 'engage in a life and death struggle which serves to establish the need for personal contest, struggle, and truces within personal relationships' (Colmer, 61). This statement seems somewhat misleading in its assertion that contest, struggle and truces are needs. They are not needs, but are in Western societies common components in relationships between males, where competition and aggression are seen as proofs of masculinity. The relations between Birkin and Gerald and between Philip and Gino

---

* Forster added to this, as Nicola Beauman notes: 'The "hurt by him", by the way ought to be written in fainter ink. Although it is on my ticket, it is not as vivid as "perfect union", and it is not underlined by the desire to be trodden on or shat on which characterises extreme cases' (Beauman 1993, 302).

have strong homoerotic overtones, and both are between individuals of differing national origin, but neither Lawrence nor Forster felt able to write publicly
of pleasurable homosexual contact. Lawrence supressed his 'Prologue' to *Women
in Love* where Birkin's homosexuality is declared, but both novelists could
write of physical contact between males when the reason for such engagement
had such social acceptability as fighting. Fight scenes would also serve to impress upon the first readers of those novels the virility of the combatants, and
help to deflect any suggestion of effeminacy or 'vice'. Whereas post-Freudian
readers could observe that part of their aggression might have its origin in the
conflicting desire within each character simultaneously to embrace, and to
repress, personal homoerotic desires; such a proposition would seem of rel-
evance to both Lawrence's and Forster's male couples.

Whenever he places his male characters physically close in his public
writings, Forster is careful to establish clearly their reasons for joining together,
and a frequent excuse he employs for male physical contact is sport. Examples
of this can be found in the bathing scene in *A Room with a View* and the polo
scene in *A Passage to India*. Only in *Maurice* and Forster's other 'private' writings can males openly enjoy direct physical contact with one another. In the
fight between Philip and Gino there is violence but then also a tenderness.
Forster, like others, may have felt a cretain sexual frisson at roughnes, but
continual violence can only lead to terror, and in his fantasy Forster wants it to
lead to love. Philip fells Gino with a blow, however:

> Then he was seized with remorse, and knelt beside his adversary and
> tried to revive him. He managed to raise him up, and propped his body
> against his own. He passed his arm round him. Again he was filled with
> pity and tenderness. He awaited the revival without fear, sure that both
> of them were safe at last (WAFT, 136).

Just as Lilia acts as a conduit in bringing together Philip and Gino for the
first time, so is Caroline a factor in their reconciliation, for it is she who urges
Gino to give the milk intended for his dead baby to Philip to drink; and in a
mock ceremony, part communion and part rite of blood brotherhood, the men
share the milk; the jug they drink from is then deliberately smashed to pieces
(WAFT, 139). Forster describes this whole scene of 'bodily punishment' and its
aftermath as 'sacramental' (Lago and Furbank 1, 84), and it was certainly intended as a ritual act designed to demonstrate their being united to each other
by friendship — almost a 'marriage'. Gino's new concern for Philip is later described as 'a vision of perfect friendship', and Philip declares that whereas Miss
Abbott could 'slide away from the man [Gino] so easily':

> For his [Philip's] own part, he was bound by ties of almost alarming
> intimacy. Gino had the southern knack of friendship. In the intervals of
> business he would pull out Philip's life, turn it inside out, remodel it,
> and advise him how to use it for the best. The sensation was pleasant,

for he was a kind as well as a skilful operator. But Philip came away feeling that he had not a secret corner left (WAFT, 140).

The language used to describe the changed relationship between the two men clearly denotes their intimacy; the words evoking a physicality, even a sensuality, to their interaction. Gino urges that Philip marry Caroline as a refuge from domestic difficulties if for no other reason, unaware that male chauvinism has more opposition in England than in his native Italy. Later when Caroline admits that she loves Gino and misses him, Philip adds that he too cares for him: 'Rather! I love him too! When I can forget how he hurt me that evening. Though whenever we shake hands — ' (WAFT, 145). What Philip feels exactly when he shakes Gino's hand is not given, for his sentence remains incomplete; but we may surmise that the feeling is not purely one of relived past agonies.

At the close of the novel, Caroline and Philip — the two 'suitors' for Gino — are reconciled. Their rivalry abates, for, unlike Lilia, Caroline presents now no real threat to Philip's position with Gino, and neither does Gino's new wife. Philip, following Gino's injunction, declares that he also loves Caroline, but is careful to add that he had reached this love by 'the spiritual path' (WAFT, 141), and had not himself felt any physical attraction towards her. Having realised that she is no rival, he 'could even be glad that she had once held the beloved in her arms' (WAFT, 147). His new-found interest in her was clearly occasioned by her closeness to his beloved Gino; 'beloved' being an epithet employed here by Forster for a male loved by another male, and utilised again many years later in *A Passage to India*.

Were Caroline to have married Gino, by the Fosterian scheme of things such a union would have been doomed. As Philip observed, such a coupling would have met with 'the cruel antique malice of the gods, such as they sent forth against Pasiphaë' (WAFT 146). Pashiphaë was the wife of Minos, a ruler of ancient Crete. Minos had affronted Poseidon, the god of the sea, by failing to sacrifice to him a dazzling white bull which the god had sent to him for that purpose. In his revenge Minos made Pasiphaë fall in love with the bull, and she anxious to consummate this love, entreated Daedalus to make for her a hollow wooden cow, upholstered with cow-hide and set upon wheels. Pasiphaë entered the cow via folding doors at the back, slipping her legs inside its hollow hind legs, and waited for the bull to mount her, which it did, and Pasiphaë 'had all her desire' (R. Graves 1, 293). The child of this coupling, the Minotaur, was a deformed creature with the head of a bull and the body of a man; Forster rather coyly hinting at the Italian's sexual prowess, as well as suggesting that Gino and Caroline's union could have a monstrous outcome.

Returning to Forster's assertion that the novel was about the achievement of the 'sentimental' and noting that his definition of sentimental was rooted in his appreciation of the values and civilisation of ancient Greece, it is perhaps not suprising that at the close of the novel the main protagonists are linked, through Philip's eyes, within the framework of another Greek legend.

Adoption of the ancient Greek ideal serves not only therefore to unite man to man but also man to woman. Caroline enters into the closest part of her relationship with Gino when she is seen to adopt the aspect of the Greek moon goddess Selene, significantly shown here in adoration of the beautiful youth Endymion, as equated by Philip in the following passage with his Gino:

> As she [Caroline Abbott] spoke she seemed to be transfigured, and to have indeed no part with refinement or unrefinement any longer. Out of this wreck there was revealed to him [Philip] something indestructible — something which she, who had given it, could never take away.... Philip's eyes were fixed on the Campanile of Airolo. But he saw instead the fair myth of Endymion. This woman was a goddess to the end. For her no love could be degrading: she stood outside all degradation. This episode, which she thought so sordid, and which was so tragic for him, remained supremely beautiful (WAFT, 147-8).

At the very start of the novel Philip had predicted for Caroline that the Campanile of Airolo, which would burst on her when she emerged from the St Gotthard tunnel, would be one 'of the supreme moments of her coming journey' (WAFT, 2), and so it proves to be. When Caroline, as a woman, ceases to represent the conventional and the respectable, when she has 'no part with refinement or unrefinement' and goes beyond 'feminine criticism' or 'feminine prejudice', then she too can be with Gino; she can also comprehend, and herself realise, that love towards which, in Forster's work, true male friendships tend. As a goddess, for whom 'no love could be degrading', including no doubt homosexual love, she adopts a role played by other female characters who are close to bonded males in Forster's works. Her transformation, for example, shows parallels to that undergone by Mrs Moore in *A Passage to India*, who likewise assumes the aspect of a goddess after having become the closest female to the male protagonist's beloved and who, subsequently, is invoked after death at the celebrations of universal love in the Krishna temple at Mau.

In 'The Story of a Panic', the behaviour of Eustace and Gennaro is explained by their being possessed by the Greek god Pan. This god makes frequent appearances in the work of Forster, often in relation to attractive, active males, and stands as a symbol of unrestrained sexual exuberance. Forster's use of the myth of Endymion and his connection between Caroline and Selene also point towards a connection between Gino and Pan. For Pan's greatest success in love was his seduction of Selene, which 'he accomplished by disguising his hairy black goatishness with well-washed white fleeces'. Selene, unaware of his identity, rode on his back and 'let him do as he pleased with her' (R. Graves 1, 102). Instead of Gino, the fair Endymion, Caroline was duped into accepting Pan. As Gennaro seduced Eustace, or rather, as both were seduced by Pan, so Gino seduces both Caroline and Philip, leaving Philip feeling that 'he had not a secret corner left'.

The ending of *Where Angels Fear to Tread* has evoked differing responses. Trilling, who, though aware of the closeness of Philip and Gino's relationship, nevertheless describes the close of the novel as having 'an almost intentional weakness, petering out in a sad discourse', noted in particular that Caroline 'condemns herself to a life that is at best endurable' (Trilling, 66). The surface comedy of manners does not terminate with a wedding, the traditional happy ending of the genre, but with a separation. Rahman, however, describing the homosexual under-plot, observes that this ends on a 'note of temporary parting rather than the complete parting the heterosexual plot articulates', for Philip is merely temporarily separated from his Gino and their friendship promises to enter a new phase of greater intimacy (Rahman 1988, 69). Caroline cuts herself off from Italy and what it signifies when she declares that she will never return there, whereas Philip plans to return the following spring and join Gino in painting the town of Siena red for a day or two with his new wife's money (WAFT, 141). Cross-national heterosexual relationships in the novel end in sterility or death, male love has overcome national boundaries and promises continuance and fruition.

Whilst *Where Angels Fear to Tread* has been read by generations as a romantic comedy and for many the focus of attention has been on the relationships between Gino and the Englishwomen, nevertheless the work has always been replete with enough textual evidence to show that the writer's own focus of interest was in the relationship between Gino and Philip. In order to get his work accepted by a publisher, however, Forster had to tailor it towards a specific market by presenting it as primarily a heterosexual romance. Indeed, at this early stage of his writing career his sexual naivety probably meant that he was not yet capable of knowingly formulating a work which dealt with non-heterosexual themes; Forster having admitted that at this time he was unaware of the full import of what he was writing. In the novel the balance between surface heterosexual plot and homosexual under-plot is delicately poised. The surface comedy of manners predominates, and consequently the under-plot is muted, so as to engage the possible interest of a publisher and to play down, both consciously and unconsciously, those homoerotic elements which would leave the author open to the kind of attack he could not easily withstand.

Apart from Forster's tailoring of his text, one further reason, perhaps, why the male relationship has escaped more insightful scrutiny until the recent past, has been due to the general acceptability of 'manly love' as a theme in fiction during the period in which Forster wrote the novel. This acceptability would also serve in part to explain Forster's own apparent ignorance of the sexual overtones of some of his work, for just as manly love could be described, in ignorance as well as in innocence, without reference to manly sex, so too could Forster believe that when he wrote of manly love he was not thereby also writing about manly sex; though clearly, as he later realised, he was.

THE LONGEST JOURNEY

The first surviving manuscript draft of *The Longest Journey* is a plot outline dated 17 July 1904 (LJ, xlviii). Forster worked on the novel intermittently over the following two years, giving it priority over *A Room with a View*. The final draft was ready by the end of 1906 (LJ, liv) and the novel was published on 16 April 1907, to some enthusiastic press coverage; though not all reviewers were impressed, nor were the opinions of Forster's Bloomsbury friends entirely favourable (Furbank 1, 149-50); T. E. Lawrence however felt it 'great... just great without qualification' (Lawrence 1992, 368).

The book opens in a Cambridge University college with a 'symposium', the word immediately recalling the famous *Symposium* of Plato, where the nature of love — specifically love between males — was the central topic of metaphysical discourse. The focus of argument for the Cambridge debaters is the nature of reality and how any number of realities might occupy a similar location. The novel, however, whilst dealing initially with the philosophical concepts discussed by Forster and his friends in his student days at university, also specifically addresses issues similar to those raised long ago in Plato's work.

Forster's dedication for the novel was *'Fratribus'*, meaning in Latin 'to the brothers', and the work is an exploration not only of the relationship between two brothers — Rickie and Stephen — but also of the possible nature of 'brotherly' relationships between men. His choice of a Latin dedication was no haphazard one, for *'frater'* carries with it a subtle extra meaning, which its English equivalent 'brother' does not. The historian James Boswell, in his study of same-sex relationships in the early Christian Church, notes that, in the discussion of male homosexual friendships in the work of certain early Roman writers, *'frater'* is frequently employed by a male lover to address and describe his male beloved. Boswell cites the works of Petronius Arbiter, Cattulus and Calpurnius to support his assertion (Boswell, 67-9), and significantly (as shall be seen in a later discussion in this chapter), he links this use of the term 'brother' to a subtext derived from the overtly homoerotic relationships depicted in the works of Theocritus (Boswell, 67 n74). Forster, an amateur student of the classics and close friend of the noted classicist Goldsworthy Lowes Dickinson, would certainly have been aware of this additional meaning, and that the use of the word in a homoerotic context was continued long after the decline of ancient Greece and Rome in Latin works produced in Europe during the Middle Ages (Boswell, 182-3).

Both the *Symposium* and *The Longest Journey* are concerned with the respective merits of heterosexual and homosexual love and their differing offsprings. G. L. Dickinson, in his study *Plato and his Dialogues*, notes that the 'first and most remarkable thing in Plato's treatment of love is that he regards it always as a relation between persons of the same sex' (194). In Plato's view, the aim of relations between the opposite sexes was the production of good children, and 'he did not think mutual love had anything to do with the securing of that result' (195). In the *Symposium*, male love is seen as ennobling, and it is accepted without question that only such a love could satisfy man's highest spiritual aspirations. Carnal love between the sexes is seen as inferior, for the concept of heterosexual marriage as a partnership covering all aspects of a person's life was an alien concept to the ancient Greeks.

So it is with Forster's novel, where in essence the love of one man for another is shown to be, potentially, greater than the narrow, wedded love between a man and a woman. This theme is carried over from *Where Angels Fear to Tread* where the developing love between Gino and Philip Herriton promises to be profounder than the relationships between Gino and the Englishwomen. Likewise the procreation of children, whilst obviously necessary for the continuation of humanity, is not seen as greater than other acts of creation and, like Gino, in this novel Rickie too loses a child. Similarly the novel discusses the constraints imposed on individuals by the institution of marriage and by the concomitant demands of social custom and convention.

Although Forster condemns 'modern' marriage as restrictive, he does not propose its replacement by promiscuity. In his esssay 'My Books and I', he referred to *The Longest Journey* with 'its meagre moral (we oughtn't to like one person specially)' (LJ, 305). What Forster attacked is the common romantic notion of love and marriage whereby it is assumed that a married person will find in their partner a person who is able to complete their life and meet all of their needs; whatever religious pundits may espouse, relationships based purely on the need of the human species to reproduce are not per se the high point of human love. Unlike the characters in *Where Angels Fear to Tread*, those in *The Longest Journey* do not have the advantage of being in Italy, that 'beautiful country where they say "yes", and the place "where things happen"'. Forster nonetheless establishes a link between England and Italy (and through her to ancient Greece) for, as Rickie views the Wiltshire landscape, he compares it to Italy, referring to it as 'the spiritual fatherland of us all' (LJ, 126). Unlike Italy, however, which is conceived of as an exotic place to be admired and reverenced, the unostentatious fields of England are to be loved. The way in which Forster commends human love to proceed, both in English fields and elsewhere, and the origin of the title of the novel, is revealed to the reader by Rickie's reading of Shelley's poem 'Epipsychidion':

The book was Shelley, and it opened at a passage that he had cherished greatly two years before, and marked as 'very good'.

I never was attached to that great sect
Whose doctrine is that each one should select
Out of the world a mistress or a friend,
And all the rest, though fair and wise, commend

To cold oblivion — though it is the code
Of modern morals, and the beaten road
Which those poor slaves with weary footsteps tread
Who travel to their home among the dead
By the broad highway of the world — and so
With one sad friend, perhaps a jealous foe,
The dreariest and the longest journey go. (LJ, 126-7)

What Rickie strains to find during the course of this novel is not a companion who would later have become, in Shelley's words, 'one sad friend', but a love which would lead him to something greater.

Forster's acquaintance with the works of Shelley was most likely mediated through his reading of John Addington Symonds's writings on the poet, and by his friend Dickinson, whose own work was dominated by Shelley's influence (GLD, 34 & 45). When we look at the origin of 'Epipsychidion', it becomes even clearer why Forster felt drawn to it. Shelley wrote the poem during his sojourn in Italy in 1821. Its subject, Lady Emilia Viviani, was a beautiful woman whose father kept her imprisoned in a convent until he found a husband for her that he could approve of. Symonds, in his biography of Shelley, noted that she too was something of a poet, having composed 'a rhapsody... on the subject of Uranian Love — "Il Vero Amore"' (Symonds 1895, 138). Shelley visited her in her 'dreary prison' and 'was struck by her amazing beauty, by the highly cultivated grace of her mind, and by the misery she suffered in being debarred from all sympathy'. Eventually she was married to a man chosen by her father, but after six years of misery she left her husband, subsequently 'dying of consumption in a dilapidated old mansion in Florence' (Shelley, 149). The poem celebrates Shelley's 'lifelong search for the eternal image of Beauty, in the earthly form of his various wives, mistresses, and female friends'; the work is 'passionately sexual as well as Platonic', attacks conventional marriage and in its place proposes 'Free' or 'True' Love (Drabble 1993, 322).

Shelley sent the poem to his publisher requesting that it be printed anonymously and limited to 100 copies 'for the esoteric few'. As the poet noted in a letter written in October 1821, the poem was not well received and some readers were inclined to approximate the poet 'to the circle of a servant girl and her sweetheart'. Shelley retorted by declaring his intention to write a 'Symposium' of his own 'to set all this right' (Shelley, 152-4). In his Preface to the poem Shelley stated that it had been written by a person who had 'died at Florence, as he was preparing for a voyage to one of the wildest of the Sporades... where it was his hope to have realised a scheme of life suited, perhaps, to that happier and better world of which he is now an inhabitant, but hardly practicable in this' (Shelley, 152-3). The island in the Sporades described by Shelley is an Elysian paradise, recalling those depicted in the bucolic poetry of ancient Greece with its woods, 'sylvan forms', fountains, glades, caverns, and even a 'rough shepherd'.

Forster no doubt saw parallels between his own situation and that of Emilia Vivani. Restricted by a viciously homophobic society in the aftermath of the Wilde trials, as much as by his own shyness and reticence, he felt that, like Vivani, he too would be unlikely to be free to choose whom he wished to love. Social convention would have urged him to marry, preferably a woman of his own class, but were he to have done so, he could be certain that the union would be as disastrous as Viviani's. His sympathies were obviously with Shelley in commending the virtues of the *Symposium* in preference to the 'dreariest and longest journey' of conventional marriage. And like Shelley's 'anonymous' poet, he dreamed of leading a life which he knew would be 'hardly practicable in this'. Shelley's paradise in the Sporades, which offered the putative poet some hope of a happier existence to come, matched Forster's own romantic idyll of a better life lived long ago in ancient Greece.

Symonds went on to point out that in 'Epipsychidion', the poet's 'identification of Intellectual Beauty with so many daughters of the Earth, and his worshipping love of Emilia, is spurious Platonism'; Shelley acknowledging that his 'error consists in seeking in a mortal image the likeness of what is, perhaps, eternal' (Symonds 1895, 142). Forster, perhaps, falls into a similar error in *The Longest Journey*, where, to most readers, the character of Stephen Wonham cannot live up to his creator's idealisation of him; no more than Gino, in *Where Angels Fear to Tread*, seems to warrant Philip's commendation. Perhaps it was this over-eager seeking of the eternal amongst the mortal which Mr Pembroke, in *The Longest Journey*, had in mind when he recalled that he had known endless trouble result from boys who had attempted Plato 'too soon, before they were set' (LJ, 46).

Both Shelley and Forster found in Plato's work an ethic and a philosophy which commends the transcendence of particularity in human affections. Whilst Shelley recorded in his 'Essay on Friendship' that as a youth he had felt attracted to a fellow schoolboy, as an adult he was predominately heterosexual; Forster, however, could identify much more directly with the situation of Plato's lovers.

In the *Symposium* male love is exhorted not to limit itself to physicality, nor to the kind of possessiveness which characterises a 'modern' marriage, but to move from the admiration of the mortal shell of beauty to the immortal; the transition being achieved by the eschewing of long-term particularity towards one person, and ultimately replacing it with a veneration of those qualities best exemplified by the loved one. Such a man, Plato asserts, will achieve an immortality greater than that of those who simply produce children of the flesh. In *The Longest Journey* Forster gives Rickie Elliot, ironically a character whose crippled body would ordinarily exempt him from being an 'example of beauty', the vision to apprehend 'absolute beauty'. And, like his creator, Rickie's criteria for beauty are derived from Hellenic sources. 'Modern marriage,' however, with its insistence on exclusivity, interferes with such developments.

Whilst Forster approved in general of certain values he saw commended by the ancient Greeks, he did not ultimately accept Plato's eschewing of the physical, as Trilling explains:

> We know of Forster that he is a Hellenist but not a 'classicist', that he
> loves Greece in its mythical and naturalistic aspects, that Plato has
> never meant much to him, perhaps because he mistrusts the Platonic
> drive to the absolute and the Platonic judgment of the body and the
> senses (Trilling, 19).

Trilling was speaking of the Forster he knew in the 1940s, but at the time
he was writing *The Longest Journey* Forster was actually living a life characterised by sexual naivety, frustration and, by today's standards, a gross ignorance
of the practicalities of sexual behaviour. Physical sex (whether homo or hetero)
was experientially unknown to him; masturbation still viewed, as in early pu-
berty, as a 'beastliness' he ought to avoid. The subjugation of sexual feeling to
an ideal that negates it is a common experience of adolescence. So too Forster,
who was quite ignorant of sexual matters, felt his own body unattractive and
others far beyond his reach. Ancient Greece embodied his sense of the ideal
and in early manhood he interpreted his burgeoning sexuality within the framework of his reading of its classics. It is hardly suprising therefore that he saw
the ideal of celibacy propounded in Plato's work as a worthy goal to follow; it
seemed for a while, paradoxically perhaps, the only positive moral guide by
which he could grow into adulthood. What explanations he knew of his homosexuality, from the science of his day, commended only sterility to those
'afflicted' by personal homosexuality. When Forster did indeed mature, and
had acquired direct sexual experience, he then learnt, as Trilling averred, to
mistrust 'the Platonic judgment of the body and the senses'. Within this context *The Longest Journey* can be seen as Forster's attempt to delineate, and
perhaps thereby to exorcise, the influences of both Platonic thought and scientific ideology at the start of his adult life; only after such a purgation could
he have written *Maurice*. And in *The Longest Journey*, he depicts what disasters
might befall someone like himself, or his friend Hugh O. Meredith, if they
chose marriage in a mistaken bid to escape their homosexual orientation.

In *The Longest Journey*, as in other Forster novels, the freedoms enjoyed in
male relationships are frequently absent in relationships between men and
women, especially in the institution of marriage, where a man and a woman
are joined in a socially predetermined relationship. Predictably perhaps, when
Rickie's mother and her lover, Robert, attempted by elopement to escape social convention, they were ultimately doomed to failure. To these lovers the
class difference meant very little, but this difference meant much to their
wider society and was the reason for their flight to Stockholm. It is highly
significant that in endeavouring to present such a heterosexual relationship,
Forster's narrator does not seek a heterosexual parallel to comment on their
love, but utilises lines from the homosexual poet Walt Whitman's 'Song of
Myself' as being most appropriate to describe their feelings for the natural
world whilst being in love. In fact Forster's whole description of their love

across class boundaries, their love of 'work and living in the open' and 'their love of beauty... [which] grew not from the nerves but from the soul' seems to use a vocabulary derived from Whitman (LJ, 237). The reason perhaps is obvious, for in general in Forster's day, the words generally associated with heterosexual relationships outside of marriage and across class boundaries were not positive and rarely celebratory. To find the right words for a 'forbidden' relationship, Forster turned to a poet whose vocabulary was inspired by, and devised to celebrate, another socially unacceptable form of love.

Conventional marriage turns out to be a disaster for both Rickie and his wife, Agnes. Rickie in particular feels deflated:

> [h]e was a husband.... The crown of life had been attained, the vague yearnings, the misread impulses, had found accomplishment at last. Never again must he feel lonely, or as one who stands out of the broad highway of the world and fears, like poor Shelley, to undertake the longest journey.... But as the term passed he knew that behind the yearning there remained a yearning, behind the drawn veil a veil that he could not draw (LJ, 167).

This 'yearning' is at first unidentified, but it becomes clear that it is for 'another helpmate' — for his, and Agnes's, earlier love, Gerald. Rickie's desire for another, male partner in his life recalls the same plea from Birkin in D. H. Lawrence's *Women in Love*, and Forster's interest in this aspect of Lawrence's novel recurs in his creation of *A Passage to India*. Birkin feels dissatisfied with his exclusive relationship with Ursula and wishes for 'a man friend' to make his life 'complete', 'really happy'; he 'wanted eternal union with a man too: another kind of love' (D. H. Lawrence, 541). It is intriguing that the men who exemplified both Birkin's and Rickie's ideal bore the same name, Gerald. Unlike Birkin's 'marriage', however, in which he and Ursula seem likely to remain together even should an extra male partner become involved, in Rickie's marriage there is no room for those others, who are in Shelley's words condemned 'to cold oblivion'. Subsequently, Rickie tells Agnes that he can see no future in their relationship. When she asks him what he means by this, he explains:

> He meant that the relations between them were fixed — that there would never be an influx of interest, nor even of passion. To the end of life they would go on beating time, and this was enough for her.... But he had dreamt of another helpmate, and of other things (LJ, 190).

Marriage is shown to be a potentially satisfying institution for Agnes, but for Rickie, whose truer passion was for Gerald, it becomes a prison, as deadening as that pre-nuptial one endured by Shelley's Lady Viviani.

Forster's view of the dangers of too restrictive a relationship in marriage is reflected in his distaste for the conventional use of the topic in fiction. He relates his viewpoint in *Aspects of the Novel*:

Love, like death, is congenial to a novelist because it ends a book conveniently. He can make it a permanency, and his readers easily acquiesce, because one of the illusions attached to love is that it will be permanent. Not has been — will be. All history, all our experience, teaches us that no human relationship is constant, it is as unstable as the living beings who compose it... if it is constant it is no longer a human relationship but a social habit, the emphasis in it has passed from love to marriage (AN, 38).

Forster's main complaint is of 'that idiotic use of marriage as a finale' (AN, 26), but it is evident from the passage quoted that he sees 'love' as dynamic, whereas conventional marriage is a separate 'social habit' which has 'the illusion of permanence'; readers do not object, for this illusion is their own dream also (AN, 38). *The Longest Journey* sets out to disabuse readers of this illusion, and of their 'dream'; perhaps this is why it was, in Forster's own view, the least popular of his novels (LJ, lxvi).

But why did Forster in 1906 rush to deal with the subject of marriage, giving *The Longest Journey* priority over his 'Lucy' novel, and what influenced his viewpoint? The subject of marriage had occupied his thoughts considerably during the writing of the novel for, during that period, Forster's first real love had abruptly announced that he intended to marry. This news disturbed the writer and forced him to consider the origins of his own homosexuality and how this would almost certainly preclude any future marriage and children of his own. The friend concerned was Hugh Owen Meredith (1878–1963) and it was on him that Forster modelled in part the character of Stewart Ansell.

The relationship between them was undoubtedly significant; in Forster's own words, from his New Year's review of 1911, Meredith had been 'the ground work of my life' (Furbank 1, 205). According to Furbank, the character of Ansell is, in its externals, a portrait of A. R. Ainsworth, a minor Cambridge acquaintance of Forster, but when it comes to Ansell's role as Rickie's conscience, there one finds the influence of Meredith (Furbank 1, 77). That the novel was indeed based in part on Forster's relationship with Meredith was a fact commented on very soon after its publication. In a letter to Duncan Grant of 30 April 1907, Lytton Strachey wrote that Forster, 'a queer King's brother', had just written his second novel, which contained an amusing account of Cambridge life but that the rest was a 'dreary fandango', adding that the principal figure, Ansell, was Meredith and the 'hero' based on Forster himself (Furbank 1, 150; Holroyd, 353).

Forster's friendship with Meredith had flourished during his second year as a student at King's College (1898–99). Meredith was the son of an Irish legal shorthand-writer; his father was socially ambitious and had sent him to good private schools, where he had earned a brilliant reputation prior to his departure for Cambridge (Lago and Furbank 1, 26). Their relationship was initially rewarding to both parties. Furbank, drawing upon Forster's own memories of this period, recorded that Meredith was 'tall, goodlooking and athletic', 'rather noble in his appearance, and intellectually impressive in his quiet-voiced manner' (Furbank 1, 61). Forster seems to have fallen for him on their first meeting and very soon the two became inseparable.

The degree of his impact upon Forster can be seen in the fact that not only did he serve in part as a model for three of Forster's fictional characters — Ansell in *The Longest Journey*, Clive in *Maurice* and George Emerson in *A Room with a View* — but the latter novel was also dedicated to him. He profoundly affected Forster's religious development, demolishing what remained of his adolescent Christian beliefs, though these were not deeply held convictions in the first place (Furbank 1988, 62). Along with Goldworthy Lowes Dickinson and the Cambridge Apostles, Meredith was also influential in fostering his friend's interest in the culture and ethics of ancient Greece.

In February 1901, as a result of Meredith's sponsorship, Forster became a member of the Cambridge Conversazione Society, generally known as the Apostles — it is a similar group who are shown at the opening of *The Longest Journey*). Furbank describes the Apostles as the 'most exclusive intellectual coterie in Cambridge'; its purpose being defined by one of its then most devoted members, Henry Sidgwick, as 'the pursuit of truth with absolute devotion and unreserve by a group of intimate friends' (Furbank 1, 75); for some critics, it is this group to whom the dedication '*Fratribus*' was, in part, meant. That the intimate friends were all male, and many seem to have been homosexual, is perhaps obvious to the reader.

During the winter of 1902–03 Forster's relationship with Meredith became intense. Though their emotional ties to each other were strong, Forster seems to have been the more deeply affected partner. Forster told P. N. Furbank that his relationship with Meredith did not involve sex, and that physical contact, by mutual agreement, went no further than kisses and embraces. Forster told him also that the affair was an 'experiment' for Meredith who had already had affairs with girls (Furbank 1, 98).

Their relationship however was not destined to retain this high plateau. Meredith was in emotional turmoil and in 1903, shortly after the development of his affair with Forster, he had a nervous breakdown. According to Furbank, the cause, or symptom, of his distress seemed to be his getting engaged to a Cambridge friend, Caroline Graveson (Furbank 1, 140). Whatever the circumstances, this engagement was short-lived, though Meredith did get married in 1906, to Christabel Iles; the marriage was a disaster for them both. Not surprisingly, the whole situation badly affected Forster, who became severely depressed, and in his diary entry for 22 June 1906 wrote that he had even contemplated suicide (Furbank 1, 141).

Meredith's difficulties in reconciling his homoerotic feelings with his desire to settle into a conventional heterosexual relationship are issues reflected upon by Forster, not only in *The Longest Journey* but also in *Maurice* and in *A Room with a View*, the three novels within which Meredith's influence is clearly recognisable, and openly acknowledged, by their creator. The notion that conventional heterosexuality is the only orientation to be viewed as in healthy conformity with the development of the human species, is similarily explored.

In his search for an understanding of his own sexuality, Forster could turn to science. The then dominant scientific philosophies were developments either from the work of Charles Darwin or from works which specifically set out to refute Darwinism. Forster, though, seems to have learned about the scientific speculation about heredity less from his own reading of scientific theses than from his study of the works of Samuel Butler. In the years during which he wrote *The Longest Journey*, Forster had poured over Butler's works (Stape 21, 22; Furbank 1, 159n), and in a later essay, 'A Book that Influenced Me', he praised Butler's novel *Erewhon* for its impact on his own intellectual development (TCFD 222-6). Initially Butler had embraced Darwin's ideas, eschewed his own Christian upbringing, and sought the great scientist's company. Later though his adulation of Darwin gave way to severe doubts, and Butler became one of his most bitter critics. He attacked Darwin personally and disparaged his work, utilising the ideas of an earlier scientist, Jean Baptiste de Lamarck and his theory on the inheritance of acquired characteristics (Raby 166). Butler wrote books and articles to disseminate his views, subsequently proposing a concept of evolution which accorded almost a mystical sense of purpose to the world, something which Darwin had rather belatedly excluded.

By the time Forster was writing *The Longest Journey*, Lamarck's notion of the inheritability of acquired characteristics had been disproved by the German scientist August Weissman, one of the founders of modern genetic theory. No doubt Forster would have been aware of the limitations of both Darwin and Butler's ideas, and so the way was paved for his later acceptance of Edward Carpenter's more revolutionary approach to the subject of evolution and on the role of homosexuals in that process. Even as late as 1913 however, when Forster had turned to Carpenter as his 'saviour', he also consulted Butler's book *Life and Habit*, with its praise of instinct as the basis of right conduct, during his writing of *Maurice* (Furbank 1, 257-8).

In Darwinian theory, species are said to develop by natural selection which is accomplished through the survival of the fittest offspring in the struggle for existence; sexuality is the means of propagating the species and has no purpose beyond procreation. In this context, as will be seen below in Iwan Bloch's view, homosexuality inevitably represents an inability to contribute to the development of human society. Such ideas however, were directly challenged by Forster and his Cambridge friends, who proposed that human progress is sustained not by any crude biological mechanism of natural selection, but by the development of civilised values

Forster's concern throughout was not for ideas which sought to explain comprehensively the 'great world', which he denounced in his own 1960 Introduction to *The Longest Journey*, many years after his completion of the novel (LJ, lxviii) — the sort of world-view which scientific theorising sometimes entails — but for 'good societies'. Furbank pointed out that in matters of conscience Ansell is the voice of Meredith, and, by comparing the following speech by Ansell with Forster's Introduction, we can see that it is also the writer's voice:

> There is no great world at all, only a little earth, for ever isolated from the rest of the solar system. The little earth is full of tiny societies, and Cambridge is one of them. All the societies are narrow, but some are good and some are bad — just as one house is beautiful inside and another ugly.... The good societies say, 'I tell you to do this because I am Cambridge'. The bad ones say, 'I tell you to do that because I am the great world' — not because I am 'Peckham', or 'Billingsgate', or 'Park Lane', but 'because I am the great world'. They lie. And fools like you listen to them, and believe that they are a thing which does not exist and never has existed, and confuse 'great', which has no meaning whatever, with 'good', which means salvation (LJ, 62-3).

In *The Longest Journey* modern marriage is shown as the means whereby Rickie is trapped in the illusion of the 'great world'; his wife Agnes keeping him from Cambridge 'society' and its values until one night he dreams that she lay in his arms which displeased him and he determines to think about Gerald instead. When he does this however 'the fabric collapsed' (LJ, 66). Once Rickie thinks of Gerald, and realises that by marriage he may lose all hope of any meaningful friendship with such a man, then his relationship with Agnes crumbles. He 'knew there was nothing shameful in love. But to love this woman!... the crime was registered in heaven' (LJ, 66). The 'great world' had commended marriage, and Rickie had listened to it. If he had listened instead to the 'tiny society' of his Cambridge friends he would have realised that as a homosexual a conventional marriage could only end in disaster for both husband and wife. Rickie learnt this lesson too late.

In coming to an understanding of his sexuality Forster felt the need to grapple with the question of heredity, and its effects on the formation of human beings is one of the main themes of the book. Elizabeth Heine, in her Introduction to the Abinger edition of *The Longest Journey*, puts forward the view that Rickie's inherited lameness is parallel to Forster's speculation that his homosexual orientation was an inherited trait (LJ, xxiv).* Rickie's father was also lame (LJ, 22), as is his aunt. Not insignificantly, his bad foot is on the same side of his body as his heart and the thematic link between foot and heart is made in the text (LJ, 23).

Forster's specific interest in heredity was clearly influenced by his belief that at least three of his relatives, including his father,** shared his sexual

---

* Forster's friend Goldsworthy Lowes Dickinson compared his own homosexual orientation to that of being crippled. On 7 September 1910, in his 49th year, he wrote in his private papers: 'I am like a man crippled; will and character may make more of such a life, through the stimulus of the defect, than many normal men make of theirs' (Dickinson 1973, 11).

** cf. *Maurice* where the protagonist recounts to Mr Lasker Jones his night of love with Scudder: 'When all was detailed, the perfection of the night appeared as a transient grossness, such as his father had indulged in thirty years before' (M, 197).

orientation. Forster's recent biographer Nicola Beauman asserts that Forster believed his father to have been homosexual, and that 'Ted' Streatfeild, a distant cousin of his father, had been his lover (Beauman, 16). Their relationship however was quite covert compared to those of his Uncle Percy. Percy James Wichelo (1858–93), known as 'Pucky Ruby', had been the young friend of General Guy Philips. One day in the 1870s when he and his brother Harry were on the train and 'dressed in their white cricketing things... they caught the eye of an elderly dundreary-whiskered military gentleman', the general. Philips took a particular fancy to Percy, who was 'a handsome and dashing young fellow, and eventually he more or less adopted him'. Looking back on the relationship, Forster told Furbank that 'the implication was obvious'. When the general died in the late 1880s, he left Percy his entire fortune, which was considerable and included part of a palazzo in Venice. He does not seem to have been in mourning for very long for in addition to travelling widely, Percy held uproarious parties on his houseboat, the *Doris* (another part of the general's legacy). And 'occasionally discarded sweethearts of Percy's would come slowly rowing by the *Doris* for a sight of him' (Furbank 1, 31-2).

The specific assumption of an hereditary basis for homosexuality was, during Forster's early life, widely accepted as scientific fact. The most notable work supporting this notion was that of the German doctor Richard von Krafft-Ebing. In 1886 he published his masterwork *Psychopathia Sexualis* and swiftly became the leading world authority on sexual pathology. The English translation of the work appeared in 1892. In his book he examined numerous case histories of those whose sexual lives were at that time considered abnormal.*

In discussing homosexuality Krafft-Ebing made a clear distinction between what he described as 'acquired contrary sexual instinct' and 'congenital contrary sexual instinct'. The 'acquired cases' were characterised as follows: 'The homo-sexual instinct appears secondarily, and always may be referred to influences (masturbatic neurasthenia, mental) which disturbed normal sexual satisfaction' (Krafft-Ebing, 319). These 'cases' could ordinarily be treated back into heterosexuality, usually by a course of hypnotic therapy. In his book Krafft-Ebing describes the precise methods used in his work with homosexuals, and in *Maurice* the protagonist is similarly treated by Mr Lasker Jones for his 'contrary sexual instinct' by the use of hypnotherapy (M, 168-9).

Where the 'contrary sexual instinct' was not seen to have been 'acquired' by the incidents or circumstances of a person's life, then Krafft-Ebing viewed the instinct as 'congenital' in origin. To him such cases were signs of 'degeneration', the result of an hereditary defect manifesting itself in a succeeding generation (Krafft-Ebing, 225). In attempting to explain his view he wrote:

An explanation of congenital contrary sexual feeling may perhaps be found in the fact that it represents a peculiarity bred in descendants,

---

* cf. *A Passage to India* where Aziz has a dislike of the European tabulation of the facts of sex, for 'It didn't interpret his experiences when he found them in a German manual...' (PTI, 94).

but arising in ancestry. The hereditary factor might be an acquired abnormal inclination for the same sex in the ancestors... found fixed as a congenital abnormal manifestation in the descendants. Since, according to experience, acquired physical and mental peculiarities, not simply improvements, but essentially defects, are transmitted, this hypothesis becomes tenable (Krafft-Ebing, 228).

In his chapter on 'Therapy', Krafft-Ebing makes it clear that for those whose 'contrary sexual instinct' was congenitally determined the prognosis was extremely poor, hence the need for firm preventative measures to stem this hereditary 'defect': 'The prophylaxis of these conditions becomes thus the more important, — for the congenital cases, prohibition of the reproduction of such unfortunates' (Krafft-Ebing, 320).*

The dominant medical advice was thus clear: homosexual men must not marry for fear of passing on their degenerative traits. This advice finds an echo in Agnes's initial observation that Rickie ought never to marry: 'He says he can't ever marry, owing to his foot. It wouldn't be fair to posterity.... He thinks that it's hereditary, and may get worse next generation' (LJ, 50). Such was the background against which Forster strove to understand his own sexual orientation and within which he attempted to comprehend his friend Meredith's desire to marry, and such was the power of those ideas in the 'great' world that their influence could never be ignored.

But in *The Longest Journey* heredity is not quite all. Rickie's friend Ansell appears to have overcome any inherited limitations and his family circumstances, for 'To be born one thing and grow up another — Ansell had accomplished this...' (LJ, 29). Rickie's emotional bond with him is made plain throughout the novel. In one scene the two men engage in playful wrestling, Ansell pleading with Rickie not to leave him to go and see Agnes. Ansell takes hold of Rickie's ankle, observing that 'It's amusing you're so feeble. You — simply — can't — get — away. I wish I wanted to bully you'. Suddenly they overbalance and fall on to the grass where 'Ansell, with unusual playfulness, held him prisoner'. Ansell's good humour turns swiftly to anger however when he realises Rickie is going to leave him to meet Agnes (LJ, 64-5). Rickie is half-aware of the threat she will pose to his male friendships, but is not yet fully aware of his true feelings and can do nothing to prevent disaster. Later at lunch with Agnes and Mrs Lewin, he quickly becomes embarrassed and defensive when questioned about his proposal to breakfast with his friend, fearing

* The theme of a prohibition on the reproduction of 'unfortunates' is echoed in Forster's short story 'The Machine Stops'; the protagonist, Kuno, is informed that his request to become a father had been refused by the Committee, for 'His was not a type that the Machine desired to hand on' (CS, 135). In the future society depicted in the story, athletes are eliminated, for 'it would have been no true kindness to let an athlete live; he would never have been happy in that state of life to which the Machine had called him; he would have yearned for trees to climb, rivers to bathe in, meadows and hills against which he might measure his body' (CS 133). Perhaps by killing off athletes, the Committee also hoped to kill off 'athletic love'?

that the women may be noting more of him that he wishes them to know. When he mentions the name of Ansell, 'It seemed as if he was making some great admission. So self-conscious was he, that he thought the women exchanged glances. Had Agnes already explored that part of him that did not belong to her? Would another chance step reveal the part that did?' (LJ, 68-9).

Unlike his friend, for Rickie there is no transcendence of his inheritance, and he does delude himself with the idea that marriage may save him. Any such notion is doomed from the start; indeed, his bride-to-be was the first person in the novel to point out that he was ill-suited to matrimony when she spoke of his inherited deformity and cruelly contrasted it with the perfection she saw in her lover Gerald (LJ, 9). Later it is left to Ansell to argue by letter with his friend why, for important reasons other than heredity, he ought never to marry:

> You are unfitted in body: that we once discussed. You are also unfitted in soul.... I have read in books — and I cannot afford to despise books, they are all that I have to go by — that men and women desire different things. Man wants to love mankind; woman wants to love one man. When she has him her work is over. She is the emissary of Nature, and Nature's bidding has been fulfilled. But man does not care a damn for Nature — or at least only a very little damn. He cares for a hundred things besides, and the more civilized he is the more he will care for these other hundred things, and demand not only a wife and children, but also friends, and work, and spiritual freedom. I believe you to be extraordinarily civilized (LJ, 81).

Key phrases from this letter of Ansell's are clearly applicable to Forster's own situation — 'not a person who ought to marry', 'Man wants to love mankind,' etc. — and may well be similar to the arguments employed by Forster himself to dissuade his friend Meredith from matrimony. Familiar also is the argument that a woman's role is decreed by Nature as settling a man down and child-bearing, said to be in conflict with the desire for 'friends, and work, and spiritual freedom'. Significantly Ansell proposes that the more civilised a man is the more he will care 'for a hundred things besides' a family — the idea being that the advancement of humanity is not simply effected by the propagation of the species. It is not suprising after such a comprehensive warning that Rickie writes back urgently to his friend to assure him that his future wife 'will never come between us' (LJ, 83).

When Ansell wrote his letter he clearly had in mind an earlier discussion between Rickie and himself, when Rickie had expressed his wish to live in a society of true friends; the homoerotic nature of this friendship is quite obvious:

> He [Rickie] was thinking of the irony of friendship — so strong it is, and so fragile. We fly together, like straws in an eddy, to part in the

open stream. Nature has no use for us: she has cut her stuff differently. Dutiful sons, loving husbands, responsible fathers — these are what she wants, and if we are friends it must be in our spare time. Abram and Sarai were sorrowful, yet their seed became as sand of the sea, and distracts the politics of Europe at this moment. But a few verses of poetry is all that survives of David and Jonathan.

'I wish we were labelled,' said Rickie.... he wished there was a society, a kind of friendship office, where the marriage of true minds could be registered.

'Why labels?' [asked Ansell]

'To know each other again'* (LJ, 64).

Rickie's 'friendship office' recalls a passage from the autobiography of his friend G. L. Dickinson. Dickinson's editor, Dennis Proctor, points out that fifty years ahead of his time, Dickinson wrote an attack on the prevailing law against male homosexuals, and condemned the prevailing prejudice against marriage between men, arguing that two male lovers 'ought to be able to meet and love and publicly and permanently evince their relation' (Dickinson 1973, 11). Doubtless he discussed the proposal with Forster.

In his depression Rickie reviews the negative opinions of his sexuality with which the 'great world' has assailed him. The point is made that with regard to male friendships, 'Nature has no use for us: she has cut her stuff differently' and what is required is that men take on roles which relate to women and to the rearing of children; friendships 'must be in our spare time'. The reference to 'the open stream', and why friends part in it, will become clearer later in this chapter in discussing the stream of generations.

If Rickie was unfitted by heredity for propagating the species, a childhood acquaintance of his was not. Rickie's first real view of the adult Gerald Dawes comes when he is reintroduced to him by Agnes, then Gerald's fiancée, and his response is clearly homoerotic:

Agnes was leaning over the creosoted garden gate, and behind her there stood a young man who had the figure of a Greek athlete and the face of an English one. He was fair and clean-shaven, and his colourless hair was cut rather short. The sun was in his eyes, and they, like his mouth, seemed scarcely more than slits in his healthy skin. Just where he began to be beautiful the clothes started (LJ, 35).

---

* Rickie alludes here to the history of humankind as related in a speech by Aristophanes in Plato's *Symposium*. Aristophanes tells of Zeus having divided each of the original inhabitants of the earth into two parts, two different entities who yearn for reunion and constantly search for their other half; love being simply the name for 'the desire and pursuit of the whole'. Mrs Moore, in *A Passage to India*, makes a similar allusion in her comment that 'The human race would have become a single person centuries ago if marriage was any use' (PTI, 192).

His sexual attractiveness to Rickie, perhaps (and without doubt to Forster), is added to by his chosen career in the army; 'our naughty soldier' is Mr Pembroke's description of him (LJ, 47).

Although physically perfect, the result of a fortunate heredity, his character is not without defect. Gerald at school was a bully (LJ, 38) and remained so into adulthood (LJ, 39). Clearly Gerald's bodily perfection is not joined to an equally attractive temperament; he is violent towards Agnes (LJ, 39), crude, 'ungramma-tical and bumptious', dismissive of university men and 'full of transparent jealousy and petty spite, nagging, nagging, nagging, like a maiden lady who has not been invited to a tea-party' (LJ, 37). Rickie recalls how Gerald had asserted that 'He [himself] was the right kind of boy' and Rickie was the wrong kind (LJ, 38). This discrepancy between beauty of form and ugliness of spirit dismays Rickie who wonders 'whether, after all, Ansell and the extremists might not be right, and bodily beauty and strength be signs of the soul's damnation' (LJ, 37). Heredity may produce the appearance of physical perfection but perfection of the soul is differently acquired.

It is noteworthy that often when Forster introduces an attractive male character, beauty and cruelty seem invariably to be mixed. Here Gerald, and — earlier — even Ansell had spoken of wishing that he wanted to bully Rickie. Later in this novel, Stephen Wonham shows his capacity for brutality, just as Gino did in *Where Angels Fear to Tread* and the subaltern in *A Passage to India*. No doubt this points us towards Forster's penchant for rough trade, leading back to 'The Story of a Panic'.

For all his classical beauty, Gerald's marriage was to conform to conventional Christian ideals. When Rickie and Mr Pembroke discuss Plato and the influence of ancient Greece on the civilisation of Europe, Rickie proposes an alternative relationship, which seems to him more worthy an ideal than the modern marriage. The fact that marriage involves a man and a woman, and Rickie's ideal involves two men, is unremarked on in the novel. In a humorous reference to, possibly, homosexual friends, Mr Pembroke questions Rickie about the 'men who found Plato not difficult', but here Rickie 'kept silence' (LJ, 46), and the conversation is quickly turned to the proposed union of Gerald and Agnes. To Mr Pembroke, her brother, Agnes has found in Gerald 'a worthy help-meet for life's journey' (LJ, 48) and he feels sure their union will prosper. Rickie though, countering Mr Pembroke's commendation of matrimony, declares, in an argument reminiscent of Plato's, that it is quite possible to imagine a better arrangement, quoting from Aristophanes' *Clouds* in support of his assertion:

> 'How could you get a better?' he cried. 'Do you remember the thing in "The Clouds"?' And he quoted, as well as he could, from the invitation of the Dikaios Logos, the description of the young Athenian, perfect in body, placid in mind, who neglects his work at the Bar and trains all day among the woods and meadows, with a garland on his head and a friend to set the pace; the scent of new leaves is upon them; they

rejoice in the freshness of spring; over their heads the plane-tree whispers to the elm — perhaps the most glorious invitation to the brainless life that has ever been given. (LJ, 47)*

Significantly, whilst finding an exalted classical parallel for Gerald in the Dikaios Logos, Rickie could not easily think of a similar classical parallel for Agnes, for 'She was not born in Greece, but came overseas to it — a dark intelligent princess' (LJ, 47). Later however, when Rickie is married to her, she could be characterised (by Jackson) as 'Medusa in Arcady' (LJ, 178).

Before he can marry and propagate the species though, Gerald unfortunately dies; despite his athletic prowess, 'He was broken up in the football match' (LJ, 51). Rickie, forgetting his earlier espousal to Mr Pembroke of the superior life of the young and single Athenian athlete, marries Agnes in a vain attempt to restore him to life by taking upon himself the role that Gerald was to have fulfilled in marriage. Rickie convinces himself it is the right path to follow, and that a man ought to marry, though when he realises it was Gerald that he loved, despite his brutality towards him, and not Agnes, then the whole 'fabric collapsed'.

With Rickie deformed by his heredity and Gerald, despite his appearance of physical perfection, not actually fit enough to survive, the way is made clear for Stephen Wonham, who appears eminently qualified to contribute to posterity. Predictably, as befits a male love object in a work by Forster, he is powerful, physically attractive and, ostensibly, in a lower-class position for those males who would ultimately admire him; as with Gerald, references comparing him to the men of ancient Greece litter Forster's description of him. Stephen is 'a powerful boy of twenty, admirably muscular, but rather too broad for his height' (LJ, 87), who can prove his athletic prowess on the cricket field (LJ, 214). He has 'astonishingly blue eyes' (LJ, 87). He is rugged — 'Water trickled over his unshaven cheeks' — yet has the aspect of a classical statue for his hair was 'so wet that it seemed worked upon his scalp in bronze' (LJ, 87).

Aggressively heterosexual, he enjoys a drink with soldiers, and though he likes to read, he does not hold with books in the open and none of his older workmates read (LJ, 88). His link with ancient Greece is made explicit throughout; to Ansell, he gave 'the idea of an animal with just enough soul to

---

* Rickie's opening questions in this passage clearly recall a similar passage from an earlier homoerotic work by Edward Fitzgerald, *Euphranor; A Dialogue on Youth* which first appeared anonymously in 1851. In that work the character Euphranor asks the narrator: 'Do you remember that fine passage in Aristophanes' *Clouds*...' (Fitzgerald 2, 43), before eulogising the scene of the young athletes in terms similar to Forster's. What neither Fitzgerald nor Forster add to their allusions to Aristophanes' play are the references to homosexuality, and to the sexual desires provoked in some by well-formed Athenian youths, which follow the description of the boy athletes (Aristophanes, 152-4). In Alan H. Sommerstein's translation of the play, the character representing 'Old Athens' who describes the athletes (given here the name of 'Right') abandons his asexual stance towards the youths when he realises that most of the best people in society are gay and, commending paederastry to all, wholeheartedly embraces it (Aristophanes, 156-7).

contemplate its own bliss. United with refinement, such a type was common in Greece' (LJ, 212). That he lives with Mrs Failing at Cadover, built in a classical style, chiefly a version of the architecture of ancient Rome (LJ, 96), stresses his link with the classical past, albeit now slightly degenerated. His reading of anti-Christian literature further underlines his pagan aspect (LJ, 89). To Mrs Failing's fancy, Stephen was likened to 'the young pagans who were said to lie under this field guarding their pagan gold' (LJ, 128), and for Rickie, as Meredith had done for Forster, he eagerly 'overthrew the Mosaic cosmogony' and pointed out the discrepancies in the Gospels (LJ, 109).

His hero-like status however is compromised by his nickname of 'Podge', an unflattering reference to his body weight. Like Gerald, he is also a bully, although Rickie tries to excuse this as due to his poverty in childhood: 'He behaved badly,' said Rickie, 'because he is poorer than we are, and more ignorant. Less money has been spent on teaching him to behave' (LJ, 107). He can also enjoy the company of a drunken soldier, whereas Rickie cannot (LJ, 112).

Stephen's roughness is part of his attraction for Rickie, and for Forster himself, just as Gino's roughness had charmed Philip in *Where Angels Fear to Tread*. In many ways Stephen is an alter ego for both Rickie and Foster, exemplifying characteristics which they would like to have owned for themselves.

The room Stephen occupies at home is irregularly shaped, unlike the other 'classical' rooms at Cadover (LJ, 117-8); significantly, it is dominated by a picture of the Demeter of Cnidus hanging from the ceiling by a string. This was a statue of the goddess found at Cnidus, in what was once part of ancient Greece. According to Walter Pater, at her shrine there was also found a statue of 'the mystical or Chthonian Dionysus' (Pater, 124). In Greek mythology Dionysus, like Rickie Elliot, was effeminate (R. Graves 1, 104; 107) and also lame (R. Graves 1, 108 & 2, 389). Robert Graves notes that one legend makes Demeter the mother of Dionysus (R. Graves 1, 56), and Demeter, says Pater, is the goddess who guides the shepherds in an Idyll of Theocritus (Pater, 110). Given Stephen's association, discussed below, with the shepherds of Theocritus, it can be seen how both he and the lame Rickie sprang from the same mother, not only in the physical sense, but in a spiritual one as well.

Demeter's picture continually calls attention to itself, 'For she was never still... and would sway and tap upon the rafters until Stephen woke up and said what he thought of her' (LJ, 118). The Cnidian Demeter reappears later in the novel when Ansell at the British Museum sees the original statue on which Stephen's picture is based; the figure affects him for 'he knew that here were powers he could not cope with, nor, as yet, understand (LJ, 182). Furbank discloses the meaning this figure held for Forster, for the famous Demeter of Cnidus, 'in her exile at the British Museum, was already a private cult with him'. To him she was 'the benevolent mother-deity, giver of "corn and tears"', and, Furbank surmised, represented for Forster 'the reconciliation of male and female in his own nature' (Furbank 1, 102-3).

The picture calls attention to the fact that Stephen's masculinity is not of a conventional kind, societal gender norms do not constrain him. In the British Museum the figure is behind a railing, 'with "No Admittance," so that she cannot be touched' (AH, 172), but in Stephen's irregularly shaped room she is given pride of place, although Stephen is unaware of her true powers. Being the goddess of spring her arrival brings fecundity back to the earth after the sterile winter months, as Stephen is destined to be fruitful, and his fertility is not compromised by this touch of femininity. In his essay 'Cnidus', Forster describes the goddess as receiving 'prayers of idolatry from suffering men as well as women, for she has transcended sex' (AH, 172). And in addition to being a centre of worship, it is significant that the ancient city of Cnidus was also the place where every four years athletes gathered for competitive games held in honour of Apollo by the Dorian Greeks, 'among whom comradeship became an institution' (Carpenter 1984, 256); Forster neatly finding in Cnidus a home for androgyny, male comradeship and sporting prowess.

The very word 'Cnidus' also conveys a meaning not available to the average reader of Forster's work. The historian Alan Bray notes that 'cinaedus' was a term employed in past centuries to denote a homosexual (Bray, 13). Likewise, Sir Richard Burton identifies 'cinaedus' (alternatively spelt as 'kinaidos') in his list of names used to denote homosexuals in history, as a word meaning the active male lover in homosexual sex (Burton, 182). Some recent writers have defined 'cinaedus' as referring to a male person who takes a passive role in homosexual sex. Will Roscoe takes such a view (Murray and Roscoe 58), as does Arno Schmitt, who defines 'cinaedus' as an 'effeminate singer, one who gets fucked (for money)' (Schmitt and Sofer 173). Their modern interpretation of the word, however, contrasts markedly with the depiction of cinaedic activities given by the ancient Roman writer Martial, and it is his description which seems to accord with Forster's understanding of the term. Martial recorded that 'cinaedi' acted as dancers and entertainers, but added that they also sold their sexual favours, taking the active role for adult homosexual clients, and 'often serviced their wives as well' (Dynes 1124). Both Burton and the historian K . J. Dover note that the origin of the word is unclear (Dover, 17),* but it derives from ancient Greek, and as such would surely have been known to Forster. Whilst 'cinaedus' might not derive from 'Cnidus', it is close enough for Forster to exploit its associations.

Returning to Forster's essay on Cnidus, we can, perhaps, see something of his original inspiration for the character of Stephen Wonham. In the essay the writer describes a rain-sodden visit to Cnidus, which was formerly a great city of Dorian Greece, but is now a provincial town in Turkey. Towards the close of the trip, Forster's party was joined by a local man, whose face 'was young, and it did not look unkind', and the man made a gesture to indicate

---

* The *Oxford Classical Dictionary* says of 'Cinaedic Poetry' that the poems 'were of a satirical and scurrilous character', and lists Sotades and Timon of Phlius as writers of such verse (Hammond and Scullard, 241). Sir Richard Burton took his name for the 'Sotadic Zone' from Sotades; this geographical zone was said to be characterised by a higher incidence of buggery (Burton, 175). Timon of Phlius wrote, amongst other things, a satyr-play entitled *Kinaidoi* (Hammond and Scullard, 1077).

that 'his brain and his heart were ours'. 'His manners were perfect' but 'there was a general tendency to avoid his attentions'. Despite the dreary weather, Forster noted that the place obsessed his imagination and he often tried to imagine it with 'a blue sky' and 'a mid-day sun that never moves'. In the last sentence of the essay he returns to the young local who had offered his services to the visitors, noting that 'over that extra person the brain will not keep steady' (AH, 173-4).

Forster made his trip to Cnidus on 6 April 1903, and although the essay indicates he left after a few hours, in reality, because of the poor weather conditions, he actually spent the night there (Stape, 16). Whether during his overnight sojourn Forster came to know the young man more intimately or not is largely immaterial, but the young man clearly remained a vibrant figure in the writer's imagination. The 'Cnidus' essay was published in March 1904, and the first draft of *The Longest Journey* followed in July that same year; Stephen Wonham's link with the Demeter of Cnidus points towards his being linked also with the dark young man of that same city about whom Forster's brain would 'not keep steady'. In the writer's imagination, the dark young man so typical of his landscape setting is transplanted to England, where, in a different setting, he becomes a blond-haired Saxon type. Vestiges of his Greek heritage remain, however, for the text is replete with examples that recall it, and in fantasy he becomes a potential 'Cinaedus', that is, an active male lover, to both Rickie and to Forster.

In *The Longest Journey*, Stephen draws many of his virtues from his closeness to the land. The Wiltshire countryside has a latent power to transform itself into the landscape of ancient Greece and to contain its values (LJ, 109-10). Mrs Failing asserts that the original inhabitants of the countryside were 'decent people', 'soldiers and shepherds', who 'worshipped Mars or Pan — Erda perhaps; not the devil', unlike their present-day equivalents from Bulford camp who rob the chickens (LJ, 129). The reference to 'soldiers and shepherds' implies a highly masculinised pastoral democracy, and the linking of those two occupations by Forster is significant.

John Addington Symonds noted that 'Greek love was originally a Dorian and soldierly passion; it had grown up in the camp' (Symonds 1893, 78); and it was a passion they shared with their contemporary herdsmen. Rickie is an avid reader of Theocritus, 'whom he believed to be the greatest of Greek poets' (LJ,5).* The poet spent part of his life in Alexandria, and Forster in his guide to that city declared his own high regard for his poetry (35-8). Theocritus wrote in the Dorian dialect (as spoken in Cnidus in its heyday), and his most distinctive poems evoke the life and rustic arts of the shepherds on his native island of Sicily (Drabble 1993, 974). Whilst his work does deal with hetero-

---

* One of the Uranian poets, Edward Cracroft Lefroy, published a series of homoerotic sonnets in 1883 under the title *Echoes from Theocritus*; its popularity led to reprints in 1885 and 1897 (d'Arch Smith, 247). J. A. Symonds included an essay on Lefroy in his *In the Key of Blue* (Symonds 1893, 87-110). And Edward Carpenter included two of the Idylls of Theocritus (12 and 29) in his *Anthology of Friendship: Ioläus*.

sexual relationships, many of his Idylls also deal with homosexual love. Examples of this can be found in Idyll 29, where the poet addresses his young male lover; likewise Idyll 30 is addressed to a young man; Idyll 5 speaks of anal sex between a shepherd and a goatherd, the herdsmen boasting of both homosexual and heterosexual conquests; and Idyll 7 relates the love of Aratus for the adolescent Philinus. Stephen is clearly linked by Forster to these shepherds of Theocritus. Mrs Failing, when speaking of Doric lays and Arcady, imagines Stephen as a 'pensive shepherd, twitching his mantle blue', instead of the rain-sodden wretch he appears to be (LJ, 88). His drunken singing with a soldier (LJ, 111-4) recalls the singing contests between shepherds and goatherds in a number of Theocritus' Idylls. And just before their singing, Stephen tells the soldier of a 'sordid village scandal' which 'sprang from certain defects in human nature, with which he was theoretically acquainted'. The 'defects of human nature' phrase seems to refer obliquely to homosexuality. Rickie hearing the scandal however, immediately recalls 'a parallel in a beautiful idyll of Theocritus' (LJ, 111-2).* It is noticeable that where Stephen sees a defect, Rickie thinks of beauty.

If any Greek god seems to rule Stephen, Pan would seem the likely candidate. In an earlier draft of the novel Forster had written a fantasy chapter about Stephen, although at that point of the work's development the character was actually known as 'Harold'. In this excised passage, Harold, having been hit on the head by an empty soda-water bottle thrown from a passing train, wanders naked into the darkened woods. In a letter to E. J. Dent of late April 1907, Forster termed it 'a long "Panic" chapter' (Lago and Furbank 1, 87). The writer's deliberate use of the word 'Panic', notably beginning the word with a capital letter, is revealing and indicative of the homoerotic content of the chapter. Forster's early short story, 'The Story of a Panic', had dealt with the sodomitic experiences of a English youth, Eustace, in an Italian wood whilst being possessed by the nature god Pan. In a similar anarchic guise Pan appears as a Faun in Forster's subsequent story 'The Curate's Friend'. The Faun, having come to England from Italy — probably, says the narrator, with a group of Roman soldiers — saves a local Wiltshire curate from an ill-advised marriage. In *The Longest Journey* Rickie reads an invocation to Pan to the boys at school, asking them, 'is it not beautiful?' (LJ, 160). Unfortunately Pan later answers this invocation and his presence is blamed in part for enthusing the same boys with brutality in their bullying of Varden (LJ, 185). Pan, a rural god, represents those aspects of nature which are wild and terrifying, and implicit in Forster's deployment of the god is the fact that he represents an uncontrolled sexuality which revels in sex as pleasure, rather than restricting its role to a mere part of the reproductive process, to be experienced only within marriage. There is, Forster argues, more to nature than simple continuance of the species; reproduction will ensure physical survival, but alone will never guarantee the character of a future society. In the version of the

*The allusion here could possibly be to Idylls 29 or 30.

novel he presented to his publisher, Forster played down Stephen's 'Panic' quality, though his close ties to nature and to sexual licence remain.*

The excised fantasy chapter is revealing, showing the basic themes of the work and how Harold, that is, Stephen, would develop if left unchecked by social convention. There is also a harder edge to the atheistic stance of the narrator than in the final published version of the novel, where the existence of a deity is doubted; in the early drafts, perhaps under Meredith's influence, the absence of a god, in the Christian sense, is accepted. In the excised chapter, Harold, in a delirium occasioned by his being struck on the head, runs naked through the woods at night and dives into 'a pool swollen by the rains' (LJ, 335). The pool recalls the Sacred Lake bathed in by George Emerson and his friends in *A Room with a View*. Naked and 'being himself a god', 'Heaven did open' (LJ, 336):

> Harold [Stephen] saw the whole <tyranny> \ tangle / of convention, to which most men are unconscious slaves. He too must <enter it again> \ re enter it. / But his <ens> slavery should be conscious. Never again would he pretend that he enjoyed it, or that it was universal, like the light or air. It was an arrangement — a temporary device to keep things goings [sic]. Behind it lay no immortal sanction (LJ, 336).

Elated by the freedom of this revelation, he returns home and throws into the fire grate his collection of sixpenny reprints, including, significantly, an abridgement of Darwin (LJ, 337).

The earlier drafts also demonstrate more strongly what the final version only hints at, Rickie's physical attraction to his half-brother, whom he kisses (LJ, 374 and 376), the discovery of which leads Agnes to confide to her brother, Herbert: 'I feel we're on the edge of something too big for us' (LJ, 374).

Forster hints that were England to be closer to its inherently pagan roots, its future inhabitants would be more likely to emulate Stephen's best characteristics. Agnes however can see little to praise in Stephen's character, even at one later point declaring him to be 'illicit, abnormal' and 'worse than a man diseased' (LJ, 261). For a while she had successfully persuaded her husband not to associate with him. But this break in their relationship led to a breakdown in Rickie's health; once reunited with Stephen his constitution improves dramatically (LJ, 267).

Their renewed intimacy leads Rickie to muse on romance and to their discovery of the stream of generations. Stephen, like Rickie earlier, is uncertain as to whether or not he should marry, and his reasons for not doing so echo Rickie's. Whilst driving back to Cadover in a trap at night, he confides to Rickie that although he may find a woman who will take him, 'she should

---

* Eustace's mysterious encounter with the goats in 'The Story of a Panic' has its parallel in *The Longest Journey* with Stephen's boyhood encounter with a flock of sheep which similarly leaves him 'in convulsions' (LJ, 117).

never have all my thoughts. Out of no disrespect to her, but because all one's thoughts can't belong to any single person' (LJ, 271). He adds later that, 'it's something rather outside that makes one marry, if you follow me: not exactly oneself.... We want to marry, and yet — I can't explain' (LJ, 272). Suddenly he breaks off the conversation and announces that they had arrived at 'our stream' (LJ, 272). The scene is a magical one, and the narrator speaks of romance, but Rickie 'thought of his brother's future and of his own past, and of how much truth might lie in that antithesis of Ansell's: "A man wants to love mankind, a woman wants to love one man"' (LJ, 272).

By the stream Stephen is transformed, for in his 'transfigured face... a new spirit dwelt there, expelling the crudities of youth'. Rickie 'saw steadier eyes, and the sign of manhood set like a bar of gold upon steadier lips' (LJ, 272). Together at Stephen's suggestion they place a lighted piece of paper 'flower-like on the stream' which carries the light away. Symbolically the flame is ignited by Stephen and its light is seen longer by him than by Rickie, for it is revealed as the stream of generations and, the text declares, Stephen 'governed the path between them' (LJ, 289):

> the flower sailed into deep water, and up leapt the two arches of a
> bridge. 'It'll strike !' they cried; 'no, it won't; it's chosen the left,'
> and one arch became a fairy tunnel, dropping diamonds. Then it
> vanished for Rickie; but Stephen, who knelt in the water,
> declared that it was still afloat, far through the arch, burning as if
> it would burn for ever (LJ, 273).

The light vanishes for Rickie as he is doomed not to have children to follow on after him, whereas Stephen sees the light 'burning as if it would burn forever', for he will have issue. When Rickie and Agnes do have a child, she is born lame and soon dies, and Rickie recognises that no child should ever be born to him again (LJ, 184). His brother is the one who will ultimately be fruitful in life, for Stephen would have children and he, not Rickie, 'would contribute to the stream; he, through his remote posterity, might be mingled with the unknown sea' (LJ, 192).

After the death of his daughter Rickie's bodily sterility is further mocked in references to the constellation of Orion, when in his misery he sees 'above mean houses the frosty glories of Orion' (LJ, 193). Elizabeth Heine, in her general notes to the Abinger edition of *The Longest Journey*, refers to a short story by Forster, 'The Point of It', to explain the author's symbolism. In that story, Orion is 'the central star of whose sword is not a star but a nebula, the golden seed of worlds to be' (LJ, 428) and the sight of its 'frosty glories' crushes Rickie. Before his final disintegration in a sterile marriage, the symbols of the stream and of Orion reappear, but Rickie is beyond their influence (LJ, 282).

One night as he endeavours to take the drunken Stephen home, Rickie crosses a railway line. A train comes and Rickie pushes his friend away, but fails to avoid being struck himself, and is killed. By sacrificing himself Rickie ensured that Stephen would continue to live and propagate, believing in his misery that his own life would anyway be doomed to sterility, whereas the future would belong to Stephen and his descendants. In this Rickie, and Forster, were merely reflecting the scientific opinion of the time.

The conventional negative view of science towards homosexuality and reproduction during the period of Forster's writing of this novel, can be found in Iwan Bloch's *The Sexual Life of Our Time*, which first appeared in an English translation (from German) in September 1908, just over a year after *The Longest Journey* had been published:

> The greatest spiritual values we owe to heterosexuals, not to homosexuals. Moreover, reproduction first renders possible the preservation and permanence of new spiritual values.... However obvious it may appear, we must still repeat that spiritual values exist only in respect of the future, that they only attain their true significance in the connexion and the succession of the generations, and that they are, therefore, eternally dependent upon heterosexual love as the intermediary by which this continuity is produced. The monosexual and homosexual instincts permanently limited to their own ego or their own sex are, therefore, in their innermost nature dysteleological and anti-evolutionistic (Bloch, 534).

Forster's view in this novel stands in sharp contrast to Bloch's disparaging view of homosexuals, and he earnestly maintains the notion that, whilst not reproducing, they can make a positive contribution to 'the succession of the generations' which is not 'anti-evolutionistic'. Indeed, later, under the influence of Edward Carpenter, Forster even attempted to show that the 'intermediate' state of homosexuality was actually a progressive development of the process of evolution itself, rather than a regressive one. If homosexuals are prohibited by Nature, by science, by social convention and by their 'congenital' contrary sexual instinct from entering into the stream of generations, how then are they supposed to contribute positively to their society?

Mr Jackson, Rickie's fellow teacher at Sawston, and known as 'my queer cousin' by Widdrington (LJ, 178), tries to 'express all modern life in the terms of Greek mythology, because the Greeks looked very straight at things, and Demeter and Aphrodite are thinner veils than "The survival of the fittest", or "A marriage has been arranged", and other draperies of modern journalese' (LJ, 174). Likewise, in 1897, Havelock Ellis had proposed in his *Sexual Inversion* that his homosexual contemporaries adopt the ethical values of the Greek paederasts (Broome, 99). Returning to Plato's *Symposium*, we can see exactly what procreativity is commended for male lovers, and ultimately expounded by Forster in *The Longest Journey*. In Plato's work, Diotima's words, approved of by Socrates, set out the nobler acts of creativity:

Men whose bodies only are creative, betake themselves to women and beget children — this is the character of their love; their offspring, as they hope, will preserve their memory and give them the blessedness and immortality which they desire in the future. But creative souls — for there are men who are more creative in their souls than in their bodies — conceive that which is proper for the soul to conceive or retain. And what are these conceptions? — wisdom and virtue in general. And such creators are all poets and other artists who may be said to have invention.... And he who in his youth has the seed of these implanted in him and is himself inspired, when he comes to maturity desires to beget and generate. And he wanders about seeking beauty that he may beget offspring — for in deformity he will beget nothing — and embraces the beautiful rather than the deformed; and when he finds a fair and noble and well-nurtured soul, and there is union of the two in one person, he gladly embraces him, and to such an one he is full of fair speech about virtue and the nature and pursuits of a good man; and he tries to educate him; and at the touch and presence of the beautiful he brings forth the beautiful which he conceived long before, and the beautiful is ever present with him and in his memory even when absent, and in company they tend that which he brings forth, and they are bound together by a far nearer tie and have a closer friendship than those who beget mortal children, for the children who are their common offspring are fairer and more immortal. Who, when he thinks of Homer and Hesiod and other great poets, would not rather have their children than any ordinary human ones? (Plato, trans. Jowett)

That was the perspective familiar to Forster through his study of the Greek classics, but there were contrary and negative views, like those of Bloch, to contend with. To Krafft-Ebing, for instance, such 'fairer' and 'immortal' children produced by individuals suffering from 'congenital homo-sexuality' were not always to be admired, for 'In the majority of cases, psychical anomalies (brilliant endowment in art, especially music, poetry, etc., by the side of bad intellectual powers or original eccentricity) are present, which may even go so far as pronounced conditions of mental degeneration (dementia, moral insanity)'; Krafft-Ebing urges that such 'anomalies' be recognised as yet further symptoms of hereditarily acquired degeneration (Krafft-Ebing, 225-6). Forster however, supports Diotima's argument in Plato and discloses that, although he will not leave children behind him, Rickie's contribution to 'the stream of generations' will not be insignificant.

The notion that the master works left by great artists are their children was not a new one to Forster's generation. Earlier writers had taken up the same Socratic notion. The poet Shelley, for example, who had translated Plato into English, spoke of his own poems as his 'intellectual children' (Shelley, 153), and J. A. Symonds, in discussing male love, wrote of its 'immortal progeny of high thoughts and generous emotions' (Symonds 1893, 70); even later, in 1924, Havelock Ellis observed that if society destroyed the 'invert' (his choice of word for 'homosexual') then it 'may, perhaps, destroy also those children of the spirit which possess sometimes a greater worth than the children of the flesh' (Broome, 99).*

Rickie's legacies as an artist, his 'children', are his writings. Pembroke gives a collection of his stories the name of 'Pan Pipes', marking the source of its inspiration. According to Walter Pater, Pan passed his flute to the shepherds of Theocritus (Pater, 9), and Theocritus is clearly one of Rickie's literary mentors, as well as an inspirer of Stephen's character. Both of them receive this legacy from an ancient past. In the closing scene of the novel between Stephen and Mr Pembroke, the true value of Rickie's legacy is revealed, although Rickie's success had earlier been predicted by his bed-maker at Cambridge who had been certain that 'The world... will be the better for him' (LJ, 9). Stephen, though physically fruitful, for he has a son and daughter, lacks any real appreciation of the true value of Rickie's bequest, whereas Mr Pembroke, the classical scholar, is sure that 'the world will be the gainer' (LJ, 283).

Towards the end of the novel, in Mr Failing's essay 'The True Patriot' we can see a commendation of a better world where these spiritual and physical children unite. Mrs Failing asks Rickie to read her the essay:

He took the book and found: 'Let us love one another. Let our
children, physical and spiritual, love one another. It is all we can do.
Perhaps the earth will neglect our love. Perhaps she will confirm it, and
suffer some rallying-point, spire, mound, for the new generations to
cherish' (LJ, 274-5).

Mr Failing died unhappy, uncertain his work would mean anything, but as Mrs Failing declares, his legacy has been passed on, for Rickie is regarded as his 'spiritual heir' (LJ, 195).

In an earlier draft of *The Longest Journey* Forster had written that Rickie, though realising he can never have children, does not see it as leading to his extinction; 'it is not really darkness', he says, 'for those I loved are handing the torches on' (LJ, 385).** Sadly this reassurance seems missing from the final published version. Had Rickie read the Uranian poet E. C. Lefroy's *Theocratic Idyll* (no. lxvi), he might have gained some comfort, for in that poem the 'Torch Bearer' of the title bears the light of a poetry which 'is but the soul's light cast upon the world for other souls to see' (Symonds 1893, 106).

---

* cf. Fielding's comment to Aziz, in *A Passage to India*: 'I'd far rather leave a thought behind me than a child' (PTI, 110).

** cf. *Maurice*, where the narrator says of the mothers of Maurice and Clive, 'they had handed on the torch their sons would tread out' (M, 88).

Returning to Elizabeth Heine's observation concerning the 'frosty glories' of Orion, whose centre star containing 'the golden seeds of worlds to be' so dispirited Rickie, had he not been so blinkered by depression he could have realised that the Orion legend had in fact asserted that creation did not invariably depend upon heterosexual intercourse. Orion, also known as Uroin, who was 'the handsomest man alive' (Graves, 151), had no mother; his mortal father Hyrieus bore him with the help of divine intervention. Robert Graves in *The Greek Myths* relates the story:

> Hyrieus, a poor bee-keeper and farmer, had vowed to have no children, and he grew old and impotent. When one day, Zeus and Hermes visited him in disguise, and were hospitably entertained, they enquired what gift he most desired. Sighing deeply, Hyrieus replied that what he most wanted, namely to have a son, was now impossible. The gods, however, instructed him to sacrifice a bull, make water on its hide, and then bury it in his wife's grave. He did so and, nine months later, a child was born to him, whom he named Uroin — 'he who makes water' (R. Graves 1, 152-3).

Forster no doubt appreciated the irony of the Orion legend, for who would have thought that the carrier of the 'seeds of worlds to be' should have been born without a mother, his father being assisted solely by two male deities.*

Having shown in *The Longest Journey* that it is possible to contribute to posterity without raising children of the flesh, Forster returned to his 'Lucy' novel, and concentrated on exploring the subject of love (divorced from any demands of procreation) in all its manifestations.

In the last of his short 'unpublishable' stories, 'Little Imber', written in 1961, Forster made a humorous return to the theme of children produced, like Orion, solely by males. Set in the 'lamentable future' (AS, 226) in a world where women predominate, males are dying out. The few men who remain are in demand for sexual services, but only daughters are being born to the women they impregnate. Two male studs, Warham and Imber, whilst arguing over their own respective merits, begin to fight and this leads to their sharing of sexual climax: 'Their hatred passed into wrestling which presently quietened, and they parted without looking at each other or at the seed they had both dropped onto the Birth House floor' (AS, 230). Their seeds unite to produce life, but they fail to keep the 'enigmatic mass' alive. Warham believes their 'child' might have been a new strain of human being, one 'that's supposed to get into the human bloodstream and start it breeding'. So Warham and Imber

---

* Of the gods attending Orion's conception, Zeus loved the boy Ganymede and Hermes was both the 'patron of flocks and herdmen' in the Idylls of Theocritus (Rist, 25) and the father of Pan (Hammond and Scullard, 773).

have sex again and produce a baby, 'the first of the new strain', closely followed by another child, its brother (AS, 234-5). Their homosexuality humorously enters into the 'stream of generations', not by contributing 'spiritually' to human civilisation, as Plato and the Greek paederasts had commended, but by a biological process which neither Krafft-Ebing nor Iwan Bloch could have imagined, directly usurping the role of women.* And significantly, their issue, conceived in 'a pagan grove', possess the feral natures of Harold in the excised 'Panic' chapter of *The Longest Journey* and, by implication, thereby of Stephen Wonham; the subsequent behaviour of these offspring recalls the sexual anarchy of Eustace and the Italian waiter in 'The Story of a Panic':

> Retiring to a pagan grove... they perfected their technique and produced Romuloids and Remoids in masses. It was impossible to walk in that country-side without finding a foundling, or to leave two together without finding a third. The women were stimulated and began to conceive normally as of old, their sons got raped by the wild boys and buggered their daughters who bore sons, the pleasing confusion increased and the population graph shot up until it hit the jackpot. Males had won (AS, 235).

The new offspring of 'Romuloids and Remoids' are evisaged as founders of a great future civilisation, their names obviously alluding to Romulus and Remus, the reputed founders of ancient Rome.

Returning to *The Longest Journey*, it should be of little suprise, given the identification of Forster with the character of Rickie, that Rickie adores Stephen, for Forster himself adored the character of Stephen Wonham. In an interview in 1952 Forster was asked what degree of reality his characters had for him after he had finished writing about them. His reply was clear: 'There are some I like thinking about. Rickie and Stephen, and Margaret Schlegel [from Howards End] — they are the characters whose fortunes I have been interested to follow. It doesn't matter if they died in the novel or not' (Dick, 14).

Similarly during a return trip to Wiltshire in 1964 to meet with the writer William Golding, Forster accompanied him on a walk. Seeing a Chalk Blue butterfly Forster suddenly began to chase it, and according to Furbank, 'His private thoughts were all of gratitude' and he felt at last in fantasy that a long-held secret yearning was fulfilled. Forster wrote:

> I exclaimed several times that the area was marvellous, and large — larger than I recalled. I was filled with thankfulness and security and glad that I had given myself so much back. The butterfly was a moving glint, and I shall lie in Stephen's arms instead of his child (Furbank 2, 319).

---

* cf. Gino's assertion in *Where Angels Fear to Tread* that Philip is to be the godfather of his next child (WAFT, 124). Also Forster's comment that he 'conceived' the idea for *Maurice* when touched on the buttocks by George Merrill (M, 235).

ROOMS WITH VIEWS

Appearing in 1908, *A Room with a View* was the third of Forster's novels to be published, but work on it had commenced much earlier. The writer began the book, initially known as his 'Lucy' novel, in the winter of 1901–02 during his first visit to Italy. Clear thematic parallels exist between this work and an unfinished novel of Forster's, begun sometime in the year 1900 (AS, viii) and now known as 'Nottingham Lace'. The incomplete manuscript was untitled at Forster's death; the present title being derived from the opening line of the work, 'They are Nottingham Lace!' (AS, 1). It is possible to examine the thematic links between this early work and *A Room with a View*, tracing the novel's evolution from an incomplete story centring on the isolation of a young male protagonist who desires to escape his situation, to a completed work centring on the rescue of a young woman and a young man from unhappiness and 'muddle'. Discussion of the links between Forster's work and that of the New England Transcendentalists, as well as the writer's older contemporary, Edward Carpenter, can also be utilised to mark out some of the homoerotic, political and visionary elements in the final text; and additional reference to Carpenter's work will elucidate Forster's own ambivalent attitude towards the novel.

A Room with a View opens in the Pensione Bertolini in Florence with Mr Emerson, an elderly English traveller and his son, George, offering new rooms with new views to two women, Lucy Honeychurch and her older cousin Charlotte Bartlett. When Lucy and Charlotte complain that their own allocated rooms have no views, Mr Emerson, direct and insistent, to the unease of his genteel auditors, calls in an effort to assist them, that he has a view, adding that his son too has a view, which they would gladly give to the ladies. It is not simply the offer of a new room, but more significantly the offer of a new view with which the novel is concerned, and it is by their response to this new view that the characters in the novel are to be judged. Exactly what this new view is will be discussed later, but in the minor social contretemps at the Pension Bertolini occasioned by Mr Emerson's undiscriminating geniality, Lucy is perceptive enough to realise that the subject of rooms and their views has a significance beyond the mundane:

> Lucy... had an odd feeling that whenever these ill-bred tourists spoke the contest widened and deepened till it dealt, not with rooms and views, but with — well, with something quite different, whose existence she had not realized before. (RV, 4)

As a theme in the writer's work 'rooms and views' was not new for it appeared in his very first mature piece of writing, 'Nottingham Lace', the commencement of which Furbank dates to late 1900 or early 1901 (Furbank 1, 73). Forster worked intermittently on the story until abandoning it during a stay in Naples in March 1902. Subsequently he turned his attention to his 'Lucy' novel (Furbank 1, 91). Work began on 'Lucy' sometime between December 1901 and February 1902 (Lucy, 3) and Forster produced two incomplete versions of the novel — the first known as 'Old Lucy', and the second or 'New Lucy' begun in December 1903. Progress on the novel proved irregular. In addition to work on several short stories, essays and articles, Oliver Stallybrass notes that after the publication in October 1905 of *Where Angels Fear to Tread*, Forster diverted his attention from work on 'Lucy' towards work on the novel that was eventually to become *The Longest Journey* (RV, viii). Once that novel was published in April 1907, Forster turned to the completion of 'Lucy' which he accomplished towards the end of that year when the novel acquired its new title of *A Room with a View*.

Like *The Longest Journey* and *Maurice*, 'Nottingham Lace' contains a main character, here Sidney Trent, who was based on one of Forster's earliest loves, Hugh Owen Meredith, the H O M to whom *A Room with a View* was dedicated. According to Furbank, Meredith was an important influence in the creation of the novel, for Forster regarded him as his personal emancipator, and in both 'Nottingham Lace' and *A Room with a View*, he took him as the model for 'the Deliverer, coming to rescue the hero or heroine from muddle and self-deception' (Furbank 1, 97-8).

The story of 'Nottingham Lace' concerns the relationship between Edgar Carruthers and Sidney Trent. The character of Edgar clearly contains aspects of Forster's own personality, and Sidney aspects of Meredith's. Their relationship, as Furbank notes, also prefigures in part that of Lucy Honeychurch and George Emerson in *A Room with a View*. As Lucy is shown to be in need of rescue by the Emersons from the emotionally stifling, 'medieval' aspects of Summer Street society, so Edgar is seen to stand in need of deliverance from Sawston society. Sidney promises to be his deliverer, but in the fragment of the work that remains, he fails to act in this capacity; indeed he is shown to be similarly in need of an escape route from the same society.

Had Edgar, like Forster, read the work of John Addington Symonds, he would have become aware of what might provide deliverance, and how in ancient Greece, youths with a similar ailment to his own had been rescued from depression and muddle, for those in suffering had found themselves new horizons in the teachings of the sage: 'Socrates... pitying the state of young men, and wishing to raise their affections from the mire into which they were declining, opened a way for the salvation of their souls through the very love they abused' (Symonds 1893, 67). In Socratic teaching, Symonds explains, the admired young man was known as the 'hearer', who responds to his older lover, the 'inspirer'. It was the duty of the inspirer to guide and instruct his beloved through the action of their love towards an ideal of 'Passionate friends, bound together in the chains of close yet temperate comradeship, seeking always to advance in wisdom, self-restraint, and intellectual illumination' (Symonds 1893, 69).

Forster had found his 'inspirer' in Meredith, though their relationship seemed inevitably doomed to failure in the long run. Nevertheless Meredith's intervention proved decisive when he led Forster to the two 'grand discoveries' of his late adolescence, his break with Christian dogma and the recognition of his homosexual identity. Such an inspirer Edgar Carruthers yearns to discover in 'Nottingham Lace', but the search for a soul like his seems, at first, to be hopeless. Edgar, a middle-class, eighteen-year-old youth, lives with Mr and Mrs Manchett, his uncle and aunt. Rather like Forster, Edgar is unathletic, thought to be physically weak by his relatives, and was bullied at his minor public school (AS, 6). He soon ceased to attend that school, whose prime aim according to his uncle was to 'bring up manly boys' (AS, 16), and subsequently, in an effort to ensure the continuance of Edgar's manly development, his uncle buys him a cricket bat, a tennis racket and a Sandow's exerciser (AS, 37). Sport holds little attraction for Edgar, though sportsmen are another matter entirely.

As the result of an earlier sojourn at the home of a maiden aunt, Edgar has a developed taste for literature, including, significantly, the writings of Walter Pater on ancient Greece, and the Persian poetry of Omar Khayyam .* For Edgar, poetry provided a refuge from the world without, 'and into that refuge, where no one in the house could follow him he would retire day after day' (AS, 7). His usual refuge, however, like that of most adolescents, was his room. He entered literature, as he entered his room, in order to escape, but, like Charlotte Bartlett in *A Room with a View*, who locked her door at the Bertolini to keep out imagined dangers, the refuge is little more than a prison; freedom beyond the room proving elusive.

Edgar's life begins to be transformed when he meets his inspirer, Sidney Trent. Sidney is slightly older, being twenty-three years old, when he arrives in Edgar's home town of Sawston to become a teacher at that very public school for the raising of manly boys which Edgar had recently left. Despite being a schoolmaster, he is looked down upon by Sawston society in general, and by Edgar's aunt, Mrs Manchett, in particular, because of his lower-class origin as the son of a Newcastle draper. Sidney's masculinity is very evident, for he is 'brown, athletic and good-looking' (AS, 15). Being a successful athlete however does not preclude him from having artistic inclinations, for he reads literature, paints water-colours (AS, 28) and can play Wagner upon the piano (AS, 29). Nonetheless, he was perfectly aware that to some he is seen as either vulgar and ill-bred, a rough diamond, or as one of nature's gentlemen (AS, 17). In his undoubted virility, youth, physical beauty and lower-class origins, and in the discomfort he occasions in polite society, he is a clearly an early prototype of George Emerson. And both George and Sidney, like the hero athletes of ancient Greece, prove their manhood in sporting successes; Sidney is good at rugby and George in *A Room with a View* proves adept at tennis.

* See below, in the chapter on *A Passage to India*, for a discussion of the significance to Forster of Edward Fitzgerald's translation of *The Rubaiyat of Omar Khayyam*.

Also like George, Sidney is to prove the agent by whom another is to be rescued from social and emotional suffocation. The person rescued (the hearer) is similarly destined to play a major part in the transformation of the rescuer (the inspirer). Sidney begins to rescue Edgar as George rescues Lucy. It is a theme in which Forster in his early work delighted, as he noted later in his *Commonplace Book*: 'Two people pulling each other into salvation is the only theme I find worthwhile... It takes two to make a Hero' (CB, 55). What is also similar about Sidney and George is that both of them occupy marginal positions in society, so that whilst they both endeavour to lead their respective partners from their rooms, it is not clear as to where exactly they may be leading them. This is a recurring problem for Forster in both his work and, as we shall see, in his personal life; even the fictional pair of lovers he perhaps was most intimately concerned with — Maurice and Alec — simply disappear into the greenwood, but where that is or how they live is not adequately explained, although as male lovers the reason for their disappearance from contemporary society can be more easily understood.

What is also clear about both works is the importance of the underlying theme of salvation, which the rescue will effect. The narrator of 'Nottingham Lace' informs the reader that Edgar and Sidney's story 'would not be a drama of action but one of the Soul's Awakening, so dear to the modern mind' (AS, 26). The 'Soul's Awakening', as Elizabeth Heine notes, is a reference to the painting of that name produced in 1879 by James Sant, once Painter-in-Ordinary to Queen Victoria. According to Heine it is a picture of a young girl holding a prayer-book, gazing towards heaven (AS, 322). Clearly there is a humorous identification here between the young girl's hope of salvation and that of Edgar's yearning for release. And, as will be seen later in the discussion of the 'New Lucy' draft, here Forster freely attributes similarity of feeling to both genders. He does however preserve clearer distinctions between those viewed as essentially passive in a relationship and those viewed as dominant; gender is frequently ambivalent in his work, class and wider social power relationships are by contrast always carefully differentiated.

Significantly Edgar and Sidney meet in the month of May. In *A Room with a View*, Mr Emerson, misquoting the poet Lorenzo whilst defending the amorous behaviour of the Italian driver and his woman friend, warns Mr Eager of the hopelessness of fighting against the spirit of spring, essentially that of physical love, which according to Mr Emerson is at its strongest in May (RV, 63). Edgar's uncle Mr Manchett meets Sidney at the first cricket match of the year at Sawston school and, impressed by his athleticism, invites him to his home where he meets Edgar. After Manchett sarcastically criticises his nephew for not taking sufficient exercise, Sidney readily volunteers to take Edgar on long country walks. At first Manchett resists the offer, but later he urges Edgar to accept the proposal, telling him with unconscious irony, that: 'I look upon it as your last chance of becoming a man' (AS, 24). Intimacy with Sidney becomes a turning point in Edgar's life and promises to make him a very different kind of man from that which his uncle had envisaged, leading

him to a new realisation that, 'The life he liked leading and the life his relatives led were incompatible' (AS, 26). Survival seems to depend on his leading
a double life:

> He would lead two lives. His artistic interests and youthful impulses —
> all the things he cared for should be on one side, shut up in his room.
> His everyday behaviour should be on the other. There had been little
> connection between them in the past and there should be none in the
> future (AS, 26).

Significantly 'the things he cares for' are kept solely for his room, uncon-
nected to the mundane, artificial life outside of it. His decision was, and is, a not
uncommon one for a closeted homosexual to make. During Forster's lifetime it
was practically the norm for homosexuals to lead double lives, clearly marked
into two separate areas: a safe private area (visible amongst one's friends, perhaps), where sexual feelings were openly acknowledged, and a potentially
dangerous public area where they decidedly were not. The fact that Edgar seems
obviously based on Forster and Sidney on Meredith, suggests that the relationship between Edgar and Sidney was at least homoerotic, if not actively
homosexual. Forster himself felt released by Meredith's friendship, as if all the
greatness of the world had been opened up to him by their meeting (Furbank 1,
98). Likewise, it is Sidney's role as the agent of rescue to lead Edgar to a new
view, which asserts that his life need not be restricted to his room and that a
greater life may flourish outside its walls, even, perhaps, finding a place within a
wider society.

The friends' intimacy develops as Edgar symbolically admits Sidney into
his room and begins to share his inner thoughts with him. Sidney however will
not confine himself to rooms and he alerts Edgar to the beauty outside of his
home (AS, 19). Predictably, perhaps, Sidney had not recognised the value of the
view from his room before. But before Sydney can elucidate further, their conversation is interrupted by Manchett, who, unable to share in Edgar and Sidney's
outlook, sees the view as something to be limited and controlled, proposing to
enclose it with 'a brick wall, so that we shall be more secluded. We must get
privacy at all costs. An Englishman's home, you know, is his castle' (AS, 20).
His plans to fence off the view echo Charlotte's response to the view across the
Arno from the room given to her (RV, 12-13). And whereas in England a
man's home is private, in Italy no one has the least idea of privacy (RV, 33). As
noted earlier in the discussion of *Where Angels Fear to Tread*, in some parts of
Italy during the earlier part of this century, homosexual men from England
did not need to strive so earnestly to keep the private and public areas of their
life rigidly separate.

Later Edgar and Sidney, alone in Edgar's room, look at the view through
the window and see in the distance a ridge and pine-woods beyond. Sidney
wonders if the people beyond it are nicer than people in Sawston (AS, 27) and

proposes that they cycle there to find out. Had they explored those pine woods they might have come across the Sacred Lake which figures so prominently in *A Room with a View*, but such a discovery is not to be. Edgar protests that he cannot ride a bicycle; his inspirer, Sidney,can of course teach him.

The two aspects of Edgar's life are sustained by a necessary deceit; his relatives are ignorant of Sidney's true influence and Edgar's ability to cope with this situation is conditional: 'He felt his new formula of life was working well. It would not be difficult to be two people after all. He did not realise that it was easy because at the moment the two persons coincided' (AS, 29). As long as the 'two persons' can exist in separate worlds all will run smoothly, at least, on the surface; problems will arise should the two worlds collide or should Edgar choose to try to connect his separate existences; connection might have proved possible in Italy, as Philip Herriton was to discover in *Where Angels Fear to Tread*, but Edgar is trapped in England. Sidney promises to provide the key to this connection, but the promise remains unfulfilled.

As so often in Forster's work, male friendships are shown to suffer from the interference of women. In 'Nottingham Lace', Edgar's aunt Mrs Manchett, once she discovers that Sidney is the son of a lowly draper,tries to undermine the friendship between the young men. At first Edgar had resisted the promptings of his relatives to accept Sidney's friendship; in order to placate them he had aquiesced. He had been pleasantly suprised by his new friend, finding a robust and sensitive companion with whom he could share the two, still separate, aspects of his life. Having refused his aunt's request to cease association with Sidney, 'his new system had broken down' (AS, 34). In his anger at the Manchetts' snobbery Sidney 'launched into two orations, one against the rules of English society, the other against the imperfect education of women' (AS, 34). It is an outburst which invigorates Edgar who was startled by his friend's zeal, 'and finally carried away by it, and in company they endeavoured to build the sorry scheme of things anew, according to the habits and duties of young men' (AS, 34). Sidney leads Edgar to accept the validity of his inner thoughts and feelings, partially freeing him from some of the adverse effects of the homophobic society they dwell in.

Edgar's family are incapable of changing things, for, in truth, they can construct no real alternative view, nor can Edgar and Sidney transform social realities. Unlike George in *A Room with a View* they have no mentor to suggest how they ought to proceed; Sidney, the inspirer, needs further inspiration himself. This situation is evident when Edgar begins to see Sidney's weakness, failing however to realise that it was he himself who in his isolation had exaggerated Sidney's powers (AS, 35). Sidney proves as rudderless as Edgar in the move towards a more fulfilling way of life.

Later Edgar meets the wealthy Miss Logan who flirts with him, and in the affair he is depicted as 'the unsuspecting victim' (AS, 54). Though he remains oblivious to Miss Logan's stratagems, his aunt does not, yet she is content to see them united for 'she was living in that realm of modern fiction, where the love of woman for man and of man for woman can alone produce startling situations and heroic deeds, and alone bring happiness and misery to the characters concerned' (AS, 54). (This ironic observation perhaps discloses how early Forster began to be concerned about the limitations he felt were placed on his public fictional writings.) It seems that possibly marriage might resolve Edgar's isolation and his sense of social incongruity and so, forbidden by the Manchetts to associate with Sidney, he passively agrees to see more of Miss Logan, even admitting her to his room (AS, 55).

Edgar seems destined to drift towards a disastrous union, just as Lucy drifts towards marriage with Cecil Vyse in *A Room with a View*. Further plot similarities arise when Sidney reveals his jealousy regarding Edgar's walking with Miss Logan; Sidney's disquiet mirroring that of George over Lucy and Cecil. Unlike George Emerson, Sidney has no Italian driver to prompt him to 'Courage and love' (RV, 67) and he fails to act decisively when they meet. After a few minutes of 'furtive conversation' and giving Edgar what is apparently a piece of paper, he abruptly rides off (AS, 55). The paper turns out to be a bank-note and another attempt by Sidney to save Edgar from his domestic prison:

> He [Edgar] found himself imprisoned by his uncle, walled in with no outlet. No outlet. Then he thought with a shudder that there was always the front door. That was what Trent [Sidney] wanted. He wanted to see him run away and had given him money to do it with (AS 56).

The fragment of the story terminates with a long conversation between Edgar and his younger cousin Jack. Jack has been condemned by his father and his school for smoking a cigarette and for having been seen in the company of Sidney Trent's younger sister, Piggy. Jack laments that he is being punished for having committed no wrong: 'it is hard luck. You see, the school or he [his father, Mr Manchett] just says the things are wrong, but I don't see they're wrong for that'. Edgar agrees: 'Things aren't wrong because people say they are', and, 'filled with a strange excitement', it leads him to an outburst of his feelings of injustice (AS, 64-5).

Edgar's complaint, whilst in part typically that of many an adolescent, arises from his feelings of powerlessness; he had looked to Sidney to release him from the prison of his room and to provide a new view which would challenge and replace the social conventions he now rails against. Jack proposes that society itself be disdained, urging Edgar towards self-reliance, but Edgar remains doubtful. Jack half apologises for bothering his cousin, but Edgar shows his pleasure at Jack's coming:

> 'Hope you don't mind me coming', he [Jack] said, to pave the way for departure. To his intense discomfort he found his hand seized by both of Edgar's.
>   'Mind you coming! I shall bless you for it the longest day I live. There I was, sitting numb, unable to move, even to think, crushed,

beaten. You've shown me what to do, because you're strong and [...]
(AS 66)

At this point Forster's manuscript draft ends. What Edgar has really decided to do remains unclear. What is clear however is that Forster, like Edgar,
had not yet learned how to activate relationships in his work. Like Edgar, he
lacked a view, a practical perspective upon which to develop the story and within
which the friends might find salvation, and so abandoned it. Ancient Greece
had provided a starting point with 'inspirer' and 'hearer', and his relationship
with Meredith had provided a more contemporary model.

Furbank, whilst acknowledging that the plot of 'Nottingham Lace' is a
first sketch for the rescue of Lucy by the Emersons in *A Room with a View*,
argues that what is not there in the fragment is much in the way of shaping or
narrative power: 'Not only does he [Forster] not know what will happen to his
characters, he is not yet attuned to the idea that things can happen' (Furbank 1,
74-5). Furbank later adds that it was Italy which eventually freed Forster's imagination (Furbank 1, 93), and significantly, it was on his first trip to Italy in
1901 that Forster finally abandoned work on the manuscript of 'Nottingham
Lace'. He recorded the event, and his reasons for not completing the novel, in a
letter written from Perugia to his friend Goldsworthy Lowes Dickinson on 15
December 1901. Forster wrote that he had felt unable to write whilst he was
abroad as he had become very discontented with his own approach to 'Nottingham Lace'. His failure he put down to his attempts at 'realism', for instead of
copying incidents and characters that he knew, he had tried to imagine others
equally as commonplace (Furbank and Lago 1, 51).

Forster's difficulty in finding a suitable resolution to the relationship between Edgar and Sidney can be explained by this commitment to 'realism'.
Writing in a period closely following the trials of Oscar Wilde, when male friendships began to be viewed more sceptically, a commitment to realism would
inevitably militate against a happy ending for a homoerotic friendship; realism,
being often marked by pessimism, would perhaps demand a tragic ending to
the love affair. In the generally tolerant atmosphere of his life at Cambridge,
Forster could enjoy intimacy with Meredith, but where could the likes of Edgar
Carruthers and Sidney Trent find acceptance? According to 'Nottingham Lace'
their relationship is only at its deepest in the privacy of Edgar's room, but the
desire both these friends express is for a life beyond that prison.

Once Forster himself had changed his creative perspective, then new vistas of
the imagination were opened up, although his persistent diffidence (as much
as the social condemnation of homosexuality) still held him back from an
unqualified commitment to any social, political or ideological cause. Furbank
dates the moment at which Forster 'found' himself as a writer to May 1902
when the writer staying at Ravello in Italy wrote the short story, 'The Story of
a Panic'. Furbank explains that Forster had begun to realise that he possessed
the faculty of producing writing that mattered, and that it could matter was

important to a writer who 'had been born into a period when, under the influence of Flaubert and Zola, serious literature seemed committed to pessimism and to a mask of "coldness"'. Forster's impulse to write, by contrast, was inseparable from his optimism: 'That the universe was good, that life was worth living: these seemed the only messages that justified the effort of writing (Furbank and Lago 1, viii).

It is of course one thing to assert that 'the universe was good, that life was worth living', but how is that to be expressed openly in writing about friendships between men? It is a problem Forster never solved; those writings of his which dealt overtly with intense male friendships remained unpublished until after his death; homoeroticism, in his works intended for publication, was hidden behind a fragile surface heterosexuality or, mirroring marginalisation in a wider society, was pushed to the textual edges.

One of the first fruits of Forster's new approach to his work was the short story 'Ralph and Tony'. Begun in 1902, and finished during a stay in Italy in 1903, the story is set in the Tyrol, where the 'effeminate', 'delicate' and 'unorthodox' Ralph, in what appears to be another Forster self-portrait, is travelling with his mother. When he meets the 'lovable' and 'strong' Tony and his equally attractive sister, Margaret, he would like to know them both, but the brother is his obvious favourite. Tony, the 'strenuous' athlete, who was often 'faring roughly among rough men' (AS, 78), at first rejects Ralph's attempts to win his friendship. Unable to win the brother, Ralph subsequently proposes that he be allowed to marry Margaret, but adding that he especially wants Tony to live together with them in a new type of relationship:

> People say that three can't live together — that there will be jealousy.
> They don't know what love is. It doesn't deal in quantities. It's nothing to
> do with sex or relationship. It never says 'a husband's dearer than a
> brother, a wife's more than a friend'. That's the old false love, where all is
> wrecked. I know of the new love — not in metaphysics but in earthly
> life, and that alone is safe and true. (AS, 80)

After pleading his case, Ralph falls at Tony's feet, desperately entreating him to accede to the suggestion. But Tony explodes with anger and repeatedly kicks Ralph until he is out of the room. Ralph goes off into the cold mountain snows, and Tony, his anger subsequently cooling and fearing for the other's safety, decides he had better follow him as otherwise disaster is bound to befall Ralph. Tony finds him, but cannot persuade him to return, so knocks him out with a punch and proceeds to carry him back to the hotel. Exhausted by this burden, Tony stumbles on the return journey and can go no further, but fortunately Ralph awakens and summons help for them both. Back in Tony's hotel room his problem is diagnosed as 'heart disease' (clearly a coded reference to 'problems of the heart'). Ralph's heroic rescue of him begins to alter his view of the man, and he now wishes that Margaret would marry Ralph, yet feels he cannot tell his sister about his change of heart, for it would involve 'terrible, unthinkable, explanations' (91).

After an afternoon and early evening together in Tony's hotel room, the two men are reconciled. What occurs in that room is not revealed, merely that it leads to the men's decision that Ralph will marry Margaret and that all three of them will live together; a decision which Margaret herself later endorses when she allows Ralph to kiss her and embraces him in return. How their decision to live together will work out in practice is not pursued, but it is clearly based on a secret compact between the two men. Bringing in Margaret provides a useful smokescreen and a socially acceptable reason for the two men to live together. When Ralph has married Margaret, Ralph and Tony's 'manly love' would be viewed as a familial love, the two men being related by the marriage, and familial male intimacy is unlikely to raise the kind of suspicion that would attend domestic intimacy in a friendship between two unrelated males.

The idea for such a relationship may have occurred to Forster as a way in which he could continue to be close to Meredith, after the latter's marriage, and the concept of a non-sexual ménage à trois, or rather, more particularily, of a triangle of intimacy between two male characters and a female, is one Forster frequently employed in his work; examples being found in the relationships between Gino, Philip and Caroline in *Where Angels Fear to Tread*, and between Aziz, Fielding and Adela in *A Passage to India*; though in both novels, the woman is presented as a potential bar to closer intimacy between the men involved. It is perhaps for this reason that 'Ralph and Tony' proceeds no further than the proposal of marriage and, in those works where Forster develops such a triangular relationship, the concept seems unworkable in practice, for in both the novels cited the relationships between the men continue long after the woman has been discarded by the author.

In Forster's day, for a writer to resolve the relationship problems of his fictional creations by a marriage invariably implied adherence to some degree of gender stereotyping, something which as a writer of 'realism' he wanted to avoid. One particular solution to this problem which he utilised in his work is that of the free attribution of feeling to characters regardless of gender, by which is meant that in the construction of his characters, conventional definitions of gender do not dominate, although the influence of such gender stereotyping is often clearly at work upon the characters in their daily lives. This practice allows Forster to write about sexual and emotional relationships between men under the guise of a surface heterogeneity. An example of this, referred to earlier in 'Nottingham Lace', is the humorous passage in which Edgar's position is compared to that of the girl in the painting of 'The Soul's Awakening'; Edgar can be presented as sharing in a young girl's emotion, yet still be subject to conventional gender norms primarily through his uncle's disquisitions on the attainment of masculinity. This is not only true of his 'passive' characters like Edgar but also of his 'active' ones such as George Emerson, Freddy Honeychurch and Mr Beebe who can humorously be called 'nymphs' by the narrator in the bathing scene at the Sacred Lake (RV, 130). Of course in both of these in-

stances what perhaps renders the overt reference to femininity in male characters free of conventional censure is the fact that the references are on the
surface ironic; humour cloaks conventionally unpalatable observations, rendering them acceptable to a general readership.

This refusal to ascribe fixed attributes and sensibilities to characters, and
little more than a notional regard to gender conventionalities, permitted Forster
to explore the issues of sexuality and gender more freely and more creatively,
though still firmly in the closet. For example, in an early draft of *A Room with
a View* we see that an experience later given to Lucy Honeychurch was originally described as befalling a young man. Lucy's emotional distress in the Piazza
Signoria in Florence where she witnesses the murder of a young Italian was, in
'Old Lucy', originally the experience of a character known variously (in the
manuscript) as 'Arthur', 'Mr. Arthur' or as 'Tancred'. This character described
by Stallybrass as 'the somewhat unheroic hero' was, according to Forster's own
notes, based on Meredith (Lucy, 3), and some of Arthur's biographical details
mirror Meredith's own. As the hero he was still destined to 'rescue' Lucy, but
like his predecessor, Sidney Trent, and his successor, George Emerson, he is
likewise in need of the kind of awakening destined for his partner. And Arthur's
moment of awakening, like Lucy's, has overt sexual overtones, although here
the language is clearly homoerotic, indicating that the sexual awakening will
not be limited to a heterosexual one:

> Arthur hurried to the Fountain of Neptune, and... he soon clambered
> over the bronze groups of Tritons and Satyrs and reached the central
> basin. On the rim lay a young man \ of twenty /, stripped almost
> naked<, and blood\ . Blood / was dripping quickly off him into the
> water, and the people who held him were \ bathing him & / making
> frantic efforts to stop the <drip> \ flow /. « He was <an Italian> about
> twenty, one of the many handsome young » \ He was one of those
> handsome / Italians of the lower classes who may be seen by the dozen
> in any Tuscan town. He was magnificently made and his splendid chest
> swelled & contracted with every spurt of blood, while his brown sun
> burnt arms played idly upon the fountain rim (Lucy, 36).

The experience profoundly disturbs Arthur on a number of levels:

> By some subtle connection, the sight of the young Italian's perfect form
> lying on the fountain brim had led him to disbelieve in his own capacity
> for rendering beauty. <Though that> \ That / indeed was an aesthetic
> connection, intelligible if unexpected, but there was also a \ stronger /
> connection of a more subtle <and still stronger> kind. He longed to be
> more emotional and more sympathetic: to see more, and more largely, of
> the splendid people <who> with whom he should live so short a time
> (Lucy, 37).

The placing of the murder of the young Italian is significant. It occurs in the Piazza della Signoria, which long before Forster's day and right up to our own has been noted for the Renaissance sculptures which decorate it, including some of the greatest works by Michelangelo, Cellini, and other artistic masters; the Piazza and its contents symbolise those ancient values which Forster saw as Greece's finest legacy to Italy. The narrator observes in the novel's final published form that a 'Greek statue means fruition' and that the architecture of the Renaissance means light, whereas that of the Middle Ages is associated with darkness and celibacy (RV, 86-7). Both Arthur, and later, Lucy (her name deriving from the Latin for 'light'), are destined to discover the light of ancient Greece through an encounter with Italy. First, however, Arthur, like Lucy in the final form of the novel, must witness death. But for the oozing of blood, the scene wherein young friend bathes injured friend would evoke a homoerotic idyll, reminiscent of that later enacted in the episode at the Sacred Lake. The death of the youth acquires a significance, not merely that life is of the body and is fleeting, but aesthetically that the denial of the body amounts to a denial of beauty. And denial of the body, of its sensations, is not something that Art can compensate for, for 'Art was not helping him... <It was hindering>' (Lucy, 37). Only by entering into greater intimacy with others can Arthur develop his capacity as an artist. The 'connection of a more subtle <and still stronger> kind' clearly relates to sexuality, which of course is a strong determinant in all apprehensions of physical beauty. Arthur Tancred's crisis mirrors that faced by Forster himself.

If, as Furbank asserts, Forster's impulse to write was bound up with his optimism and 'That the universe was good, that life was worth living... seemed the only messages that justified the effort of writing', then from where can this view derive ideological support? Where was that life worth living to be found, and how must it be lived? Forster's purpose in creating works of art, like Arthur Tancred's, must involve the discovery of ways in which the love of beauty and its aesthetics of the body may unite with comradeship and moral excellence. What Arthur stands in need of is transformation, but, as with Edgar in 'Nottingham Lace', this does not take place; they were both abandoned by their creator. Elements of Edgar's, Sidney's and Arthur's characters are redistributed to both Lucy and George in *A Room with a View*. The abandoned drafts of 'Nottingham Lace' and 'Lucy' both indicate the difficulty Forster had in presenting a male protagonist being liberated by another male, the convention being that a man rescued a woman, not other men. It is not surprising therefore, that in order to finish his novel, and to gain a publisher, Forster sided with convention by making George, under his father's tutelage, Lucy's deliverer.

In the completed novel the turning point in both Lucy's and George's fortunes follows on from George's bathing in the Sacred Lake, which is said to have a healing capacity (RV, 198). The bathing scene brings George into contact with other men in an atmosphere of male eroticism and freedom, which serves as an example of how beauty, aesthetics, comradeship and moral excellence can (albeit fleetingly) be united. Lucy, of course, does not — indeed within the social conventions of her time, cannot — join the bathers; whereas George finds himself in a new relationship with other men, Lucy's deliverance means only that she has a new relationship with one man, George. By replacing a male protagonist with a female one, Forster was in greater thrall to the social and genre conventions of his day.

Before he could create characters whose lives were free from stultifying society, Forster needed to discover for himself a new 'view'. Ancient Greece could only go so far, contemporary society being so very different. Clues to the development of his new perspective lie in his diary; at each year end, Forster was accustomed to writing a personal review of the previous year. In the entry for New Year's Eve 1907 he notes that it had been a happy year, justifying 'optimism in life', and records in the margin some of the writers he had read that year. Included in his list are Samuel Butler, A. E. Housman, J. A. Symonds, Walt Whitman and Edward Carpenter (Furbank 1, 159). It was Forster's study of these writers which assisted in the development of this new 'view'. All of the writers listed are now known to have been homosexual or, in Butler's case, bisexual.* Carpenter had the greatest influence on Forster, but in his early years so too did Whitman.

One of the themes of *A Room with a View* is the desire for guides, whether to help one see Italy better or to discover a better way of living. Mr Eager guides the tourists towards his appreciation of Santa Croce and the values of a pre-Renaissance, medieval, world; Baedekers are useful manuals but, as Miss Lavish points out, do not direct one to the 'true Italy', nor do the rules and conventions of society in Summer Street provide satisfactory guidance. In 'Nottingham Lace' Edgar (and Sidney) had no guide but in *A Room with a View* Lucy (and George) find one in Mr Emerson. So where, in fact, did Forster find the character of Mr Emerson?

Lee Elbert Holt has pointed out the links between some aspects of Mr Emerson's character and that of the writer Samuel Butler (Holt, 1946). At the time of writing *Room*, Forster was also working on a study (unfinished at his death) of the work of Samuel Butler. Mr Emerson's education of his son is similar to that given by Ernest Pontifex to his children in Butler's novel *The Way of All Flesh*, and Mr Emerson's refusal to have George baptised mirrors a similar quarrel which divided Butler from his family. Similarly when Mr Emerson quotes a friend of his who said that 'Life... is a public performance on the violin, in which you must learn the instrument as you go along' (RV, 201), he is in fact quoting from an essay of Butler's on 'How to Make the Best of Life'. The views commended in the novel however derive not only from Butler but also from

---

* In 1890 John Addington Symonds wrote to Whitman asking if he was homosexual. Whitman replied that he was not, claiming that he had fathered children, and professed horror at the suggestion that he had commended homosexuality in his works; most scholars now accept however that his denials were intentionally misleading (See Ellis 1, 51-6).

those other, American, writers whom Forster had read in 1907. The discovery
of their views appears to have facilitated the writer's creativity, answering some
of the aesthetic difficulties raised in Arthur Tancred's crisis and allowing him
at last to find his direction in the novel.

There are complications however in Mr Emerson's role as a guide, for he is
not required in this comedy of manners to be the epitome of what he espouses;
his occasional bumbling and tedious sententiousness lie uneasily next to statements which attribute to him 'the face of a saint who understood' (RV, 204). He
can still act though as an imperfect, yet honest, messenger, gently and comically
underlining the proposed guiding viewpoint in the novel; and, for the reader, he
does not guide alone for the narrator also canvasses this new perspective.

That Mr Emerson shares his last name with the American writer and philosopher Ralph Waldo Emerson could point to him as a possible original for
the character. When Mr Emerson asserts 'that all life is perhaps a knot, a
tangle, a blemish in the eternal smoothness' (RV, 26-7), he is expressing a
similar view to that held by the writer Emerson, who in his essay on 'Fate'
urges the reader:

> to see how fate slides into freedom, and freedom into fate, observe how
> far the roots of every creature run, or find, if you can, a point where
> there is no thread of connection. Our life is consentaneous [consistent]
> and far-related. This knot of nature is so well tied, that nobody was ever
> cunning enough to find the two ends. Nature is intricate, overlapped,
> interweaved, and endless (Emerson 1888, 29).

Such a viewpoint could explain why, whilst Mr Emerson urges Lucy to
beware of muddle (RV, 201) and to discover a freer course, George can make
observations such as, 'Italy is only a euphemism for Fate' (RV, 181) and that
'Everything is Fate' (RV, 128). But earlier references to Emerson had been
made in 'Nottingham Lace', and there his ideas had been rejected. Jack had
counselled Edgar to cultivate 'Self-reliance' (the term being evocative of
Emerson, who wrote a celebrated essay on the subject), however Edgar had
rejected this advice. 'Self-reliance' as a virtue can be taken to extremes; in the
sphere of sexuality, celibacy (or masturbation) might appear to be the epitome
of self-reliance, not something Edgar (nor Forster) would appear to want.
Emerson's essay had also counselled the reader to 'stay at home in thine own
heaven' (Emerson 1906, 46); this would seem to imply staying alone in one's
room, Emerson asserting that 'We must go alone. Isolation must precede true
society' for 'Travelling is a fool's paradise' (Emerson 1906, 51). Both Edgar
and Lucy, however, find their rooms insufficient and desire to experience a
more fulfilling life outside of their own narrow sphere, but for that kind of
existence they have no guide, nor any idea as to what kind of 'true society'
their isolation might precede. And by leaving their 'heaven' at home, they find
that travelling to Italy does lead to a paradise, unpeopled by fools. The freedom proposed by Emerson is really only a limited and personal experience,

involving individual freedom from social muddle and convention, not social transformation. Forster's characters needed a direction to take once they had 'escaped' nature, home and fate, and for Forster the freedom attained must be sexual as well as social. To discover this Forster turned initially to the writings of another New England Transcendentalist, Henry David Thoreau, and subsequently to the writings of Walt Whitman and Edward Carpenter.

Having met Lucy and Miss Bartlett in Italy, the Emersons subsequently go to live in Summer Street, close to the home of the Honeychurch family. The house they occupy there has been given the name of 'Cissie' — a name clearly impling gender ambiguity — and which, noticeably, has curtains of Nottingham lace (RV, 101). Soon after arriving the Emersons receive a visit from the Reverend Mr Beebe and Freddy Honeychurch.

Mr Beebe is intrigued by the books which the Emersons have brought to Summer Street. Significant amongst them is A. E. Housman's collection of poems, *A Shropshire Lad*, though Mr Beebe says he has never heard of it (RV, 125). During the gestation period of 'Lucy' Forster spent a walking-tour with George Barger, Hugh O. Meredith and his new wife in Shropshire. His admiration of Housman's work was subsequently recorded in his diary along with the observation that he had lashed himself into a liking for Shropshire though had never 'looked out for the lads' (Furbank 1, 153). By 1907 he had rightly surmised that the poet shared his own sexual orientation, from reading Housman's work and comprehending its frequent homoerotic encoding. Forster was later to write to William Plomer that there were 'breaths' of Housman in *Howards End* (Lago and Furbank 2, 287-8), and of *A Shropshire Lad* he declared that the book 'was inexhaustible, and the warmth of the writer's heart seemed unalloyed' (Furbank 1, 153). In 1928, impressed by Housman's poem 'Hell Gate' (Last Poems, XXXI), Forster sent the poet a copy of *The Celestial Omnibus*, comparing his own second story in that collection, 'The Point of It', to the poem. The scholar Richard Perceval Graves describes Housman's late poem as a 'moving fantasy about the birth of a world in which homosexuality is not punished by "hell" or "pursuit"' (R. P. Graves, 226). And Forster observed with regret that his own tale was the nearest he felt he would ever get to the spirit of the poem (Lago and Furbank 2, 85). Both works deal with a pair of male lovers who, having been separated in life, find reunion indeath.

In 'The Point of It', Harold, 'who did not care for poetry' (CS, 160), overreaches himself in rowing a boat with his friend, Mickey, and dies by straining his heart. After his death, Mickey goes on to marry Janet, and has a socially successful life devoid of any real passion. When he, in turn, dies, he goes directly to Hell. Having abandoned, and then almost forgotten, the love he had known with Harold, he seems set to remain, and 'be lost eternally' for 'there was no second hope of salvation' there (CS, 179). Finally he hears the sound of rowing, and his long-dead friend mysteriously appears, in their boat. Hell will not release Mickey without a fight, and 'all that is evil in creation, all the distortions of love and truth by which we are vexed, came surging down the estuary'. Love however conquers all, and together the reunited friends find 'a glorious evening' as they speed 'without prelude into sunshine' (CS, 180). Here we do see Forster writing of one man's saving of another, of inspirer and hearer entering eternity together, but the story, being a piece of fantasy, does not openly suggest that such love could prove redemptive in 'real' life; if 'real' life had intruded, it is unlikely that the story could have been published. Such is the story that Forster felt came close to Housman's poem; Forster, like Housman, depicting an ideal world where male love proved redemptive.

Housman's work, inspired by male love and the Greek classics, had in turn inspired Forster in *A Room with a View*. Prior to Mr Beebe's discovery of Housman's work at the Emersons' home, Mr Emerson had quoted in Italy a poem from *A Shropshire Lad* — poem 32, 'From far, from eve and morning' — in a conversation with Lucy, urging her, despite the transitory nature of human life, to accept the proposition, 'Let us rather love one another, and work and rejoice' (RV, 26-7). According to the Housman scholar John Bayley, the poem from which Mr Emerson quotes, is addressed by the poet to a passing soldier or friend:

> in 'From afar [sic], from eve and morning', the reader receives the
> message as if on behalf of the soldier, or on behalf of the friend whose
> hand the poet asks for. On receipt of the message the hand is not given;
> and the soldier on his way out of the poet's life can be granted nothing
> but a goodbye wish (Bayley, 34).

Mr Emerson's exhortation to 'love' without the joy of permanence being assured has therefore its emotional origin in Housman's sad acknowledgement of the transitory and dispiriting nature of his contact with a soldier or a friend. Either way it arises from an expression of male love.

Returning to the scene at Cissie villa, Freddy notices with surprise that Mr Emerson's wardrobe bears the inscription, 'Mistrust all enterprises that require new clothes' (RV, 125). The quotation is actually a misquotation from Henry David Thoreau's book *Walden, or Life in the Woods*. The correct text should read: 'beware of all enterprises that require new clothes, and not rather a new wearer of clothes', and the sentence which follows this is illuminating with regard to the scene which follows in *A Room with a View*; it reads: 'If there is not a new man, how can the new clothes be made to fit?'(Thoreau, 15). In the enterprise which does follow — the bathing in the Sacred Lake* — clothes, or rather the removal of them, acquires, as in Thoreau, a symbolic meaning.

---

* The description of the scene around the Sacred Lake recalls that of the dell in *The Longest Journey*, that dell also 'became a kind of church' (LJ, 18). Similar too, perhaps, in its meaning rather than in its surrounding vegetation, to the temple tank at Mau, in *A Passage to India*, Forster stating that this novel had ended with 'a lady chapel' (Furbank 2, 109). Stephen Wonham's bathing in *The Longest Journey* is also linked to spirituality, for as he bathes in his room, the picture of the Cnidian Demeter turns to watch him. Before going out onto the roof to sunbathe in the nude, he declares that he would 'as soon follow an old stone goddess' (LJ, 118).

Freddy invites his new friend, George, to bathe with him. George agrees, Mr Beebe observing that such an invitation only works between men and not between women (RV, 126), and Mr Emerson adding that that will change, for soon, like men, they too shall be 'comrades'.

The use here of the term 'comrades' leads us to another inspirer of Forster, the works of the American poet, Walt Whitman. Whitman had made a distinction between what he called 'amative' love — that between men and women — and 'adhesiveness' which he used to describe the love of man for man (Erkkila, 177). In his *Democratic Vistas* Whitman linked the notions of 'adhesiveness' and 'comradeship', and, like Mr Emerson, saw its development as a way of improving society:

> It is to the development, identification, and general prevalence of that fervid comradeship (the adhesive love, at least rivaling the amative love hitherto possessing imaginative literature, if not going beyond it), that I look for the counter-balance and offset of our materialistic and vulgar American Democracy, and for the spritualisation thereof.... I confidently expect a time when there will be seen, running like a half-hid warp through all the myriad audible and visible worldly interests of America, threads of manly friendship, fond and loving, pure and sweet, strong and lifelong, carried to degrees hitherto unknown — not only giving tone to individual character, and making it unprecedently emotional, muscular, heroic, and refined, but having the deepest relations to general politics (in Carpenter 1929, 178).

Whitman's ideas were enthusiastically taken up by the British philosopher and socialist, Edward Carpenter, and it is his development of Whitman's work which seems to have most influenced Forster. Both Whitman and Carpenter acknowledged Emerson's influence in their work, Whitman asserting that Emerson helped him to 'find himself', adding: 'I was simmering, simmering, simmering; Emerson brought me to the boil' (Carpenter 1921, 157), and in the second edition of his *Leaves of Grass* he referred to him as his 'Master' (Carpenter 1921, 164). Carpenter's book on Whitman, *Days with Walt Whitman*, first appeared in May 1906, over a year before *A Room with a View* was finished and at a time when Forster was reading both Whitman's and Carpenter's works. It is therefore more than likely that this work formed part of his reading in 1907, and in looking at Carpenter's description of Whitman it is evident that there are numerous parallels between Whitman's philosophy and that commended by both Mr Emerson and Forster in the novel; as Forster later wrote, at this time of his life he had already come to regard Carpenter as his 'saviour' (M, 235). Carpenter writes that to Whitman:

> Always the inward, the enduring, the central, the vital, is acknowledged and honoured; the external, the temporary, the unessential thrown off.

Underneath all morals, manners, races, titles, classes, the original
human soul and its affections, greater than all. Underneath clothing,
costume, ranks, trades, and occupations, the bodily form, its needs and
physiology. Underneath all art and social life, sex and fraternity. Greater
than all houses, temples, galleries, and museums, the life of the open air
and its lessons. In such simple elementary things as these — in the
universal human soul, rediscovering itself in all forms, in the healthy and
beautiful human body, in sex and fraternity, in life with the earth and
the open air, Whitman sees the root out of which future humanity will
spring (as it has sprung in the past): out of which a society of proud,
strong, free individuals, who shall also be brethren and lovers, may easily
and naturally arise... (Carpenter 1921, 87-8).

The tone is similar to that adopted by Mr Emerson in his injunctions to
Lucy; not only in his 'Let us rather love one another, and work and rejoice' (RV,
27) but also in his urging of her to realise, 'that love is of the body; not the body,
but of the body. Ah but the misery that would be saved if we confessed that! Ah
for a little directness to liberate the soul!' (RV, 202). Also reminiscent of Whitman
is the praise of democratic ideals and democratic love and the disdain for class
distinctions and the deceit of clothing. It was Mr Emerson's words, and her
reaction to his son, George, that led Lucy to see 'the whole of life in a new
perspective' (RV, 27). Mr Emerson's genuine feeling is set in clear contrast to the
hypocrisy of the Reverend Mr Eager, who, in his lecture to the tourists at Sante
Croce, can prate ironically about St Francis' 'vision of the brotherhood of man'
(RV, 25), but lamentably fail to observe any such idealism in his own life. It is
no accident that he denounces the canoodling of the carriage driver and his
girl, nor that Mr Emerson defends their lovemaking. And Mr Eager's later
denunciation of Mr Emerson himself only serves to hasten the growth of Lucy's
affection for him.

The ideals expressed by Mr Emerson appear metaphorically to have their natural
home in the woodland glade which includes the Sacred Lake. Mr Beebe leads
the party through the pine woods to the pool. Pine woods had been the distant goal of Edgar and Sidney in 'Nottingham Lace' (AS, 27) and Thoreau's
Walden pond is likewise surrounded by pine woods (Thoreau, 210). The narrator describes the Lake:

> They climbed down a slippery bank of pine-needles. There lay the pond,
> set in its little alp of green — only a pond, but large enough to contain
> the human body, and pure enough to reflect the sky. On account of the
> rains, the waters had flooded the surrounding grass, which showed like
> an emerald path, tempting the feet towards the central pool (RV, 129).

Wilfred Stone suggested that the pond referred to in Forster's essay 'The

Last of Abinger' could well be the original model for this Sacred Lake. The description of a pond in the essay does in part tally with that of the Lake; and rather intriguingly, at Abinger, that pond lies in a 'queer clearing' for it 'is the centre of the whole affair, if affair there be' (TCFD, 362).

The main descriptive details of the bathing and the lake are found in Chapter 12, called simply 'Twelfth Chapter', just as Chapter 4 had been called 'Fourth Chapter'. In the novel these two chapters alone bear titles that do not relate to their content, and are, thereby, clearly connected. Both deal with crucially important moments in the lives of the characters. Chapter 4 relates Lucy's experiences in the Piazza Signoria and Chapter 12 the bathing in the Sacred Lake. Both Piazza and Sacred Lake are locations for male bathing and male friendships, and serve as settings for the rediscovery of those ancient Greek values which Forster held in esteem; the bathing linking this to social and sexual freedom, and to Whitman's 'comradeship'.

Turning directly to Whitman's writings we can find a scene parallel to that enacted by the Sacred Lake, and like it, the scene combines homoeroticism, nudity, the quest for freedom, brotherhood, democracy, nature and love. In a journal entry for Sunday, 27 August 1877 in *Specimen Days*, Whitman records:

> Last summer I found a particularily secluded little dell off one side by my creek, originally a large dug-out marl-pit, now abandon'd, fill'd with bushes, trees, grass, a group of willows, a straggling bank, and a spring of delicious water running right through the middle of it, with two or three little cascades. Here I retreated every hot day... It was just the place and time for my Adamic air-bath and flesh-brushing from head to foot... Never before did I get so close to Nature; never before did she come so close to me...
>
> As I walk'd slowly over the grass, the sun shone out enough to show the shadow moving with me. Somehow I seem'd to get identity with each and every thing around me, in its condition. Nature was naked, and I was also. It was too lazy, soothing, and joyous-equable to speculate about. Yet I might have thought somehow in this vein: Perhaps the inner never lost rapport we hold with earth, light, air, trees, &c. , is not to be realized through eyes and mind only, but through the whole corporeal body, which I will not have blinded or bandaged any more than the eyes. Sweet, sane, still Nakedness in Nature! — ah if poor, sick, prurient humanity in cities might really know you once more! Is not nakedness then indecent? No, not inherently. It is your thought, your sophistication, your fear, your respectability, that is indecent. There come moods when these clothes of ours are not only too irksome to wear, but are themselves indecent. Perhaps indeed he or she to whom the free exhilarating extasy of nakedness in Nature has never been eligible (and how many thousands there are!) has not really known what purity is — nor what faith or art

or health really is. (Probably the whole curriculum of first-class
philosophy, beauty, heroism, form, illustrated by the old Hellenic race
— the highest height and deepest depth known to civilization in those
departments — came from their natural and religious idea of
Nakedness) (Whitman, 150-2).

We may note the references to 'my Adamic air-bath' and to 'the old Hel-
lenic race'; Mr Beebe and Mr Emerson had earlier discussed the Garden of
Eden and in the description of the bathing scene in *A Room with a View*
reference is made to ancient Greece. And Mr Emerson, reminiscent of
Whitman, had asserted that, 'not until we are comrades shall we enter the
Garden' (RV, 126).*

George, initially apathetic to the bathing expedition, nonetheless soon
disrobes and 'followed Freddy into the divine' (RV, 129), his 'Michelangelesque'
pose on the bank recalling the Renaissance statuary of the Piazza Signoria and
further linking chapters 4 and 12 and their settings. Emboldened by their
playfulness (and the lack of any curious parishioner), Mr Beebe decides to
bathe also. Following an ironic reference to Wagner's water-nymphs he joins
their sport:

> The three gentlemen rotated in the pool breast high, after the fashion of
> the nymphs in Götterdämmerung. But either because the rains had
> given a freshness, or because the sun was shedding a most glorious heat,
> or because two of the gentlemen were young in years and the third
> young in the spirit — for some reason or other a change came over
> them, and they forgot Italy and Botany and Fate. They began to play.
> Mr Beebe and Freddy splashed each other. A little deferentially, they
> splashed George. He was quiet: they feared they had offended him. Then
> all the forces of youth burst out. He smiled, flung himself at them,
> ducked them, kicked them, muddied them, and drove them out of the
> pool (RV 130-1).**

* cf. Similar bathing scenes in *Maurice* (M, 68) and *Howards End* (HE, 216), both of which also
involve male friends. Forster, writing later of school visits as a child to swimming baths declared
them 'the vestibule of a physical glory' (Furbank 1, 35). British prudery regarding unregulated
public bathing is one of the national traits Forster attacked in his 'Mrs Grundy at the Parkers'. In
this essay Mrs Grundy approves of bathing 'provided it is so regulated that no one can enjoy it',
declaring that people 'shall bathe in an atmosphere of self-consciousness and fear'. She goes on to
describe how she had arranged for a policewoman to watch one particular male bather at Wor-
thing and feign to be offended when the hapless bather left open the door of his bathing-machine;
having signalled to her male colleage on the beach, the bather was subsequently arrested (AH, 16).
Forster was fully aware of the ubiquity of police entrapment.
** In his wartime pageant play, *England's Pleasant Land*, Forster perhaps makes a camp, self-mocking
(in his use of the word 'fairies') reference to this kind of scene, in the speech by the Second Guest:
'And that lovely wood there. *(Points)* One almost feels that fairies might be hidden in that wood, it's
so thrilling and romantic, and come out and dance in the evening. And the lake behind us — how
cool, how mysterious, how peaceful. Perhaps there are fairies in the lake too' (53).

Their sportiveness continues; they race in the sunshine, they pretend to be Indians in the willow-herbs and bracken and, utilising a bundle of George's clothes, play soccer with an imaginary goalpost. This mixture of athleticism, nudity and bathing clearly parodies a homoerotic idyll in Ancient Greece, such as that which is to be found in the *Phaedrus* of Plato (and also referred to by Carpenter), where, when male lovers meet and embrace 'in gymnastic exercises and at other times of meeting, then does the fountain of that stream, which Zeus when he was in love with Ganymede named desire, overflow upon the lover, and some enters into his soul, and some when he is filled flows out again;... watering them and inclining them to grow, and filling the soul of the beloved also with love' (Carpenter 1929, 58).

Throughout this innocent Arcadia however there is yet another presence:

And all the time three little bundles [of their clothes] lay discreetly on the sward, proclaiming: 'No. We are what matters. Without us shall no enterprise begin. To us shall all flesh turn in the end' (RV, 131).

Thoreau had warned against enterprises that required new clothes rather than new wearers of clothes, and here we see a call for the transformation of persons without resort to clothes, that is, without resort to new class barriers and spurious social distinctions which mask a common humanity. Thoreau notes how clothes disguise the wearer: 'sailing under false colors' and asks 'how far men would retain their relative rank if they were divested of their clothes' (Thoreau 1966, 15-16).* As with Whitman, scenes of Arcadian male camaraderie are presented as utopian images of a democracy yet to be realised. And in the playfulness of the bathing scene, the conventional world based on rank and class is disdained as symbolically 'Clothes flew in all directions' (RV, 131). When the revels are abruptly disturbed, by the moralistic Cecil approaching with Lucy and her mother, the spell is broken. It is noticeable that it is two women and Cecil, the advocate of the values of 'Middle Ages', who disrupt the scene. Yet again women are shown in Forster's work as interfering in relations between men. And despite being a man, Cecil's exclusion from the bathing party is symptomatic of his inhibited nature. In this he shows echoes of Charles Wilcox in *Howards End* who likewise fails to bathe in a forest lake (HE, 216):

On the morrow the pool had shrunk to its old size and lost its glory. It had been a call to the blood and to the relaxed will, a passing benediction whose influence did not pass, a holiness, a spell, a momentary chalice for youth (RV, 133).

---

*In Forster's short story, 'The Machine Stops', 'beautiful naked man was dying, strangled in the garments that he had woven' (CS, 157); a new man, not his old clothes, being needed to ensure the survival of man.

Lionel Trilling's discussion of this scene consists of a mere few lines, in which he confines himself to a simple description of the event (Trilling, 92). John Colmer however does discuss the homoerotic elements of the scene, albeit quite briefly, observing that 'This high-spirited bathing episode, like other bathing scenes in Forster's fiction, acts as a baptism into brotherhood', and that 'the essence of its eroticism is homosexual' (Colmer, 51). Whilst Wilfred Stone in his study of Forster notes:

> The Sacred Lake and the male swimming party could have been the book's symbol rather than the room with a view and the lovers in their chamber. But the Sacred Lake could not issue into the stream of the generations, and Forster quite obviously needs to talk about continuance in a social as well as mystical sense. We may lament though that George is such a rough diamond. Sex and sensibility might have made a more graceful pair (Stone, 232).

Stone may lament George's roughness, Forster does not, indeed his rough-ness is essential to the novel's theme, and in line with his creator's tastes. George's status as an outsider in genteel society is seen as an aspect of his attractiveness, like his beauty and athleticism. Stone draws attention to the similarity between the Lake and the spring in Forster's short story 'The Road from Colonus'. Awareness of this similarity makes it all the more difficult to understand Stone's assertion that in Forster's novel continuance in a social and mystical sense needs to be separated — especially as Forster wrote frequently about the point at which they intersect. From his readings of the works of Whitman and Car-penter, Forster would be well aware of a language and of concepts whereby what the Sacred Lake represents could issue into the generations without re-course to a pair of heterosexual lovers. Stone appears to imply that continuance must mean heterosexuality, and in a basic biological sense it does mean het-erosexual behaviour. But in the story Stone has cited, 'The Road from Colonus', written in 1903 whilst he was working on 'Lucy', Forster presents a situation where the influence of a sacred lake does issue into the stream of generations. In the story, a tired old man, Mr. Lucas, on holiday in Greece, bathes in flowing streams which magically appear when, by an act of will, he attempts to enter the youthful spirit of ancient Greece. Bathing in its waters he becomes aware of the stream of generations, for 'Others had been before him — in-deed he had a curious sense of companionship' (CS, 103). Forster did not need heterosexual lovers to express social or mystical continuance, indeed *The Longest Journey* shows Rickie, as much as (if not more than) Stephen, contrib-uting spiritual children to the 'stream of generations'; 'comradeship', despite Stone's assertions, obviously can have a 'continuance in a social as well as a mystical sense'.

Regrettably the bathing scene in the 1985 Merchant/Ivory film based on *A Room with a View* rang false, the problem lying, perhaps, with us, the viewers. For unfortunately we cannot share our forebears' apparently innocent attitude towards male nudity, so that for us, group adult nakedness seems invariably bound up with sexual activity, and the chaste games of boys quite incongruous amongst men.

The casting off of redundant clothing (and thereby of redundant social distinctions) prior to bathing has yet a further significance in Forster's work, as we can see from the following extract from his short story, 'The Tomb of Pletone', written some time between December 1903 and April 1904 (AS, x) during the gestation period of *A Room with a View*. Forster writes:

> The great emotions are the same in all ages. It is in questions of transition that one century differs from another. The moderns move gradually, revealing many an interesting intermediate state between joy and sorrow, hope and despair, keeping the shroud till it can be used as swaddling-clothes. But the men of the past stepped naked from one emotion to the other, caring nothing for the old garment when the reason for wearing it was over. Because of this abruptness we fancy them more inconsistent than ourselves (AS, 112).

The implication here is that, contrary to popular belief, modern society, unlike that of the past, lacks fluidity; the men of the past stepping 'naked from one emotion to the other' are the very antithesis of those moderns who live in too stultifying an adherence to the conventions of a society like that found in Summer Street. Cecil Vyse is the perfect example of this state, being compared to 'a Gothic statue... with shoulders that seemed braced square by an effort of will... he resembled those fastidious saints who guard the portals of a French cathedral' (RV, 86), and as his 'frozen' state suggests, he could not embrace Lucy as any 'labourer, navvy or young man behind a counter' could have done (RV, 108). Forster's use of the phrase 'many an interesting intermediate state' is significant here, for it directs knowing readers to Carpenter's work, 'intermediate' being used by him, both as noun and adjective, to refer to homosexuals. Its use here is part of an encoded homosexual discourse whereby knowledgeable readers, familiar with Carpenter's term, and possibly in sympathy with his work, would be alerted to the complete, and intended, meaning of Forster's words, a meaning he could not more openly express in those writings intended for public consumption.

Carpenter's work had formed part of Forster's reading list of 1907 and, like Mr Emerson, he was an ardent socialist. Forster appears to have drawn also upon his philosophy in his development of the 'view' in *Room*. In 1906 Carpenter's essay 'The Intermediate Sex' was published together with an enlarged edition of his earlier work *Love's Coming-of-Age*. In this essay Carpenter discusses modern society and the significance of what he called the 'intermediate temperament':

The subject dealt with in this book is one of great, and one may say growing, importance. Whether it is that the present period is one of large increase in the numbers of men and women of an intermediate or mixed temperament, or whether it merely is that it is a period in which more than usual attention happens to be accorded to them, the fact certainly remains that the subject has great actuality and is pressing upon us from all sides. It is recognised that anyhow the number of persons occupying an intermediate position between the two sexes is very great, that they play a considerable part in general society, and that they necessarily present and embody many problems which both for their own sakes and that of society, demand solution (Carpenter 1984, 185).

Although Carpenter was essentially referring to homosexuals as 'intermediates', he nonetheless believed that gender identities themselves (regardless of a person's sexual orientation) were in a state of transformation. In Forster's novel the bathing in the pool, the discarding of old clothing and the innocent, erotic sportiveness represent entry into such an 'intermediate' state and from it a variety of new states and conditions may emerge. Those evolving will become the 'new wearers of clothes' whose arrival Thoreau had demanded. Freddy led the way into the 'divine' and became one of the Lake 'nymphs', along with Mr Beebe and George. Lucy was barred in her early life by Aunt Charlotte from entering the Lake (RV, 107), but is slowly growing to accept the new values propounded by Mr Emerson, who had predicted earlier that both sexes would one day be together in the Garden of Eden on equal terms (RV, 126). Within the novel Lucy, George, Freddy and Mr Beebe can be said to occupy, if not the intermediate state of homosexuality (though this could apply to Mr Beebe), then at least a state where their gender positions are, conventionally speaking, highly ambiguous. Some critics have even proposed that Lucy, despite her name, may really be a boy (RV, xv); Forster's manuscript drafts of the novel however provide evidence that no conscious deception over Lucy's gender was intended.

The instability of conventional gender ideologies, where a clear distinction is maintained between masculinity and femininity, was apparent to Forster, who according to Furbank had, in writing his 1903 essay 'Cnidus', dealing with the statue of Demeter found at Cnidus in Greece, recognised his own ambiguous gender position; Furbank claiming that the Demeter of Cnidus represented for Forster the reconciliation of the male and female aspects he found in his own nature (Furbank 1, 102).

Certainly to Cecil Vyse, Lucy represents the possibility of a new and freer kind of life, when he declares to her that, 'It is a question between ideals, yours and mine — pure abstract ideals, and yours are the nobler. I was bound up in the old vicious notions, and all the time you were splendid and new' (RV, 173); and at one point he speaks of her having become 'a different person' with 'new thoughts', 'even a new voice' (RV, 172). This aspect of the progressiveness of

Lucy's new values is identified also in a reference to the bathing scene as the narrator clarifies its meaning, for 'Who could fortell that she and George would meet in the rout of a civilization, amidst an army of coats and collars and boots that lay wounded over the sunlit earth?' Lucy had bowed awkwardly to the three bathers at the Lake, but the narrator explains that, in a grotesque parody of genteel behaviour, she had really bowed across the deathly conventionalities which the cast-off clothing had signified: 'She had bowed — but to whom? To gods, to heroes, to the nonsense of schoolgirls! She had bowed across the rubbish that cumbers the world' (RV, 134).

Interestingly, in a later part of his essay, Carpenter notes: 'It may be that, as at some past period of evolution the worker-bee was without doubt differentiated from the ordinary bee-sexes, so at the present time certain new types of human kind may be emerging, which will have an important part to play in the societies of the future' (Carpenter 1984, 186). There is no evidence however that Forster was forging a connection between bees and his 'intermediates' with his use of the names Beebe, Honeychurch and the Beehive Tavern.

In 1970 the critic Jeffrey Meyers suggested that Mr Beebe is actually in love with George, a proposition which seemed confirmed in 1977 when the drafts of 'Old Lucy' and 'New Lucy' were published. In the final draft of *A Room with a View*, Mr Beebe finds George 'a nice creature' (RV, 8) while, 'from rather profound reasons', he was 'somewhat chilly in his attitude to the other sex' (RV, 32). Simon Callow's portrayal of Beebe in the Merchant/Ivory film of the novel perfectly captures the curious mixture of chasteness and knowing in the character. Fully alert to every dubious nuance, his Beebe follows the progress of the lovers with more than a partisan interest in the achievement of their union. And those gay viewers who know something of the actor can be certain that he is on the side of 'courage and love'.

Oliver Stallybrass in his Introduction to the Abinger edition of *A Room with a View* supported Meyer's assertion regarding Mr Beebe's more than friendly interest in George (RV, xviii), but conclusive evidence came from the 'New Lucy' version. In his notes on that text Forster wrote that: 'Mr Beebe feels hostility to George whom he likes' (Lucy, 106) and there is a revealing scene between the two in 'New Lucy' which was subsequently dropped from the final version of the novel. In this particular scene George and Mr Beebe meet by chance one evening in a wood — significantly a pine wood (Lucy, 107); their meeting is replete with ambiguity and is homoerotically suggestive:

> 'Is that face yours?' he [Mr Beebe] called.
> 'I'm all here tonight,' was the reply.
> The remark struck him as vaguely ominous. 'What do you mean?' he asked laughing.'
> 'Come and sit down. You may find out. '

Wild thoughts of a midnight assignation had darted through the clergyman's head. <He> \ It is true that he / dismissed them as unworthy. But nonetheless did he prepare for action.

'My dear George, you are the most romantic person. It is a wonderful gift. '
'Romantic?'
'You get into such poetic situations. \ When I retire to bed with my flat candlestick* I often think of you lying in the open, listening to the invisible water, watching the fir tops brush the stars. /' (Lucy, 106)

The scene continues with Mr Beebe's flattery of George; he calls him as strong as a lion, praises his beauty, and compares him to the hero of a novel — 'young, strong, quite good looking, sprung... from the plough, tinged with an interesting sadness' (Lucy, 107). Suddenly there is a change of mood as Mr Beebe recognises 'He was in the presence of romance' (Lucy, 107).

Why Mr Beebe should suddenly feel himself in the presence of 'romance' with George is not entirely clear, but being placed within a long panegyric upon George's beauty, strength and heroism and in the context of an ambiguous midnight encounter, this reaction would lend strong support to the idea that Mr Beebe is sexually attracted to George, at least in the draft version of *A Room with a View*, and vestiges of this aspect remain in the final published version. The conversation between the two soon resumes its tone of ambiguity, as Mr Beebe notes that George's qualities are 'paying ones'. Presumably he means ostensibly such as would guarantee George's success in life, but also perhaps he alludes that George's qualities are such that certain men might pay to be with him, as a rent-boy, that is:

'Paying?' [said George]
'Perhaps 'victorious' is a nicer word. 'He hesitated.
George, he felt, had a queer temper. Would he stand the full impertinence? He dared it. 'My dear man, I'll say to you what I wouldn't say to anyone. You're what the cads call irresistable [sic]'
(Lucy, 108).

That George has 'a queer temper'and is 'irresistable' appears to confirm the nature of Mr Beebe's interest in him. His comments are greeted with a long silence before George mumbles a reply and Mr Beebe makes to depart, Mr Beebe adding in parting: 'I knew a hint would be enough. Good night, man.' and 'You won't take it amiss, will you?' As Beebe stooped down and 'touched the prostrate figure [of George] lightly, George begins to laugh; then, 'he gripped the clergyman's hand', 'sprang up and kissed it lightly with his lips', as he de-

* A phallic allusion?

clares his love for Lucy. Mr Beebe horrified, declares to George, 'Stop! my dear
boy, stop. You've misunderstood me. I've misled you' and tries vainly to persuade George that Lucy does not love him (107-9).

It is clear from this scene, excised from the final version of the novel, that
Meyers's assertion of Beebe's homosexual interest in George is well-founded.
However, whereas the draft version can be overtly suggestive, in the published
novel such suggestiveness is carefully suppressed. Certainly the pervasive ambiguity concerning sex and gender and the fact that the central romantic
relationship in *A Room with a View* appears to be a reworking of the central
relationship betwen two men in 'Nottingham Lace' points further towards a
fluidity of perspectives relating to sex and gender in the novel and is suggestive
of Carpenter's definition of the intermediate state.

With such homoerotic influences on the text and in the making of a 'new
view', Forster clearly had a problem in finding a suitable ending for the work.
The form he had adopted in the final draft of the novel, a romantic comedy of
manners, did as a genre require a happy ending, complete with the marriage of
the leading male and female protagonists. This is what both his publisher and
the majority of his readers would have expected, and subsequently this is what
Forster provided, perhaps recalling that his previously published novel, *The
Longest Journey*, with its general pessimism, had proved somewhat unsuccess-
ful, both to the critics and to Forster's Bloomsbury friends, and consequently,
in some bookshops that novel had been remaindered (LJ, lxx). The whole
thrust of *Room*, however, was for something new, something expansive, to
replace an old, tired confined existence, something which would promise to
break down the prison walls of a narrow and self-contained room.

Mr Emerson had proposed the transformation of social structures; likewise Cecil
Vyse had noted that Lucy's ideals, unlike his own 'old vicious notions' were
'splendid and new', and so it is not unreasonable for the reader to expect something 'splendid and new' at the conclusion of the novel. Disappointingly
however, it ends on a conventional note: youthful love and romance have
triumphed over adversity and to the general reader the implication is certainly
one of happiness ever after attending the happy (wedded) couple. One anonymous and perceptive early reviewer noted that 'somehow the last chapter falls
a little flat after the high level of the rest of this book of delightful
"unexpectedness"'(P. Gardner,108).

The novel ends with the two lovers in romantic Florence, sharing the same
room: 'Youth enwrapped them; the song of Phaethon announced passion re-
quited, love attained. But they were conscious of a love more mysterious than
this' (RV, 209). Whether the river outside of their room 'bearing down the
snows of winter' is connected to the 'stream of generations' is unclear, but there
seems no hint of any new approach to marriage in Lucy and George's relationship; the enigmatic reference to 'a love more mysterious than this' is not
explained and for the general reader easily disregarded.

In an interview in 1952 Forster admitted that in his writing, endings always gave him trouble (Dick, 9) and *A Room with a View* is a clear example of his difficulty. If, as Goldsworthy Lowes Dickinson in a letter written to Forster late in life asserted, the Emersons represented all that Forster approved of (RV, xviii), it becomes easier to understand the writer's subsequent expression of his dislike of the novel's ending. The themes, characters, ideas and motifs contained in his work had indicated a multitude of progressive possibilities, but its actual ending had simply reinforced conventionality. The last chapter was audaciously entitled 'The End of the Middle Ages', but where was Forster's evidence for this? Certainly the ideology of conventional romance was far from defeated.

In his Introduction to the Abinger edition Oliver Stallybrass raises the question of why Forster himself had such a low opinion of this novel (RV, xvi), asserting that the answer may be revealed by a paper on 'Pessimism in Literature' which Forster had read to the Working Men's College Old Students' Club on 1 December 1906. Stallybrass remarks that, after stating that the end is of supreme importance in a book, Forster continues:

> This being so, let us ask ourselves — A man of today, if he writes a
> novel how will he end it? 'Happily, of course,' the optimist replies. Very
> well. In what kind of happiness?... And sooner or later he will give the
> old, old answer, marriage. Let the book end with a happy marriage. Let
> the lovers be united, to the sound of wedding bells. A hundred years
> ago, or fifty years ago, this would have seemed a very good answer...
> But the woman of today... may marry, but her marriage is most
> certainly not an end, either for herself or for her husband (RV, xvi).

Forster notes that, if the optimist advises ending a novel with a marriage, a pessimist might suggest ending it with some scene of separation. He asserts that the modern author is bound to listen to the pessimist's advice and yet asks that if he wants to end his book on a note of permanence, then where shall he find it? (RV, xvii)

An answer to Forster's question, according to his friend Dickinson, could not be found in Whitman, but Forster would have been aware of a possible answer through his reading of Carpenter.

In *Love's Coming-of-Age*, Carpenter, in a discussion of contemporary sexuality, had proposed a new approach to marriage. Close parallels are evident between the themes he discusses, the language he uses, and those employed by Forster here. Carpenter notes that in the wild and bacchanalian festivals of all the earlier nations, there is 'an element of Nature-sex-mysticism which has become lost in modern times, or quite unclean and depraved'; yet it is an element which he saw as a 'vital and deep-lying' one in humanity, and would probably reassert itself in the modern world in one form or another. He acknowledged that some of his readers may be shocked at this suggestion:

Possibly, to some, these remarks will only suggest a return to general confusion and promiscuity; and of course to some people they will seem inconsistent with what has been said before on the subject of the real Marriage and the tendency of human beings, as society evolves, to seek more and more sincerely a lifelong union with their chosen mate; but no one who thinks twice about the matter could well make this mistake. For the latter tendency, that namely 'from confusion to distinction', is in reality the tendency of all evolution, and cannot be set aside. It is the very nature of Love that as it realises its own aim it should rivet always more and more towards a durable and distinct relationship, nor rest till the permanent mate and equal is found.

But it is just the advantage of this onward movement towards definiteness that it allows — as in the evolution of all organic life — of more and more differentiation as the life rises higher in the scale of existence. If society should at any other future time recognise — as we think likely it will do — the variety of needs of the human heart and of human beings, it will not confuse them, ... It will allow in fact that there are different forms and functions of the love-sentiment, and while believing that a lifelong comradeship (possibly with little of the sexual in it) is the most satisfying form, will see that a cast-iron Marriage-custom which, as today, expects two people either to live eternally in the same house and sit on opposite sides of the same table, or else to be strangers to each other... is itself the source of perpetual confusion and misapprehension (Carpenter 1984, 171-3).

Looking closely at this passage a number of parallels with *A Room* with a View emerge. With regard to Carpenter's lament over the loss of an element of Nature-sex-mysticism in modern times, we can see in Forster's novel the expression of a similar loss and an attempt to restore its visibility. In the novel there are references to the mythology of ancient Greece, characters are identified with nature divinities; there are Arcadian woodland scenes wherein George kisses Lucy, and the men bathe in a Sacred Lake; there are many references to Nature and its effect on human love, such as the remark by Mr Emerson, who, while defending the amorous Italian driver against Mr Eager's censure, declares: 'Do you suppose there's any difference between spring in nature and spring in man? But there we go, praising the one and condemning the other as improper, ashamed that the same laws work eternally through both' (RV, 63).

There are other similarities betweeen Mr Emerson's views and those of Carpenter. As Carpenter had warned of 'confusion and misapprehension', so too does Mr Emerson warn Lucy to 'beware of muddle': 'Do you remember in the church, when you pretended to be annoyed with me and weren't? Do you remember before, when you refused the room with a view? Those were muddles — little, but ominous' (RV, 201). And, in an oblique reference by Forster to an essay by Samuel Butler, Mr Emerson quotes a friend in saying that Life 'is a public performance on the violin, in which you must learn the instrument as you go along'; Forster then takes this remark and adds: 'Man has to pick up the use of his functions as he goes along — especially the function of Love' (RV, 201) — a concept similar to Carpenter's regarding the evolution from confusion to distinction. Mr Emerson's words eventually lead Lucy to her union with George, ostensibly rescuing her from the muddle she had stumbled into in her relationship with Cecil.

Carpenter had warned that 'a cast-iron marriage custom which... expects two people either to live eternally in the same house... or be strangers to each other... is itself the source of perpetual confusion and misapprehension', so does the conventional ending of *A Room with a View* indicate that Lucy and George have fallen into another 'muddle' at the close of the novel? Certainly their creator was not so certain that they had not.

In an article entitled 'A View without a Room' published in 1958, Forster revisited his characters from the novel. He noted that this of all his novels might fairly be called the nicest and that it 'contains a hero and heroine who are supposed to be good, good-looking and in love — and who are promised happiness', but he is unable to say with certainty that happiness has been achieved (RV, 210). Where the happy couple of George and Lucy now live also presents problems: 'But where do they live? Ah, that is the difficulty, and that is why I have entitled this article "A View without a Room". I cannot think where George and Lucy live' (RV, 210). This statement highlights Forster's problem, for although a location (room), like Italy, may prove conducive to a vision (view), by implication the vision also demands a conducive location in which to materialise; consequently the new views of the Emersons, and later of Lucy, appear to remain goals to aim for, rather than present realities. This point is emphasised later in the essay when George, now a soldier in World War II, returns to Italy with the invading Allied forces. Forster writes: 'George had to report to Lucy that the View was still there and that the Room must be there, too, but could not be found. She was glad of the news, although at that moment she was homeless. It was something to have retained a View, and, secure in it and in their love, as long as they have one another to love, George and Lucy await World War III —' (RV, 212). This emphasises that the view was essentially an inner vision and potentially could occur regardless of externalities; it did not need Florentine rooms in which to materialise for it transforms ordinary rooms. In this there is yet a further link with the New England Transcendentalists: Emerson had warned that 'Travelling is a fool's paradise. We owe to our first journeys the discovery that place is nothing. At home I dream that at Naples, at Rome, I can be intoxicated with beauty, and lose my sadness... [but when I do] at last wake up in Naples... there beside me is the stern Fact, the sad self, unrelenting, identical, that I fled from' (Emerson 1906, 51). In *A Room with a View*, 'old vicious notions' such as those brought over from England by Mr Eager had found expression in the beauty of Italy, just as the Sacred Lake had been able to spring in an Edwardian English wood (as well as in ancient Greece); and whilst love began for George and Lucy in Florence it managed to prosper even in the 'medieval' society of Summer Street. No such compromised escape however was to await Sidney and Edgar in 'Nottingham Lace', and it was a number of years later that Forster, in *Maurice*, was able to show Maurice and Alec the way into the greenwood.

Much of the success of the encounters in the Sacred Lake, and that of George and Lucy, lies in the feeling of 'comradeship', the discovery in others of a shared view, which transforms one's own little room; a point which the narrator emphasises by noting that, 'Anyone can find places, but the finding of people is a gift from God' (RV, 67), and by affirming that for Freddy Honeychurch, the presence of the Emersons 'kindled the room into the life he desired' (RV, 90).

Why should Forster end the novel so conventionally? Perhaps his difficulty lay in a perennial problem — that values are easier to formulate theoretically than actually to implement in a social situation, especially if, as in Forster's case, society was something one endured or mimicked, rather than openly confronted. And how could he fully express in publishable form what was, to him, a vision infused by the work of homosexual writers? During the period in which he wrote *A Room with a View*, Forster was sexually very naive, and it was only later in *Maurice* that he grappled with the idea of expressing his apotheosis of the idea of 'comradeship'. Could it not simply be perhaps that Forster had wanted a quick and easy ending to a novel which had proved so troublesome to write?

Whatever the answer, it is possible to accuse him of timidity, of a failure to follow through his ideas to the point at which they seriously challenged social institutions, for the action of *Room*, which had promised so much that was new, ends, like many an older, nineteenth-century, novel, with a marriage which seems to confirm rather than challenge the existing social order.

On this last point it is, perhaps, revealing to note that when asked in an interview which of his characters represented himself, Forster replied that Rickie in *The Longest Journey* more than any; as well as Philip Herriton from *Where Angels Fear to Tread*, adding that 'Cecil [Vyse] has got something of Philip in him' (Dick, 14). Cecil, 'bound up in the old vicious notions' (RV, 173), would, no doubt, also have thought of conventional marriage as the only realisable goal for a young couple.

HOWARDS END

In contrast to the composition of most of Forster's other novels his writing of *Howards End*, though slow in its progression, was a relatively straightforward process. As before, people and locations known to the writer provided creative starting points, which were subsequently marshalled into an overall idea and philosophical scheme, informed initially in this instance by Forster's reading of Walt Whitman. And as with *A Room with a View*, further thematic horizons were inspired by the work of a 'disciple' of Whitman's, Edward Carpenter.

The germ of *Howards End* came when Forster met the Posten family in the summer of 1908, and as he wrote, he became impressed by Mrs Posten, seeing her as a charming and cultivated woman (Furbank 1, 142). She had recently married into the business-orientated Posten family and her temperament and position clearly suggest those the writer gave to Margaret Schlegel, while the Postens were the originals for the Wilcox family in the novel. At the same time his uncle, Philip Whichelo, visited Forster from London bringing 'squalid stories' of metropolitan life and these, coupled with his observations on Mrs Posten, led to the first rough plan of the novel being produced on 28 June 1908 (Furbank 1, 165). Earlier that month Forster had begun to re-read Whitman's *Leaves of Grass* and further reading of the poet's work in July of the same year stimulated the germinating novel (Stape, 31).

Having found his moral inspiration in Whitman, Forster, as in his earlier novels, turned to his friends and his life experience, amongst other sources, to provide the material with which he would construct his work; for example, the Schlegel household was based on that of his friend G. L. Dickinson (HE. viii) and *Howards End* itself was based on Rooksnest, a house known to Forster during his childhood (HE, vii). What is significant about this novel, however, is the fact that no specific and current, relationship of Forster's with another man seems to have directly influenced it. In *A Room with a View* and *Maurice*, for example, Meredith's influence is clear, and aspects of the relationships between some of the characters of those novels reflect this; likewise in *A Passage to India*, with Mohammed el Adl and Syed Ross Masood, but there seems no equivalent in the creation of *Howards End*. The reason for this can clearly be linked to Forster's growing wariness about his public writings. Possibly friends had alerted him to the fact that his novels betrayed aspects of his own character, that is his homosexuality, to general readers as well as to those readers who were attuned to his encoded style. Relationships which had formerly inspired him to write seem almost to have been consciously excluded, as Forster's awareness intensified about what his general audience of readers expected from him. On his writing of the novel in 1909, he observed that he had lost his inspiration, and that 'Words are more in the foreground than they were: even these I seem writing for an audience' (HE, xii). Given Forster's love of verbal irony and ambiguity, and how revealing his word-play could be, it became an urgent necessity for him, as his success as a writer increased, to pay even closer attention to his particular use of words. And a consequence of this was that, unlike his practice in previous novels, Forster felt that he had to suppress more of his own feelings and sentiments in this work. The finished novel does show that if this was his original intention, it was inconsistently executed. Nevertheless relationships between the characters in *Howards End* do not approach the intimacies of those, say, between Philip Herriton and Gino (in *Where Angels Fear to Tread*), or between George and Lucy (in *A Room with a View*). In comparison the relationships between Margaret Schlegel and Henry Wilcox and between Leonard Bast and Helen Schlegel appear cold and almost mechanical. Forster gives these relationships a degree of psychological plausibility, but no sense of love seems evident, despite the fact that love is commended by the narrator (HE, 258). Forster himself, obliquely, seems to acknowledge this in his diary entry of 19 September 1910 when he declared that he had never written anything less erotic (HE, xiii).

Progress in writing the novel was slow, but a rough draft, close to the final published edition, was forwarded to Forster's publisher in March 1910 (HE, xii). Oliver Stallybrass suggests that prior to publication the publishers, Edward Arnold, made attempts to have the incident of Helen Schlegel's sexual encounter with Leonard Bast cut from the novel (HE, xiii). Forster resisted this and a suggestion that he shorten his work, and the final version of the novel was published on 18 October 1910 (HE, xv).

With the exception of Mrs Wilcox, who lived 'nearer the line that divides daily life from a life that may be of greater importance' (HE, 74), the Wilcox family represent a section of the weathly upper-middle-class of English society, characterised, in Forster's work, by an avoidance of 'the personal note in life', hypocrisy, ruthlessness, a fear of the body, and a total unconcern for those whose lives are dependent upon their deployment of their money. The narrator observes that the personal life is of no real interest to them. The public life of social convention helps to sustain their denial of any inner life, but within each one is a state of 'panic and emptiness' (HE, 90-1), existing in a wider world marked out by 'telegrams and anger' (HE, 101). Significantly, the Wilcoxes are primarily characterised by their 'masculinity', which in Helen Schlegel's opinion (Trilling, 109) is 'far from adequate', and this is contrasted with the 'femininity' of the Schlegel household (HE, 41), both families, in part, representing a conventional division of gender characteristics. The home at the centre of the novel, Howards End itself, which Mrs Wilcox wishes to leave to Margaret Schlegel, is presented as a symbol of England. The struggle over who shall ultimately inherit the house — Wilcox or Schlegel, or an amalgam of them both — functions as an allegory as to who shall ultimately take possession of England itself.

Unlike the gestation period of his other novels, Forster's private life during the writing of *Howards End* was relatively trouble-free. The earlier emotional

upheavals involving the acceptance of his homosexuality and stressful relationships (such as with H. O. Meredith — although this still continued to
provide occasional concern) seem to have given way to a period where people
came running after him, and it was he who now ran the risk of disappointing
and jilting them. Further consolations came as his friendship with Syed Ross
Masood flourished (Furbank 1, 166-7), though by the end of 1909 his unre-
quited love for Masood had begun to create new anxieties (Stape, 33).

Tensions were not completely banished from Forster's life during this
period, but he had learned how to accommodate, if not to accept, them. His
sexuality, especially in Britain in the years which followed the Wilde trial, inevitably meant alienation from the majority. Undoubtedly this sense of alienation
was to contribute to his new novel, where Forster commends 'connection' as
an antidote to widespread social dislocation.

The key idea in *Howards End*, deriving from the work of Walt Whitman,
is declared in the novel's epigraph — 'Only connect...' — an exhortation to
build a better future based on the proper understanding of the links between
the disparate parts of oneself and of humanity. It could also, in a camp context,
be read as an exhortation to 'connect' as in sexual intercourse, Forster himself at
this time being in need of development in that area of his life. Stallybrass notes
in his Introduction to the Abinger edition of *Howards End*, that immediately
prior to commencing work on the novel Forster had specifically referred to
Whitman for a quotation to inform his work, the incident being recorded in
Forster's diary entry of 16 June 1908:

> I opened Walt Whitman for a quotation, & he started speaking to
> me. That the unseen is justified by the seen; which in turn becomes
> unseen and is justified by the other.... No more fighting, please,
> between the soul & the body, until they have beaten their common
> enemy, the machine (HE, x).

Whilst a number of Whitman's poems may be cited to show his influence
on Forster, the references to 'seen' and 'unseen' clearly point to the poem 'Song
of Myself', in the third part of which Whitman writes:

> Urge and urge and urge,
> Always the procreant urge of the world.

> Out of the dimness opposite equals advance, always substance and
>   increase, always sex,
> Always a knit of identity, always distinction, always a breed of life.

> To elaborate is no avail, learn'd and unlearn'd feel that it is so.

> Sure as the most certain sure, plumb in the uprights, well
>   entretied, braced in the beams,

Stout as a horse, affectionate, haughty, electrical,
I and this mystery here we stand.

Clear and sweet is my soul, and clear and sweet is all that is not
    my soul.

Lack one lacks both, and the unseen is proved by the seen,
Till that becomes unseen and receives proof in its turn.
               ('Song of Myself', ll.43-54)

This passage makes clear that the 'unseen' for Whitman in his poem, and likewise for Forster in his novel, is linked to human sexuality and the power it has in shaping human identities. By linking it to the 'procreant urge of the world', it is further linked to the idea of evolution — ideas which Whitman throws out in passing, but to which his British admirer, Edward Carpenter, attempted to give a more positive and concrete expression than that found in the scientific works of Krafft-Ebing and Bloch. The question Forster proposes to explore is one concerning the future inheritors of England, a land in which the machine, the petrol engine in particular, is threatening to pollute its physical beauty, especially that of its countryside, just as the Wilcox philosophy of profits before people is working to pollute the inner lives of its citizens. The 'unseen' works to enhance life; the outer polluted world, denying its procreative power, is in a state of actual decay.

In seeking to affirm the power of the 'unseen' in human life, Forster does not confuse 'unseen' with unreal, for *Howards End* also attempts to show the limitations of certain notions of what constitutes our 'real' lives: the Wilcox world of 'telegrams and anger' has a reality, but it does not exclude the 'reality' of the inner life. Forster notes, in a diary entry of 10 February 1909, a meeting with the editor of a mining newspaper who 'was prone to think "real life" meant knowledge of finance; but he made me see how wide an abyss opens under our upper class merriment and culture' (HE, xi). The attitude of the editor is reflected in that of Mr Wilcox and most of his family for whom money is of the greatest importance, and for whom its distribution determines social hierarchy and consequently all their relationships with others. Forster — himself on an, albeit small, inherited income — knew the importance of money and the misery that frequently attends the lack of it, but as a sexual dissident he also knew that finance was not, for him, his 'real life', and that alienation and self-repression were the only options life in England could then offer him. As Furbank observes during this period, Forster felt 'only half alive', a state which occasionally visited him and in which he lost any feelings or thoughts of 'passion and sensuality' (Furbank 1, 182).

The problem for Forster was how to connect his innermost thoughts and feelings, his homosexual orientation, which truly constituted for him his 'real' life, however 'unseen' by his contemporaries, with his everyday existence. And as a writer how could he 'Only connect the prose and the passion' (HE, 183) in a society which would have destroyed him (as it had earlier destroyed Wilde) should he have publicly attempted to do so. Consequently, of the works published by Forster during his lifetime, which all to varying degree mirror the concerns of their creator, none fully reflect them; all being distorted by the pressure to conform to heterosexist ideologies. Forster, a closet homosexual, could not permit his public role as a writer of social comedies to be threatened by the disclosure of all of his interests.

Whilst stressing the importance of the 'unseen' inner world Forster nevertheless does not decry the demands of the 'outer' world of social convention and material realities. He proposes that the two, apparently separate, worlds 'connect', and this connection is symbolised at the close of the novel by the union of Henry Wilcox and Margaret Schlegel. It is the connection between Leonard Bast and Helen Schlegel however, which leads to the creation of England's true heir. Whilst the 'feminine' Schlegel family love music, literature and art and can relate on an individual level to people from differing classes, their knowledge of the public world, of business and government and the uses of power, is weak. In contrast the 'masculine' Wilcoxes have pale individual lives of their own and show disdain towards the arts, allowing their identities to be shaped not by any creative 'inner' world but by a public, 'outer' world. Margaret is sensitive to the demands of both worlds for, when her sister Helen declares 'personal relations are the real life, for ever and ever', she is quick to point out the limitations of their own experience, warning her that there is a great outer life that they have never touched, a life in which telegrams and anger count far more than personal relations, and where 'love means marriage settlements; death, death duties' (HE, 25). Later, Margaret is able to detect the narrowness and insufficiency of this 'great outer life' when, sickened by the materialism of shoppers during Christmas celebrations in London, she realises, 'It is private life that holds out the mirror to infinity; personal intercourse, and that alone, that ever hints at a personality beyond our daily vision' (HE, 79).

It is, of course, one thing to suggest connection, but to decide how this should occur, or what more precisely it should achieve, was not only a problem for Margaret but for Forster also. Both needed guidance, and to obtain it Forster had to turn again to the works of Edward Carpenter. The impact of his influence on Forster has been previously noted and, although they did not meet until 1913, Forster had been familiar with his writings from at least 1907 (Furbank 1, 159). In his 'Terminal note' to *Maurice*, Forster acknowledged the considerable influence that Carpenter's writings had had on him, how he had come to his works in his loneliness, for a short time 'he seemed to hold the key to every trouble' and he had approached him 'as one approaches a saviour' (M, 235).

To Carpenter and to Forster, the 'love of comrades', the connecting with one's friends and through them to a wider society, was one of life's highest aims. Similarily for Margaret, friends are of supreme importance for 'affection explains everything' and 'she never forgot anyone for whom she had once cared;

she connected, though the connection might be bitter...' (HE, 206). For her future husband, Henry, however, though he craves friendship and affection, he is fearful of them. (HE, 161). For Forster, Whitman and Carpenter comradeship had a sexual component, and, likewise, it contains a sexual element for Mr Wilcox. However, instead of being the origin of his desire to connect, sex is the very reason for his horror of it, and it is an abhorrence which his religion supports. Far from providing a brotherly love which would unite people, Christianity in *Howards End*, as in *A Room with a View*, provides a platform from which to hate. Mr Wilcox had 'always the sneaking belief that bodily passion is bad'. By their marrying, Margaret hoped to change this:

> She would only point out the salvation that was latent in his own
> soul, and in the soul of every man. Only connect! That was the
> whole of her sermon. Only connect the prose and the passion, and
> both will be exalted, and human love will be seen at its highest.
> Live in fragments no longer. Only connect, and the beast and the
> monk, robbed of the isolation that is life to either, will die (HE,
> 183-4).

With Whitman no such repression as that of Mr Wilcox's is proposed; his ideal of religion was not based on a denial of the body, for central to it is the free exploration of its sexuality. As he writes at the start of a phallic passage in 'Song of Myself', 'If I worship one thing more than another it shall be the spread of my own body, or any part of it' (l.527). Forster, whilst welcoming the freedom expressed in such lines, nevertheless felt some constraint essential, and in line with the advice on similar matters he found in his studies of ancient Greece, proposes a middle way, connecting human experience whilst rejecting all extremes. For Forster to live as a 'beast', ignorant about one's sexuality and to behave without licence, is to be condemned as much as the extreme repression of sexuality expressed by the wilful self-denial of a monk. Carpenter likewise had dealt with this subject, and bearing in mind Forster's declaration that he had approached him 'as one approaches a saviour', it is difficult not to see his influence at work in Forster's novel. Carpenter wrote:

> what we call asceticism and what we call libertinism are two sides
> practically of the same shield. So long as the tendency towards mere
> pleasure-indulgence is strong and uncontrolled, so long will the
> instinct towards asceticism assert itself — [...] We look for a time
> doubtless when the hostility between these two parts of man's
> unperfected nature will be merged in perfect love; (Carpenter
> 1984, 101-2).

And just as Maragaret hopes that in such a connection 'human love will be seen at its highest', so too does Carpenter assert that 'these two parts of man's unperfected nature will be merged in perfect love'.

Although it is Margaret who expresses optimism in the novel, her sensibilities and her hopes are frequently those of her creator and she speaks for him. Furbank confirms that in many important ways Margaret was Forster himself and that her views were certainly his (Furbank 1, 173); like Forster, too, Margaret hated war but liked soldiers (HE, 195). Towards the end of *Howards End* she speaks to Helen on the need for the acceptance of all human diversity and her speech urging tolerance could easily have been Forster's own:

> people are far more different than is pretended. All over the world
> men and women are worrying because they cannot develop as
> they are supposed to develop. Here and there they have the matter
> out, and it comforts them. ... others go further still, and move
> outside humanity altogether. A place, as well as a person, may
> catch the glow. Don't you see that all this leads to comfort in the
> end? It is part of the battle against sameness. Differences — eternal
> differences, planted by God in a single family, so that there may
> always be colour; sorrow perhaps, but colour in the daily gray
> (HE, 335-6).

In his Notes at the end of the Abinger edition of the novel, Oliver Stallybrass comments that 'with the hindsight given by *Maurice*, it is hard to help seeing Margaret's speech as a concealed plea for charity towards homosexuals' (HE 364). Given that Forster had been writing the novel in an atmosphere in which he had been conscious of 'writing for an audience', and where at times he felt 'only half-alive', the need for a less conformist society would have seemed particularly urgent. By making the main female character of the novel articulate his own concerns, Forster was concealing not only the gender of the originator of these views (himself), but specifically locating them within the domain of the 'feminine' inner world, rather than in the outer 'masculine' world. The character of Margaret, like that of the narrator, provides a protective mask from behind which Forster may express his opinions. Further words of Margaret's similarly argue for a tolerance and understanding of sexual diversity, as in her long letter to Helen where she points out:

> the need of charity in sexual matters: so little is known about
> them; it is hard enough for those who are personally touched to
> judge; then how futile must be the verdict of society. I don't say
> there is no standard, for that would destroy morality; only that
> there can be no standard until our impulses are classified and
> better understood (HE, 255).

In an earlier draft Forster made it absolutely clear which 'impulses' were meant when he wrote 'until the sexual impulses are better understood' (HE-

MS, 265). Implied in Margaret's letter is a rebuke to those scientists, such as Krafft-Ebing, who in an effort to understand sexuality, classify it according to their own rigidly defined standpoint, and thereby declare what should, and what should not, be acceptable to society as a whole, creating further social divisions in the process. Margaret's hope, that all diversity of sexuality will find a place in the new society, is again reminiscent of a passage in Carpenter's work, where he writes, in an historical discussion on sexual customs world-wide, that 'a really free Society will accept and make use of all that has gone before... [for] historical forms and customs are the indication of tendencies and instincts which still exist among us,' adding, that 'the question is, not the extinction of these tendencies, but the finding of the right place and really rational expression for them' (Carpenter 1984, 171). Again it is difficult not to see the similarity between Carpenter's words and Margaret's (i.e. Forster's) hopes.

Further parallels are also evident between the ideas expressed by Forster in the novel and those of Carpenter. In his *Love's Coming of Age*, Carpenter predicts the future state of the relationship between men and women and discusses the reasons behind differences in gender (Carpenter 1984, 123). He argued that the advance of civilisation would involve a reduction in the diversity between the sexes. Similarly the narrator of *Howards End* admits such a trend, but also affirms that 'The barrier of sex, though decreasing among the civilized, is still high' (HE, 63). Margaret declares that a change is occurring in the sexes, even admitting the possibility of a 'biological change' (HE, 75). For her though, such a change in human sexual development is not simply to be dictated by Nature, for she asserts that 'in nine cases out of ten Nature pulls one way and human nature another' (HE 66), so that advancement is not to be left to the purely physical forces of Nature; the inner life, an improved human nature, must nourish any advance. Later the narrator continues Margaret's (and possibly Forster's) thoughts on the future development of the sexes:

> Are the sexes really races, each with its own code of morality, and
> their mutual love a mere device of Nature's to keep things going?
> Strip human intercourse of the proprieties, and is it reduced to this?
> Her judgement told her no. She knew that out of Nature's device
> we have built a magic that will win us immortality. Far more
> mysterious than the call of sex is the tenderness that we throw into
> that call; [...] We are evolving, in ways that Science cannot
> measure, to ends that Theology dares not contemplate (HE, 237-
> 8).

It is not merely the 'call of sex' which will 'win us immortality', but how we give expression to it, and 'the tenderness that we throw into that call'. Again Margaret's words echo Carpenter's, as does her linking of 'Science' and 'Theology'.

For Forster both science and organised religion were suspect and a strong anti-clericalism is clearly evident in his work. In an age, however, where religious belief was waning, science seemed set to replace it as a guide to the purposes of human life. Not only did scientists, such as Krafft-Ebing, declare Forster's sexuality invalid, and promise by selective breeding to eradicate the 'contrary sexual instinct', but science too, instead of bringing freedom, had brought slavery. In January 1908 Forster wrote in his diary that 'Science instead of freeing man... is enslaving him to machines' and that whilst 'Man may get a new and perhaps a greater soul for the new condition', it would be at the expense of a soul such as his own which would 'be crushed out' (HE x-xi, and Furbank 1, 161-2).

As could be expected, Forster's distrust of science is made plain in his novel, for science merely 'explained people', it could not understand them (HE, 328). Margaret's anger at its destructive assumptions, exemplified in the technique used by a young doctor in his examination of Helen, clearly echoes Forster own concerns about contemporary scientific notions about homosexuality. Indeed the concern with normality and heredity reflects the language used by Krafft-Ebing in his work on 'contrary sexual instincts':

> The doctor, a very young man, began to ask questions about Helen.
> Was she normal? Was there anything congenital or hereditary? [...]
> Margaret's anger and terror increased every moment. How dare
> these men label her sister! What horrors lay ahead! What
> impertinences that shelter under the name of science! The pack was
> turning on Helen, to deny her human rights, and it seemed to
> Margaret that all Schlegels were threatened with her. Were they
> normal? What a question to ask! (HE, 286)

The possibility that science wrongly used would serve simply to 'label' Helen and 'deny her human rights' is sadly an idea only too well known to us today. These questions about Helen, and the suspicion that she may have departed from normality, also serve to cast a certain light upon the nature of her relationship with Leonard Bast.

Despite Forster's consciousness of the likely homophobia of his general readership at the time of his writing *Howards End*, yet further references to homosexuality and homoeroticism are to be found in the background characters of the novel, the most obvious examples being those relating to Tibby, to Charles Wilcox, and to the young woodcutter who makes a brief appearance at the funeral of Mrs Wilcox (the latter surely clearer to present-day readers who are aware of *Maurice*).

Tibby, the only brother of the Schlegel sisters, is depicted as an effeminate and effete young man. He is part of the 'feminine' Schlegel household, Helen maintaining, ambiguously as no doubt Forster had intended, that 'Men like the Wilcoxes would do Tibby a power of good', though noting that Margaret would probably disagree with her (HE, 2). As with similar characters in other works of Forster's, parallels could be drawn between the effeminate Tibby and aspects of the real upbringing of their creator — for Forster, too, in his youth had been regarded as rather girlish (Furbank 1, 19 & 23). Tibby's effeminacy and fussiness are stressed by Helen who refers to him as 'Auntie Tibby' (HE, 40) and, in a phrase whose deliberate ambiguity requires no explanation, wishes 'we had a real boy in the house — the kind of boy who cares for men' (HE, 40). The narrator relates that he does not express his sexuality: 'He was frigid — through no fault of his own, and without cruelty' (HE, 276). Why he is 'frigid' is not explained, but as it is 'through no fault of his own', it would seem that the fault may lie elsewhere, and that, perhaps, Tibby's sexual self-repression has been forced upon him by society at large, or possibly by heredity. Because his frigidity does not arise out of a personal dislike of sexuality, he is not prone to the petty cruelties that sometimes accompany wilful repression, his frigidity being 'without cruelty'. It is noticeable that Forster permits numerous criticisms of Tibby to go unchecked or uncountered by any comparable remarks in his favour, nor is Tibby revealed as possessing characteristics which would show such criticism of him to be particularily unbalanced or unkind. Again, the assumption must be that Forster was wary of too public a defence of such a character, fearing an adverse response from his readers, and perhaps it is significant that Margaret (who, as Furbank asserts, stands for Forster) is seen by Helen as Tibby's protector. In reality though, despite his own experience of it, Forster seems to have disliked effeminacy; his own love objects were invariably masculine — soldiers, labourers, policemen, for example. Perhaps it was part of the writer's misogyny to disparage some aspects of femininity, for in his fictions it is often virile young men who attract praise.

To Helen, Tibby lacks the grit and stoicism she finds and admires in the Wilcox family. She notes in particular that Tibby has allowed his hay fever to keep him confined at home and in need of his sister Margaret's care. Charles Wilcox, however, does not allow the same condition to restrict him, and is rather touchy about the subject, becoming quite angry when it is inquired about (HE, 2). At the close of the novel, Helen refers in an optimistic outburst to the good prospects that attend their lives and are symbolised by signs of fecundity, the birth of her own son and the promise of a bumper crop of hay in the big meadow (HE, 340). The fact that the book ends with this symbol indicates its importance in the novel. And consequently the fact that Charles Wilcox, the Wilcox family in general (though not Mrs Wilcox who is associated with hay at several points in the novel) and Tibby all suffer from hay fever thereby acquires significance.

Charles is the member of the Wilcox family who most vehemently disapproves of Helen's relationship with Leonard Bast, and who eventually brings about Bast's death — he, like his family, cannot conceive of a brighter, freer future where all is connected. Although he has children who will 'inherit the earth' (HE, 182), and indeed he is due to inherit Howards End when his own father dies, none of them promises to contribute positively to the social trans-

formation that England requires. Likewise Tibby, due to his isolation and
frigidity (and perhaps his implied homosexuality), is unable to contribute to
the bumper harvest of hay, nor does he show much sign of leaving any 'spiritual children' after the Platonic model. His implied inversion precludes a
harvest of children, whereas Charles will people the country with more destructive Wilcoxes. And unlike Rickie in *The Longest Journey*, Tibby seems
unable to make any contribution in other ways to the 'stream of generations'.
If 'hay fever' is presented as a coded reference to homosexuality, it might also
hint at other reasons for Charles's wish to destroy Bast. Charles, the reader is
informed, would get 'quite cross' when questioned about his hay fever, clearly
fearful of acknowledging its influence on his life. His marriage obviously fails
to satisfy him, he abuses his wife, and his loutish masculinity may perhaps be
a consciously constructed defence against his own, and others', recognition of
his more confused sexual identity. He reacts aggressively to male beauty, getting rid of an attractive Italian chauffeur (calling him the 'little Italian beast'
— somewhat reminiscent of Gino in *Where Angels Fear to Tread*), deliberately
replacing him with one as 'ugly as sin'. Perhaps his fear of virile beauty, and an
implied hatred of his own homosexuality, turns into a hatred of Bast when he
begins to recognise that he is attracted to the clerk; and in an effort to destroy
the feeling, he destroys the beautiful object which had provoked the hated
desire?

Further evidence suggestive of a link between Charles and repressed homosexuality can be found in the bathing scene. In *Howards End*, Charles bathes
with Albert Fussel on a day that 'was still sacred to men'. Symbolically, Charles
is unable to bathe without difficulties, which Margaret (perhaps speaking as
Forster here), finds unnecessary, and not the sort of 'bathing arrangements as
they should be in her day':

> In the first place the key of the bathing-shed could not be found.
> Charles stood by the riverside with folded hands, tragical, [...] Then
> came a difficulty about a springboard... these athletes seemed
> paralysed. They could not bathe without their appliances, though
> the morning sun was calling and the last mists were rising from the
> dimpling stream. Had they found the life of the body after all?
> Could not the men whom they despised as milksops beat them,
> even on their own ground? (HE, 216)

The reference to the day 'sacred to men' and the description of two would-
be bathers as 'athletes' hint at 'athletic love' in ancient Greece. Charles would
like to bathe with Albert, but he cannot do so, even 'though the morning sun
was calling'; the sun here referring also, as in *A Passage to India*, to Apollo, the
deity most associated by the Dorian Greeks with homosexual love. The 'dim-
pling stream' recalls the 'stream of generations' in *The Longest Journey*, but is
something they are not permitted to enter. True, Charles has children, but as

Wilcox clones they are unlikely to contribute positively to posterity. Charles's inability to bathe is referred to as 'tragical', the athletes appear 'paralysed', unable to find a 'springboard' which would allow them to dive into this Sacred Lake. The references to a frozen nature seem to confirm Charles's sexual self-repression, and, when he sees those who appear to him to betray a certain femininity, that is, the 'milksops', his attitude is one of disdain. Like other male Wilcoxes, he is unable to realise his own 'inner' sexual self and so is doomed to a life of self-repression, wherein he must apply the judgements of a cruel, homophobic society to himself and to others.

As with other Forster novels, the manuscript drafts that remain disclose that the writer deliberately removed some of the more obvious homoerotic passages from his work prior to publication. One passage, excised from the final draft of *Howards End*, occurred during a discussion of Tibby's difficulties where the narrator gives his own observations on the development of young men:

> but at the close of boyhood he [the developing boy] sees, say, a
> book with a <pink> \ green / cover and <takes it up> liking the
> colour, takes it up. The book « is about <Greece or> adventure or
> philosophy or Greece » ... and from that moment the boy expands
> <and has a chance of becoming> \ into / the best kind of
> Englishman going.... And lastly — one boy more — the boy who is
> flustered. The voices of devils distract him, the voices of men
> frighten him, literature and art, for which he longs, are unscaleable
> mountains of names. For him also deliverance may be waiting; [...]
> But his case is different, he needs human aid. One does know that
> much (HE-MS, 101).

What kind of 'human aid' may be needed to help such a boy 'expand' is not clear, but it is noticeable that the narrator cites ancient Greece as initiating the expansion. When Mr Wilcox and Tibby do speak alone, they speak of Greece. However, expansion in Greece to Mr Wilcox means the development of an olive plantation in which he has shares, while for Tibby Greece perhaps has other associations (HE, 175 and HE-MS, 177). Whatever Tibby's tribulations might have entailed, Forster did not concentrate too much upon them, for as a character in his writings intended for publication Tibby's position could only be marginal; too much interest shown in the development of this character by the author might have provoked unwelcome speculation in his readers.

Ancient Greece does survive, however, as an inspiration and significantly it is Margaret who notes that 'deep and true as the native imagination can be' England has failed to produce 'a great mythology', for 'the greater melodies about our countryside have all issued through the pipes of Greece' (HE, 264). Yet she hopes that it might be possible for a rural Arcadia to be recovered even

there in the modern age, her words recalling the brotherhood and 'adhesiveness' of Whitman's philosophy:

> In these English farms, if anywhere, one might see life steadily
> and see it whole, group in one vision its transitoriness and its
> eternal youth, connect — connect without bitterness until all men
> are brothers (HE, 266).

Margaret's, and also Forster's, fear is that the pollution of the city will in
time poison the English countryside, just as the unalloyed values of the Wilcox
family threaten to continue their pollution of English society. Forster's concern
with the countryside not only relates to its physical conservation, but acknowledges that destruction of the greenwood would also signify a destruction of
those essentially idyllic values of ancient Greece which he closely associates
with the land, with its forested 'Sacred Lakes' (in *A Room with a View*) and
secluded dells (*The Longest Journey*). And ominously, in this novel the reader is
informed that preparations are already in hand to 'scythe out one of the dell-
holes' close to Howards End (HE, 334). The protagonist of Maurice found a
safe haven for his love of Alec in the greenwood, but, as Forster recorded in his
'Terminal note' to that work, eventually, in England, there was neither forest
nor dell to shelter such lovers (M, 240).

One figure who could perhaps have symbolised Margaret's longed-for
Arcadia is the woodcutter, ostensibly in the novel an even more insignificant
and marginal character than Tibby. He makes his fleeting appearance significantly at Mrs Wilcox's funeral, where his energy and virility contrast with her
death and loss and, symbolically, whilst others mourn he is hard at work,
pollarding a churchyard elm to ensure a new and vigorous growth. Forster's
erotic interest in the character is shown in a manuscript draft where the woodcutter is described as 'a powerful and agreeable youth' (HE-MS, 84), but this
description does not appear in the final published version. The woodcutter acknowledges the passing of Mrs Wilcox, but soon 'his thoughts' dwelled 'no
longer on death, but on love, for he was mating' and after the funeral he enjoys
'a night of joy' (HE, 87). It is worth noting that when Forster was contemplat-
ing an additional chapter at the end of *Maurice* showing the rural bliss enjoyed
by his pair of male lovers, Alec and Maurice, he intended to present them as
living happily together in the forest working as woodcutters (M, 239). Further
evidence, it would seem, that only in his private 'unpublishable' writings could
Forster freely explore his characters; in his 'publishable' fiction he must remain muted concerning the 'powerful and agreeable youth'.

The earliest surviving completed work of Forster's is the short story 'Ansell',
believed to have been written in 1902 or 1903 (LTC, viii). In this story, Master Edward, clearly based on Forster himself, comes home from Cambridge

University and meets up with his boyhood friend, the former garden boy Ansell.*
The story recalls a similar garden boy of the same name, who worked at Forster's
childhood home. Forster's 'greatest affection was for Ansell, his first and never-
forgotten friend' and 'he would look back on his afternoons with [him] as a lost
paradise' (Furbank 1, 30-1). In 'Ansell', the boy has become a youth who 'was
now gamekeeper to the small shooting... [Edward's] cousin had recently pur-
chased' (LTC, 3). Perhaps with the gamekeeper in *Howards End*, and with Alec
Scudder in *Maurice*, Forster was imagining what his 'first and never-forgotten
friend' would be like as an adult.

Towards the end of *Howards End* Margaret outlines what she sees as the
highest point of heterosexual love, a point which she feels Helen may have failed
to attain, and which she tentatively describes as 'the noblest way, where man
and woman, having lost themselves in sex, desire to lose sex itself in comradeship?', and returning to the failings of organised religion, she notes: 'It is those
that cannot connect who hasten to cast the first stone' (HE, 309). If religion
cannot hold society together, nor science produce a rational and functional
alternative, then what will hold 'this nomadic civilization' together? Margaret,
through the narrator, suggests 'Love' (and here she again speaks for Forster):

> London was but a foretaste of this nomadic civilization which is
> altering human nature so profoundly, and throws upon personal
> relations a stress greater than they have ever borne before. Under
> cosmopolitanism, if it comes, we shall receive no help from the
> earth. Trees and meadows and mountains will only be a spectacle,
> and the binding force that they once exercised on character must be
> entrusted to Love alone. May Love be equal to the task! (HE, 258)

Such a remedy for social malaise had also been proposed by Carpenter in
Love's Coming of Age, where he writes that 'the spirit of Truth is the life of the
whole, and only the other side of that Love which binds the whole together',
and that 'the ideal of terrestrial society for which we naturally strive is that
which would embody best these enduring and deep-seated relations of human
souls'; he adds:

> the conclusion is that the inner laws in these matters — the inner
> laws of the sex-passion, of love, and of all human relationship —
> must gradually appear and take the lead, since they alone are the
> powers which can create and uphold a rational society; and that the

---

* cf. *Maurice*, where Maurice is disturbed to hear that George, the garden boy, has left the family
home. He 'remembered George' and 'Something stirred in the unfathomable depths of his heart'
(M, 13). The departure leads Maurice to two disturbing dreams, one where he and George, both
naked, play in a haystack, and a second where he dreams of 'a friend' (M, 15). In Forster's description
of the boy Ansell in *Marianne Thornton*, he recalls their playing together in straw-ricks and records
his delight in his boyhood companion (274-5).

outer laws — since they are dead and lifeless things — must
inevitably disappear (Carpenter 1984, 176).

Yet a further dimension to the opposition of the inner to the outer world is
provided by the narrator's depiction of the Wilcoxes' public world as 'masculine' and opposed to the 'feminine' world of the Schlegels. It is Margaret who
asserts that the Schlegel household is 'irrevocably feminine, even in father's
time... our house — it must be feminine, and all we can do is to see that it isn't
effeminate. Just as another house that I can mention [Wilcoxes] ... sounded
irrevocably masculine, and all its inmates can do is to see that it isn't brutal'
(HE, 41). A connection therefore between the worlds of the Wilcoxes and the
Schlegels would entail a mingling of the characteristics of both sexes — and
Forster, perhaps mindful of his audience, is careful to point out that the 'effeminate' is to be avoided. Such a proposition again returns us to Carpenter
where, in *The Intermediate Sex* (published in full in 1908), he suggests that
when Love takes 'its rightful place as the binding and directing force of society' it would replace 'the Cash-nexus' and society would 'be transmuted in
consequence to a higher form'. Carpenter indeed goes on to declare that 'the
superior types of Uranians — prepared for this service by long experience and
devotion, as well as by much suffering — will have an important part to play
in the transformation' (Carpenter 1984, 241). They are able to play this creative role for not only have they 'put Love before everything else — postponing
to it other motives like money-making, business success, fame, which occupy
so much space in most people's careers', but also because 'indeed no one else
can possibly respond to and understand, as they do, all the fluctuations and
interactions of the masculine and feminine in human life' (240).

Replacing the 'Cash-nexus' would transform the world of the Wilcoxes
(and of the Schlegels), by abolishing the social hierarchies based purely on
wealth and inherited status, but to Carpenter, Forster, and whoever else knows
'Uranian love', such an upheaval would be nothing new, for as Carpenter
notes:

Eros is a great leveller. Perhaps the true Democracy rests, more
firmly than anywhere else, on a sentiment which easily passes the
bounds of class and caste, and unites in the closest affection the
most estranged ranks of society (Carpenter 1984, 237).

The marriage between Henry Wilcox and Margaret Schlegel unites the
'masculine' and the 'feminine', but it is through the relationship between Helen
and Leonard Bast that social classes are also brought together. Leonard Bast, a
low-paid insurance clerk, and his wife, Jacky, Henry's former mistress, live on
the fringes of middle-class society, forever in danger of falling into the abyss of
absolute poverty. Leonard is desperate for the consolation which art and culture
promise, but beneath is simply 'an ill-fed boy' (HE, 42). 'Perhaps the keenest

happiness he had ever known,' says the narrator, 'was during a railway journey to Cambridge,' 'where a decent-mannered undergraduate had spoken to him' and had hoped they could start a friendship, but Bast 'grew shy' and did not respond (HE, 120). Bast's marriage to Jacky is lifeless, devoid of any romance, but this fails to account for his relationship with Helen; the implausibility of their union being noted, Stallybrass asserts, by both readers and critics (HE, xiv).

Bast's relationships with the Cambridge undergraduate and with the Schlegel sisters are linked by the narrator, for both were seen by him as 'corners for Romance' (HE, 120). Whilst critics may baulk at the implausibility of a union between an upper-class, cultured woman and a lower-class man, the relationship would seem less implausible were both the protagonists men. Carpenter had commended cross-class male relationships, and noted their frequency amongst homosexual men, indeed he lived much of his life in such a relationship. Forster, too, like many of his male associates, enjoyed homoerotic and homosexual relationships with lower-class men. Bast's life was not only devoid of beauty, but also of 'the love of men' (HE, 47), though in a novel intended for open publication, Forster could not overtly show how this deficit might be rectified.

Two further aspects of character point towards a possible link between Bast and homosexuality. The first pertains to Bast having heart trouble — this ailment recalling Rickie Elliot's similar affliction in *The Longest Journey*, where Forster uses it as a metaphor for congenital homosexuality. The second aspect relates to A. E. Housman's *A Shropshire Lad*; the image of the lad was that of Housman's ideal rustic male, and here Forster takes up that figure, presenting him as being now debased by urban living. Though not himself from Shropshire, Bast's maternal grandfather was, his parents lived in Lincolnshire but he himself came to London and found employment. At the opening to chapter XIV he is described as the grandson of a shepherd or a ploughboy, and one of thousands of such young men who 'have lost the life of the body and failed to reach the life of the spirit'. Had Bast returned to his Shropshire roots, he could have found refreshment there, no doubt becoming firm friends with a Stephen Wonham-like companion. But in London, Bast's Shropshire 'heredity' remains unnourished in a meagre, hostile, petrol-fumed world, and he could only pass this 'heredity' to his child.

The legacy with which the novel is concerned, the house Howards End, came to Mrs Wilcox as a result of the death of Tom Howard. Tom, a bachelor soldier was due to inherit the house from his grandmother, but his early demise led to her receiving the property. He had wanted to marry Miss Avery, but she declined, choosing to remain unmarried, and so Tom produced no heir. If Bast had had a relationship with a man, he too could have produced no heir, although the relationship might have borne 'spiritual children' in accordance with the Platonic ideal. By his coupling with Helen, she and Bast together produce a child, and not merely one of their flesh, but one who promises to contribute to the stream of generations as a child of the spirit also.

The boy child that springs from Bast and Helen's affair is to be the product of many sections of society; he is to be blessed by a favourable heredity and
is to be raised by both the Wilcoxes and the Schlegels as their heir. In him,
social class, the urban and the rural unite and a further, nurtured, inheritance
will come from an amalgam of the 'masculine' Wilcoxes with the 'femininity'
of the Schlegels. As Trilling notes, the child 'is not only the symbol of the
classless society but, as he takes his pleasure among the busy workers in the
hay, he is also the symbol of the "Only connect!"' (Trilling, 116). The child's
own legacy will be the house, symbol of England itself, the hope being that he
will prove to be one of the forerunners of a new classless, democratic, and less
sexually constrained, English society.*

In a further echo of the story 'Ansell', there is yet another aspect to the novel's
ending. In the final scene, Helen 'rushed into the gloom, holding Tom by one
hand and carrying her baby on the other' (HE, 340). Tom's father is an agri-
cultural labourer, and he is linked through Helen to the baby boy, who is to
inherit Howards End. The baby boy is likely to grow up into a Mister Edward,
like the young man in 'Ansell', and young Tom is likely to assume the role of
Ansell, perhaps first as garden boy and later as gamekeeper to the estate. In the
future, in England's future, Tom and the boy are set to become friends in a
transformed society. Forster's private view of his own, now lost, childhood
'paradise' with the garden boy Ansell has become the basis for his public utopian dream of the future of his country.

The linkage of Tom, Helen, and the baby repeats a pattern found in other
Forster novels, where a woman forms a triangular relationship between two
friendly males. Examples of this can be found in the relationship between
Gino, Caroline and Philip in *Where Angels Fear to Tread*, and that between
Aziz, Mrs Moore and Fielding in *A Passage to India*.**

In recognising Carpenter's influence on Forster's work it is also noticeable
how often the fire of Carpenter's views is constrained by Forster's prose. It is as
if the problem posed by the narrator, that of connecting the passion and the
prose, is one with which Forster himself had to grapple. In *Howards End* he
appears to respond to this problem by a conscious denial of his private 'feeling',
mindful of his readers' supposed preferences, however, his self-censorship is
not complete and his desires do find expression in the work. Essentially the
novel is a hybrid affair, with evidence of restraint side by side with passages of
passionate prose. In his private world Forster felt Carpenter to be a 'saviour',

---

* cf. *Maurice*, where the narrator speaking of the relationship of Maurice and Alec says that 'England
belonged to them.... Her air and sky were theirs, not the timorous millions who own stuffy little
boxes, but never their own souls' (M, 223).

** After writing *Howards End* Forster wrote a play, *The Heart of Bosnia*. The familiar Forster triangle
of two male characters (Mirko and Nikolai) and one female one (Fanny) was repeated in the work. By
this time, however, Forster had expressed his weariness of writing on the subject of heterosexual love.
When Fanny rejects the advances of the two males, they kiss each other with 'the kiss of blood', renew
their former friendship and murder her instead (Furbank 1, 201).

but in the 'outer' public world of his writings, this 'inner' world of his own sexuality must remain 'unseen' and only covertly expressed. It is possibly this failure to write entirely in accordance with his 'inner' world which accounts for the fact that, as early as 1912, according to Furbank, Forster 'was in a mood of reaction against *Howards End* and the whole style of patient, synoptic comment on social issues which it represented' (Furbank 1, 210).

Whatever Utopian dreams Forster may still have entertained in succeeding years were, like those of countless others, severely upset by the experience of the First World War, and the period which followed *Howards End* saw Forster in crisis over his inability to write the kind of fiction that his public appeared to demand.

Perhaps it is the acute sense of creative 'constriction' Forster felt in the writing of this novel which explains his later disregard for it. In May 1958 he noted in his *Commonplace Book* that, although he felt *Howards End* to be his best novel, he did not actually like it:

> Have only just discovered why I don't care for it: not a single
> character in it for whom I care. In *Where Angels* Gino, in *L.J.*
> Stephen, in *R. with V.* Lucy, in *P. to I.* Aziz... and Maurice and
> Alec... and Lionel and Cocoa* ... Perhaps the house in *H.E.*, for
> which I once did care, took the place of people and now that I no
> longer care for it their barrenness has become evident. I feel pride
> in the achievement, but cannot love it, and occasionally the swish
> of the skirts and the non-sexual embraces irritate (CB, 203-4).

Perhaps if Forster, in this novel, had himself been able to unite his public prose with his private passion then an even greater novel might have been created?

---

* In 'The Other Boat'.

MAURICE

The genesis of *Maurice* is described by Forster in his Terminal note to the work which was published as an appendix to its posthumous publication. Forster records that the idea for the book dated from September 1913,* whilst he was staying in Harrogate with his mother and had decided to pay a visit to Millthorpe (he incorrectly spells it 'Milthorpe'), the home of Edward Carpenter and his working-class lover, George Merrill (Stape, 50). Forster declares his sincere admiration for Carpenter and his views; Carpenter seemed to hold the key to every trouble he faced and how he 'approached him as one approaches a saviour'. It was on his 'second or third visit to the shrine' that the couple made a profound impression on Forster. George Merrill touched him on the 'backside — gently and just above the buttocks', and 'The sensation was unusual... It was as much psychological as physical' and, Forster adds, 'It seemed to go straight through the small of my back into my ideas, without involving my thoughts... [and] at that precise moment I had conceived' (M, 235).

On his return to Harrogate, Forster immediately began work on the novel which was to become *Maurice*. Later he remarked:

> No other of my books has started off in this way. The general plan, the three characters, the happy ending for two of them, all rushed into my pen. And the whole thing went through without a hitch (M, 235-6).

The writing of the novel however did not quite go 'through without a hitch'. In October 1913 Forster wrote in draft the sections concerning Maurice's boyhood and his time at Cambridge, drawing on his own sexual experiences in childhood and his memories of Hugh Owen Meredith: for aspects of the relationship between Maurice Hall and Clive Durham appear based on those between Forster and Meredith. By mid-December 1913 Forster had put the manuscript to one side, discouraged from continuing by the adverse reaction of his friend Goldsworthy Lowes Dickinson to one of his privately circulated homoerotic stories. The unfinished *Maurice* joined the similarly unfinished drafts of what was to be *A Passage to India* and 'Arctic Summer'. Further discouragement came in March 1914 whilst in Ireland on a visit to Meredith, for his 'extreme dislike' of the proposed novel caused Forster again to consider adandoning it (Stape, 51). On his return to England, however, work recommenced. Progress was not easy, but by the end of June 1914 the book approached

---

* Nicola Beauman, in *Morgan: A Biography of E. M. Forster*, disputes this date, arguing that Forster first went to see Carpenter in 1910 (Beauman 1993, 234); see below.

completion. By July it was finished but Forster felt his creative energies were deserting him. The following month the manuscript was sent to Carpenter for his comments. Forster gained the approval he wanted from his 'saviour', for Carpenter wrote in reply on 23 August 1914 that he was 'very much pleased with it' though he occasionally disliked the 'rather hesitating tantalising impressionist style' adopted by Forster in his writing (Lago and Furbank 1, 223 n2).

In a letter of 6 March 1915 to E. J. Dent, (on whom the character of Philip in *Where Angels Fear to Tread* was based), Forster recorded the loneliness of his efforts in writing the work. He explained that he wrote *Maurice* neither for his friends nor for the public, but 'because it was weighing on me'. For a time he had meant to show it no one, and believed that no one would ever read it, for he felt the option of translation too depressing to accept, even though, in 1914, publication in English was deemed impossible (Lago and Furbank 1, 222).

Whatever his initial misgivings, Forster soon began to circulate the work privately to friends and continued to do so throughout his lifetime. He also ruled out the idea of publication as long as his mother was alive, and later, in a letter to Christopher Isherwood, he still rejected the idea as he feared the effect publication would have on a working-class friend and sometime sexual partner, Bob Buckingham, then a married policeman with a young son (Lago and Furbank 2, 159; Belshaw 165). Early readers in December 1914 included G. L. Dickinson and John Maynard Keynes (Stape, 54), and by March 1915 it had been read by others including Roger Fry, Lytton Strachey and E. J. Dent (Stape, 55). Another early reader was the writer Forrest Reid, to whom Forster sent a copy of the novel in January 1915, stating 'you will be glad to know I have written *something*, and am not as sterile as I am obliged to pretend to the world'; he cautiously added, no doubt as a reminder, 'you will not mention the book's existence to anyone, I know' (Lago and Furbank 1, 217).

This openness with the manuscript towards friends is attributed by P. N. Furbank to D. H. Lawrence's 'dressing down' of Forster whilst visiting him at home in February 1915. Lawrence berated Forster with an interminable diatribe against his books, his philosophy, and his whole way of life, and this left him determined to be more open in expressing his true feelings, especially in his relationships with close friends (Furbank 2, 9). He found an excuse later however to refuse the suggestion made by Leonard Woolf that he lend the manuscript of *Maurice* to his wife Virginia (Furbank 2, 18).

Future private readers included Siegfried Sassoon in 1920 (Stape, 73), T. E. Lawrence in 1927 (Stape, 98), Christopher Isherwood in 1933 (Stape, 114). Gore Vidal saw the manuscript in the late 1940s (Vidal 1965, 158; Vidal 1996, 191) and Benjamin Britten and Peter Pears in 1951 (Stape, 151). And in 1960 the actor Charles Laughton read a copy lent to him in Los Angeles by Isherwood (Isherwood 1996, 857-8).

Forster's concern for the novel continued throughout most of his life. In 1932 he decided on a revision and added the 'hotel' chapter (Stape, 113). And later, after permitting him to read the work he asked Christopher Isherwood,

'Does it date?', to which Isherwood answered, 'Why shouldn't it date?' From then on it became 'a favourite occupation of theirs to devise endings to the novel' (Furbank 2, 208; Isherwood 1977, 99-100). Later, in 1958, suggestions by O. W. Neighbour led Forster to revise the work (Furbank 2, 304), and further changes were made the following year based on comments made to the writer by J. R. Ackerley (Stape, 157).* The final addition to *Maurice* came in 1960 when, at the suggestion of William Plomer, Forster added his Terminal note (Stape, 157). The novel comes to us now in this final version, untouched by Forster since 1960. His diffidence concerning the work attended its creation and continued right up to the final draft with the comment he inscribed on the completed typescript: 'Publishable — but worth it?' (M, ix)

The writing of *Maurice* occurred during a time of crisis in Forster's creative life. Following the success of *Howards End* he entered a period in which he felt sterile, unable to write further fiction. His writing of the novel was meant to free him from this, but it failed to do so. It only confirmed his dilemma, that is, what he most wanted to write was deemed unpublishable, and what was publishable no longer satisfied his personal creative ambitions. Generally speaking, prior to *Howards End*, the homoerotic content of his work was visible for those who knew where to look (and, as has been demonstrated earlier, it abounds in those early novels). *Howards End* itself has comparatively little of such content, for Forster seems to have intensified the degree to which he policed what he wished the public to read. The creative expression of his own interests therefore had to go into writings not intended for the general reading public. And it is perhaps to be expected that *Howards End*, a novel which is heavily concerned with women, should lead Forster to feel acutely in need of a way of expressing his own more personal concerns about men.

The ambiguities in those earlier novels had clearly been recognised by their creator. The double nature of such works and of the works of other homosexual artists is directly alluded to in *Maurice* itself in the discussion between Clive and Maurice concerning art and sexuality, which was occasioned by their looking at a picture of a man by Michelangelo:

> He [Clive] did not change the subject but developed it into another
> that had interested him recently, the precise influence of Desire
> upon our aesthetic judgements. 'Look at that picture, for instance. I
> love it because, like the painter himself, I love the subject. I don't
> judge it with eyes of the normal man. There seem two roads for
> arriving at Beauty — one is in common, and all the world has
> reached Michelangelo by it, but the other is private to me and a few
> more. We come to him by both roads. On the other hand Greuze
> — his subject matter repels me. I can only get to him down one

* A description of Forster's progress in his writing of the novel can be found in Philip Gardner's essay 'The Evolution of E. M. Forster's *Maurice*' in *E. M. Forster: Centenary Revaluations*, edited by J. S. Herz and R. K. Martin (204-223).

road. The rest of the world finds two' (M, 83).

In Clive's criticism, with the mention of 'Desire', it is clear he is referring to sexual desire; his 'private road' alludes to his homosexuality, which leads him to a particular apprehension of Michelangelo's presentation of Beauty — an apprehension implicitly placed there by Michelangelo himself. By contrast, Greuze's work, characterised in his later years by 'titillating semi-draped figures of young girls' (Murray, 190),* repels Clive because of its cheesecake heterosexuality, and he 'can only get to him down one road', that of its purely artistic merits, though its depiction of sexuality is the very reason why 'The rest of the world finds two'. During Forster's lifetime the public and private roads were carefully separated in the lives of homosexuals; only in heterosexual life do these roads openly meet, as, for example, in the institution of marriage.

In *Maurice* there is also a later reference to another work of art which was reached by two roads. Maurice attends a performance of Tchaikovsky's 'Symphonie Pathique' (sic)** and Risley wastes no time in telling him the story of the work's origins. Tchaikovsky, whose own homosexuality had caused his marriage to fail disastrously, had shortly afterwards 'fallen in love with his own nephew', in whom he found 'his spiritual and musical resurrection', and had, subsequently, dedicated the symphony to him. The narrator informs us that 'The episode of the composer's marriage conveys little to the normal reader... but it thrilled Maurice', and Risley is delighted 'to see all respectable London flock' to hear the work (M, 148-9). For 'respectable London' and 'the normal reader', Tchaikovsky's work is apprehended without regard to his sexuality (which when Forster wrote the novel was practically unknown to them), but for Risley and Maurice, the knowledge of their shared sexuality with the composer provides a second road by which the work is known and appreciated.

This critical perspective could easily be applied to a Forster novel, for, in his universally acknowledged success as a writer, there is clearly a road by which 'all the world' has reached his work, but as his writings also demonstrate, there is yet another road, that of its covert homoeroticism, recognised by only a comparative few. Forster's preference for the private road can be noted in relation to his comments in *The Longest Journey* where he asserts the primacy of the private world over that of the 'great world' (LJ, 62-3). And this also reveals how damning in Forster's eyes is Clive's later comment in the novel that, 'These

---

* According to Peter and Linda Murray in *A Dictionary of Art and Artists*, Jean Baptiste Greuze was an artist who, at the height of his popularity, produced works characterised by 'turgid colour, strong chiaroscuro, and a heightened rendering of the gamut of the passions, displayed in vivid facial expressions and gestures in a mountingly high moral tone'. When his fame receded however, during the late 1770s and in the 1780s, 'to offset his dwindling popularity', he 'produced increasing quantities of titillating semi-draped figures of young girls, grossly deficient in drawing and of mawkish sentimentality' (Murray, 190).

** The Tchaikovsky symphony referred to is his Symphony no 6, known as the 'Pathétique', and not 'Pathique' as given by Forster here. The change of name is clearly intentional however, for 'Pathique', usually spellt as 'pathic', is an old term for a 'passive' homosexual (given as 'pathic' in Bray, 13 and as 'pathikos' or 'pathicus' in Burton, 183). The *Oxford English Dictionary* defines 'pathic' as a 'man or boy upon whom sodomy is practised; a catamite'.

private roads are perhaps a mistake' (M, 83).

If we apply the idea again to Forster's work, we can see in relation to *Howards End* how much of the private road has been squeezed out in favour of the world's road, and we can see in part how, with his preference for the private road, Forster's creative crisis arose. In *Howards End* the gamekeeper is a marginal and shadowy figure, almost excised from the final draft, but he is still an important object of Forster's sexual interest. To foreground such a character, however, to present him as he really saw or would wish to see him, Forster could do only in a piece of work which was wholly private and not intended for the 'great world' of 'normal readers'. To Forster, however, it became increasingly difficult to stick to the world's road and, in his writing of fiction, only the private road seemed viable. In practice, the roads separated in his fictional work, only the completion of homoerotic stories was effected, and possible publishable works, (notably his 'Indian novel' and 'Arctic Summer') lay unfinished. It was not until the early 1920s that Forster managed to bring the two roads back together in his last major piece of fiction, *A Passage to India*.

These 'roads' of course do not merely provide two viewpoints from which to view Art, but also from which to view Life. Clive abandons the private road when he takes the common one of marriage, but for Maurice, the confirmed 'invert', every part of life is coloured by the two roads; his sexual orientation influences every perception and every relationship. We see this in his viewing of Dickie Barry:

> The boy [Dickie] ... lay with his limbs uncovered. He lay
> unashamed, embraced and penetrated by the sun. The lips were
> parted, the down on the upper was touched with gold, the hair
> broken into countless glories, the body was a delicate amber. To
> anyone he would have seemed beautiful, and to Maurice who
> reached him by two paths he became the World's desire (M, 134).

Maurice's sense of the aesthetic is inextricably bound up with what excites him physically, just as Forster's creative output is inextricably linked to his sexual orientation. The two roads exist separately for him, for homosexuality is an essence and not merely an aspect. Philip Toynbee, however, in his review of the novel criticised Forster's assertion that the 'roads' were so separate as 'surely too simple, for we all, mercifully, have enough sexual ambiguity to enable us to lend a bit of our minority impulse whenever the occasion demands it' (P. Gardner, 464).

The theme of *Maurice*, male homosexual love in a homophobic society, is of course based in part on the author's own experiences, and the aspects of male love which he presents likewise reflect his own concerns on the subject. Maurice, a shy and diffident lover, attracted by lower-class males but wary of actual contact with them, mirrors the early life of his creator. Forster asserts in his Terminal note that, 'In Maurice I tried to create a character who was completely unlike myself or what I was supposed to be' (M, 236). Nevertheless, the parallels between the author and his fictional creation can be easily discerned; similarities in class background, education, aspects of their past lives (for example, in 1902 Forster experienced 'singularly intense dreams about friendship' which according to J. H. Stape (12) are recalled in the novel), reading (specifically their knowledge of the classics), and in their everyday life experiences and hopes for the future. And Clive, too, as indicated earlier, was based on Forster's first adult love, H. O. Meredith.

The novel deals primarily with two contrasting modes of male love. The first mode, that of Maurice and Clive which involves men of similar social standing, is based in the main on ancient Greek models and is in practice fundamentally celibate. The second mode, that of Maurice and Alec, involves men of very dissimilar backgrounds brought together by a love which does not shy away from physical expression.

At first the love of Clive and Maurice promises, rather idealistically, a freedom previously unknown except only to a few. It pays little regard to contemporary society, for society has prescribed no acceptable modes for its expression; their love has 'the inestimable gain of a new language', for 'No tradition overawed the boys. No convention settled what was poetic, what absurd. They were concerned with a passion that few English minds have admitted, and so created untrammelled' (M, 83-4). Needless perhaps to say, this ideal state proves impossible to sustain.

Clive, as mentor or 'inspirer', does however attempt to guide their relationship by one tradition at least — that embodied in the writings of ancient Greece — and schools Maurice, his ephebe or 'hearer', in its philosophies. Maurice confesses early on that his religion, that is, Christianity, means a lot to him and so Clive begins his education by an attack on the meaning of the Trinity which severely shakes his faith (M, 38). This scene echoes an incident in Forster's relationship with Meredith who undermined the adolescent writer's own Christian beliefs by attacking this point of theology (Furbank 1, 62). Furbank refers to Meredith's freeing of Forster from his confused faith as his emancipation from Christianity which paved the way for what Forster termed 'the second grand "discovery" of his youth' (his homosexuality) (Furbank 1, 98). Clive's effect on Maurice is similarily progressive.

Despite the efforts of their university tutor Mr Cornwallis, who in a Greek translation class advises them to omit references to 'the unspeakable vice of the Greeks' (M, 42), Clive nourishes his friend's developing sensibilities and readily informs him that not all religious philosophies have condemned homosexuality. 'The Greeks, or most of them, were that way inclined,' he remarks and recommends a reading of Plato's *Symposium* (M, 42). Here their friendship recalls that of Rickie and Ansell in *The Longest Journey* — Ansell, like Clive, being based in part on Meredith, just as Rickie was based in part on Forster himself. Maurice's study of ancient Greek values paves the way for Clive to declare his love (M, 50) and for Maurice to accept it, as 'the horrors the Bible had evoked for him were to be laid by Plato' (M, 61). Maurice's declaration of love has an unforeseen result, however, for when confronted with the truth of his own physical desires Clive withdraws. Later, when contact is re-established, Clive insists that their relationship remain chaste, denying physical contact, for 'It had been understood between them that their love, though including the body, should not gratify it' (M, 139).

The platonic model for their love, deriving from Socratic philosophy, is ultimately one which eschews physicality, for the carnal love of beauty is seen merely as a base starting-point from which may later develop the spiritual appreciation of Beauty for itself as an absolute and entirely metaphysical ideal. When Clive and Maurice are reconciled, their love tends towards this Socratic ideal, for 'The love that Socrates bore Phaedo now lay within his reach, love passionate but temperate, such as only finer natures can understand' and, true to that Hellenic model, it was a love which meant that the lovers 'could take their place in society' as 'they proceeded outwardly like other men'. By avoiding the expression of sexual contact, their relationship poses no real threat to social structures, and the reward of this self-repression is social acceptance; 'Society received them, as she receives thousands like them' (M, 89). This mode of love satisfies Clive, who tells Maurice that 'the sole excuse for any relationship between men is that it remain purely platonic' (M, 228); in this way he can suppress the full acceptance of his sexuality and later rationalise his affair with Maurice as a passing youthful phase. For his part, once he recognises the inherent celibacy of the platonic ideal Maurice 'had no use for Greece', and 'The stories of Harmodius and Aristogeiton, of Phaedrus, of the Theban Band were well enough for those whose hearts were empty, but no substitute for life' (M, 100). Significantly, when Maurice later tells Clive of his relationship with Alec Scudder, he taunts him with the revelation that they have shared 'All I have. Which includes my body' (M, 228).

For Maurice, love must include an element of physicality to be satisfying and this combination is found in the concept of 'athletic love', alluding euphemistically to homosexuality. The term seems to have come into common usage after Whitman used it in his first 'Calamus' poem, entitled 'In Paths Untrodden'. There the poet, having 'Escaped from the life that exhibits itself', 'rejoices in comrades' and resolves to sing no songs but those of 'manly attachment, Projecting them along that substantial life, Bequeathing hence types of athletic love'. The phrase, employed by the narrator, appears on a number of occasions in *Maurice*, such as in the reference to 'the impossibility of vexing athletic love' (M, 101). And, as in other Forster novels, the closeness of two males, here Maurice and Clive, is expressed in their bathing together (M, 68). Athletic love also recurs as a concept in Forster's writing, muted as in the tennis match in *A Room with a View*, or more visibly, as in *A Passage to India* where Aziz and the army subaltern sense a kinship, reminiscent of Whitman's 'adhesiveness', through a game of polo. In *Maurice* a similar connection occurs between Alec and the protagonist through a game of cricket:

When he went out to bat, it was a new over, so that Alec
received the first ball.... Lifting his eyes, he met Maurice's and
smiled.... He was untrained but had the cricketing build, and the
game took on some semblance of reality. Maurice played up too.
His mind had cleared, and he felt that they were against the whole
world, that not only Mr Borenius and the field but the audience
in the shed and all England were closing round the wickets. They
played for the sake of each other and of their fragile relationship
— if one fell the other would follow. They intended no harm to
the world, but so long as it attacked they must punish, they must
stand wary, then hit with full strength, they must show that when
two are gathered together majorities shall not triumph (M, 187).

The connection between this cricket game and the athletics of ancient
Greece is later further emphasised by Clive who refers to the match as the Olympic Games (M, 188).

Ironically it is when he goes to view contemporary Greece that Clive becomes disillusioned, not only with the country and its literature in which he had
previously found so much solace, but also with that love commended by its
ancient writers. He sees 'only dying light and a dead land... and knew that the
past was devoid of meaning like the present, and a refuge for cowards' (M, 106).
And in a despairing letter to Maurice he confides, 'Against my will I have become normal. I cannot help it' (M, 106).

A recourse to ancient Greek models is not the only way by which Clive and
Maurice seek to make sense of their sexual predicament. In a bewildered effort
to understand himself, Maurice looks to the scientific and medical opinion of
his time, and finds it is heavily compromised by theology. Part of Forster's
purpose in the novel was to challenge such a usage of religion in support of
homophobia. In a letter to Forrest Reid about the book he wrote that he wanted
to raise the subject of sexuality 'out of the mists of theology: Male and Female
created He not them' (Furbank 2, 14). Dr Ducie (the schoolmaster) informs
Maurice, however, that men and women were created by God in order that the
world be populated, and that it is therefore his duty to marry and have children (M, 7). Sadly Dr Barry, his medical advisor, later provides similar advice
from a secular standpoint when he warns Maurice that 'Man that is born of
woman must go with woman if the human race is to continue' (M, 20). After
the collapse of his relationship with Clive, Maurice accepts his dissent from
this norm as an illness declaring: 'With the world as it is one must marry or
decay' (M, 156) and he seeks medical help to 'cure' himself.

The fiction that homosexuality is a tangible disease rather than merely an
(equally fictitious) 'immoral' condition is referred to throughout the novel. When
Maurice reads Plato's *Phaedrus*, 'He saw there his malady described exquisitely'
(M, 61) and at one point Clive alludes to his condition as 'criminal morbidity'
(M, 51). Later Maurice even asks Dr Barry, 'Am I diseased?' but, as he knows

Maurice to be a 'decent fellow', the doctor refuses to discuss the subject (M, 145-6). The narrator conveys, however, what the reader has already surmised, that Dr Barry knew nothing of the subject. In his medical training homosexuality had never been broached; he 'had read no scientific works on Maurice's "condition" for 'None had existed when he walked the hospitals, and any published since were in German, and therefore suspect'. He 'endorsed the verdict of society gladly; that is to say, his verdict was theological. He held that only the most depraved could glance at Sodom, and so, when a man of good antecedents and physique confessed the tendency, "Rubbish, rubbish!" was his natural reply' (M, 147). An earlier tentative enquiry to the young Dr Jowitt about 'unspeakables of the Oscar Wilde type' similarly failed to elicit any information except the reply that such persons were generally found in 'asylum work' (M, 142). When Maurice does find 'medical' help from Mr Lasker Jones his diagnosis of him as a 'young invert' (M, 199) and a sufferer from 'congenital homosexuality' (M, 167) appears to derive from those German scientists, such as Krafft-Ebing and Iwan Bloch, whose works were unknown to Dr Barry. Such is the prejudice of contemporary medical opinion that it is readily understandable why, later in the novel, Maurice yearned for 'spaces no science could reach' (M, 178).

At this time, deprived of consolation from the classics, Maurice finds help from his reading of a life of Tchaikovsky; it was 'the one literary work that ever helped him' (M, 148-9). The downfall of Tchaikovsky is linked to his wife and, as in other Forster novels, women are presented here too as enemies to the 'natural' freedom of men. The narrator informs the reader that both Clive and Maurice are confirmed misogynists (M, 91) who saw women 'as remote as horses or cats; all that the creatures did seemed silly' (M, 91). Marriage itself is even referred to as part of women's strategy to control their menfolk. The friendship between Clive's mother and Maurice's mother is threatening, for Mrs Durham was looking to Maurice's sisters for a possible wife for her son. Her designs are given a sinister aspect for she 'believed she could best manage Clive through his wife' (M, 92), and it is through their influence that he himself senses that he ought to marry and provide 'an heir for Penge' (M, 87). Similarily it is also part of Mr Borenius's plan to control Alec's 'sensuality' by inducing him to marry before he leaves for South America. Once Clive is married, the observation of the narrator betrays the cynicism of his creator, seen perhaps in such comments as that which asserts Clive was suffering from a 'mental vagueness induced by his marriage' (M, 228). The final chapter of the work shows Clive's marital life as sterile and false, harking back, ironically perhaps, to the supposed physical sterility promised to male love in an earlier part of the novel (M, 87).

Such is the pressure to conform to social convention that, in his depression at the end of his affair with Clive, Maurice even comes to view marriage as the only course open to him also. Once Clive announces that he will marry, his place in Nature's plan is confirmed: 'Nature had caught up this dropped stitch in order to continue her pattern (M, 124); Maurice, however, contemplates suicide. The marriage of Clive and Anne, though built on Clive's denial of his true nature, is welcomed by his family and 'Beautiful conventions received them.' His former lover's fate is less attractive, for, 'beyond the barrier Maurice wandered, the wrong words on his lips and the wrong desires in his heart' (M, 152). Later, however, on a trip to see Clive, Maurice having acknowledged 'The indifference of the universe to man!' realises, by looking at different blossoms, that Nature is filled with diversity, not conformity, and that there is no overall blueprint whereby all are supposed to exist. 'Scarcely anything was perfect,' Maurice rails: 'The indifference of Nature! And her incompetence!'; he leaned out of the window 'to see whether she couldn't bring it off once, and stared straight into the bright brown eyes of a young man' (M, 165-6). That young man, Alec Scudder, is also homosexual, but unlike Clive who was the 'dropped stitch of Nature', Alec is possibly its perfection.

Maurice gradually realises that the love he had with Clive was too easily subject to the demands of family and society, and speculates that such a love can only continue to flourish outside of usual social controls. In a letter to Forrest Reid, Forster makes it clear that it is society itself which threatens Maurice, and all but destroys him, for 'he nearly slinks through his life furtive and afraid, and burdened with a sense of sin' (Furbank 2, 14). Maurice wonders whether in the past some did escape into the free zone of the greenwood: 'two men like himself — two. At times he entertained the dream. Two men can defy the world' (M, 125). He wavers however, between acceptance of this dream, and a belief in its impossibility. He feels cut off from 'the congregation of normal men' yet has the conviction that 'After all, the forests and the night were on his side, not theirs; they, not he, were inside a ring fence.' Almost immediately, however, he limits his own freedom by adding, 'But I must belong to my class, that's fixed' (M, 199).

This conviction, that he must stick to his class, is one which Maurice is slow to abandon; to him his love for Clive flourished in part because of the similarity of their class background. Divorced from physicality, what united them was a shared sensibility and outlook which was essentially based on class unity. Initially Maurice can see only one reason for male love to cross class barriers and that is lust: 'The feeling that can impel a gentleman towards a person of lower class stands self-condemned' (M, 139), complains Maurice, for to him such contact could not be based on anything but the exchange of money in prostitution. His prejudice complements that of Clive to whom 'intimacy with any social inferior was unthinkable' (M, 227).

Alec and Maurice first join together when Maurice is staying at Clive's house. Significantly on this occasion Maurice is placed in the Russett Room (M, 163), red, of course, being a colour associated with physical passion. When Maurice had stayed previously with the Durhams, he had been placed in the Blue Room, 'The one with no fireplace' (M, 78).

In his collection of prose essays published in 1893, *In the Key of Blue*,

John Addington Symonds had associated homoerotic love with the colour blue.*
The title essay of the collection lovingly describes a young Venetian gondolier,
his friend Augusto, whom Symonds made pose as a 'mere model or lay-figure'
in various locations about the city, dressed in various shades of blue (Symonds
1893, 1-16). Symonds invariably wrote about homosexuality using the ancient Greeks as a model, and blue is linked to Italy, the heir to Greece's legacy,
and this may be, in part, why, when Clive and Maurice are friends together,
Forster places Maurice in the Blue Room, the physical relationship with Alec
appropriately taking place later, in the Russet Room.

Blue as the colour of paederastic, 'Greek' love was also being established
at the same time as Symonds was writing, by the painter Henry Scott Tuke,
and subsequently by the Uranian poets. Neil Bartlett, in his essay on Oscar
Wilde, notes that Tuke made his name with open-air studies of Cornish boys,
who posed for him pretending to be young ancient Greek heroes such as
Endymion, Leander or Perseus. Tuke's 'most famous painting was August Blue
(1893) whose soft-focus rough trade inspired a whole school of white-on-blue
"Boys Bathing" homoerotic poetry' (Bartlett, 245).

Forster himself associated the colour with homoerotic love and ancient
Greece in at least two of his short stories, 'The Story of the Siren' and 'The
Tomb of Pletone', and when Mrs Failing in *The Longest Journey* fantasises
about Stephen Wonham as a shepherd in ancient Greece, she imagines him
clothed in a mantle of blue (LJ, 88).

In Forster's 'The Story of the Siren', an English academic on a visit to
Capri accidentally drops the notes for his Fellowship dissertation on the Deist
Controversy into the Mediterranean. The academic, who also narrates the story,
describes its waters:

> Let us call them blue, though they suggest rather the spirit of what
> is clean — cleanliness passed from the domestic to the sublime, the
> cleanliness of all the sea gathered together and radiating light. The
> Blue Grotto at Capri contains only more blue water, not bluer
> water. That colour and that spirit is the heritage of every cave in

---

* Symonds specifically links the colour with Venetian working-class males: 'it is just among the working
people — fishermen, stevedores, porters, boatmen, artizans, *facchini* — that the best opportunities
are offered for attempting symphonies and harmonies of blue. Whole classes of the male population
attire themselves in blouses, sashes, and trousers of this colour' (Symonds 1893, 3-4). Likewise,
'Baron Corvo' in his *Venice Letters* describes youthful male beauty in shades of blue, which he declares
only the artist Henry Scott Tuke could properly record: 'of young Venetians poised on lofty poops out
on the wide lagoon, at high noon, when all the world which is not brilliant is blue, glowing young
litheness with its sumptuous breast poised in air like showers of acquamarines on a sapphire sea with
shadows of lapis-lazuli under a monstrous dome of turquoise — of young Venetians poised... at
sunset, glowing magnificent young strength dominantly illumined, poised in an atmosphere of lavender
and heliotrope in tremendous stretches of sea and sky all cut out of jewels, limitless amethyst and far-
reaching turquoise, or, all burnished copper splashed with emeralds and streaked with blue, the insistent
blue of borage (20).

the Mediterranean into which the sun can shine and the sea flow (CS, 197).

The English academic is left alone by the Grotto with a Neapolitan sailor, Giuseppe, who is to dive into the sea to rescue the lost notes. The sailor prepared to enter the water and disrobed, 'For a moment he stood naked in the brilliant sun', before diving in (CS, 197):

> His effect was that of a silver statue, alive beneath the sea, through whom life throbbed in blue and green.... I was delighted with him for thus falling into the key of his surroundings. We had been left together in a magic world, apart from all the commonplaces that are called reality, a world of blue whose floor was the sea and whose walls and roof of rock trembled with the sea's reflections (CS, 197-8).*

This passage suggests a link with Symonds's *In the Key of Blue*, for like Augusto who posed in blue in Venice, Giuseppe falls 'into the [blue] key of his surroundings', Forster's use of the word 'key' echoing Symonds's earlier use in a similarly charged homoerotic situation.

The Tomb of Pletone in Forster's short story of that name is notably covered with blue clematis flowers (AS, 113). Pletone, who was also known as 'Gemistus Pletho', was the subject of an essay of that name by Forster, in which he was described as a fourteenth-century Byzantine philosopher who 'looked for his religion among the half-forgotten rites of ancient Greece' (AH, 177). In the story Pletone's friend Sismondo kneels by his tomb and addresses his companions:

> 'Do you not see our master?' He [Sismondo] bowed his head and kissed one of the little blue flowers. 'His body has made this plant and his spirit has filled it. His eloquence has passed into its tendrils, his wisdom into its leaves, and the blue flowers are his soul which has contemplated heaven. For he has awoken the gods, and year by year they will renew him and increase him, till the flower which is his covers the whole earth. I will take it to Italy, this flower, and there he shall grow, as a sign that Greece has risen from the dead' (AS, 114).

Here Forster links the colour to the ancient Greek heritage, which flourished in Renaissance Italy, and which, together with the freer sexual atmosphere

* cf. 'The Bather in the Blue Grotto at Capri' by the Uranian poet Rev. E. E. Bradford (Bradford, 29). Also E. F. Benson's novel *Colin*, 'wherein the author dwells with sensual pleasure upon the charms of young Nico', an inhabitant of Capri (Masters, 185).

of their contemporary Italy, made Forster's, Symonds's and many other male homosexuals' own trips to that country so memorable.

Returning to *Maurice*, the link between homosexuality, the Blue Room and ancient Greece is further demonstrated in the narrator's comment concerning Clive: 'He hated queerness, Cambridge, the Blue Room, certain glades in the park * were — not tainted, there had been nothing disgraceful — but rendered subtly ridiculous'; this is immediately followed by his turning up of an old poem by Maurice beginning, 'Shade from the old hellenic ships' (M, 161-2).

At night, in the Russet Room, Maurice calls 'Come!' (M, 163), but does not know whom he has called. Later in the same room he is tortured by a dream which clearly relates to the sexual confusion engendered by his treatment from Mr Lasker Jones. Maurice longs for a 'darkness where he can be free', and he 'had the illusion of a portrait that changed, now at his will, now against it, from male to female, and came leaping down the football-field where he bathed...' He dreams of 'passion', 'woods', a 'majestic sky and a friend', before awakening to call out again 'Come!' — which acts as a summons to his 'friend' Alec to mount the ladder to his bed (M, 178). The word 'Come' is significant, especially in its being repeated. Not only is it ambiguous — it could refer to ejaculation in sexual intercourse — but also, it is used by Forster specifically to invoke a homosexual love. In his short story 'The Life to Come' exactly the same word is used by Vithobai to call out to his lover, and in *A Passage to India* it is similarly used in repetition by Professor Godbole to invoke the god Krishna.

Maurice's falling in love with Alec challenges all his former class prejudices, though later, when he fears that Alec is trying to blackmail him, his old suspicions reappear. Again, Maurice in his ignorance mirrors aspects of his creator, for Forster's first-hand experience of the working class at this time was severely restricted. His real knowledge of working-class men was only acquired later in his life. In a letter to Christopher Isherwood in 1938, Forster noted that in 1914 he was ignorant of this way of class, though it stimulated his imagination, and referred to Alec as 'the dream which turned into the scare and then into the mate', recording that it was his own later contacts with working-class young men which gave him 'knowledge, and stuffed the form of Alex [sic] out in places suitable to his physique' (Lago and Furbank 2, 158-9). And, as with the recognition of their homosexuality, both Maurice's and Forster's ambiguous feelings regarding class are transformed by a reading of Greek literature. Both find affirmation of their dream of cross-class male bonding in the story of the Theban Band and, during consultation with Mr Lasker Jones, Maurice asserts the unifying potential of this love:

> It strikes me there may have been more about the Greeks —
> Theban Band — and the rest of it.... I don't see how they could

---

*According to Furbank, Forster was familiar with 'certain glades in the park', for, about the time he was working on *Maurice*, 'he spent much time in erotic day-dreaming and, on his visits to London, would loiter in Hyde Park or visit public lavatories, half-heartedly hoping to make a pick-up' (Furbank 1, 255)

have kept together otherwise — especially when they came from
such different classes (M, 196).

In Edwardian Britain, however, no such public approbation could mark
the love of Maurices for their Alecs. The only hope for the continuance of
their love was to escape from urban society, for all that belonged to them in
England was an outlaw life in the greenwood:

> He [Maurice] had brought out the man in Alec, and now it was
> Alec's turn to bring out the hero in him. He knew what the call
> was, and what his answer must be. They must live outside class,
> without relations or money; they must work and stick to each other
> till death. But England belonged to them. That, besides
> companionship, was their reward. Her air and sky were theirs, not
> the timorous millions' who own stuffy little boxes, but never their
> own souls (M, 223).

This model for their love is clearly drawn in part from the work of Carpenter, who in *The Intermediate Sex* expounded its virtues and looked towards
the social future of homogenc love, as 'a great leveller:

> It is noticeable how often Uranians [homosexuals] of good position
> and breeding are drawn to rougher types, as of manual workers,
> and frequently very permanent alliances grow up in this way, which
> although not publicly acknowledged have a decided influence on
> social institutions, customs and political tendencies — and which
> could have a good deal more influence could they be given a little
> more scope and recognition (Carpenter 1984, 237).

Forster however, is unable to set and keep his lovers within society, for he
cannot demonstate how such a relationship could be fully realised unless it were
free from social constraints.

Throughout Forster's work 'the woodland' is presented as a free space
where the homoerotic may flourish; examples of this are to be found in the
'Sacred Lake' scene in *A Room with a View*, the woods in which Eustace meets
Pan in 'The Story of a Panic' or where, in 'Arthur Snatchfold', Conway and
Arthur have sex. Perhaps it was Whitman who gave Forster the theme, for 'In
Paths Untrodden' (in the poem of the same name) the poet's thoughts turned
to 'athletic love' and 'the need of comrades', or Shelley, who in his
'Epipsychidion' wrote of love in an island Arcadia; though much earlier than
both these poets, the homoerotic idylls of the Dorian Greek poet Theocritus
(referred to by Forster in *The Longest Journey*) had spoken of sexual passion in
a pastoral retreat.

Returning to *Maurice*, the reader is soon alerted to the links between 'queerness' and 'certain glades in the park' (M, 161). So true to this principle, for a happy ending to be sustained, Maurice and Alec must discover a rural refuge in order to enact the earlier dream of 'love — nobility — big spaces where passion clasped peace... full of woods some of them... arched with majestic sky and a friend' (M, 178). By a denial of sexual feeling, the love between Maurice and Clive could find a mutilated existence within society. However the love between Maurice and Alec, because it crosses class boundaries and involves taboo sexual behaviour, is deemed publicly unsustainable, and consequently must withdraw to a fictive sylvan idyll. In his Terminal note Forster adds, with regret, that today there is nowhere to escape society's intrusiveness (M, 240). This later acknowledgement of the inability of male love to find a space in which to flourish is reminiscent of the ending of *A Passage to India*, where the friendship of Fielding and Aziz can find no place to prosper, as the narrator intones, 'they said in their hundred voices, "No not yet," and the sky said, "No, not there"' (PTI, 312).

As in *A Room with a View*, one further enemy of male love, indeed of any other loves which celebrate the body, is 'medievalism' (M, 81), by which is meant the type of denial and disdain of the body which characterised the medieval Christian church. It also stands condemned in *Howards End*. In *Maurice* the proponent of this aspect of religion, and of the kind of Christianity rejected by Maurice under the tutelage of Clive, is Mr Borenius, who, shortly after his first appearance in the novel, is swiftly at work in denouncing Alec before his employer with the accusation that 'he has been guilty of sensuality' (M, 222). Borenius condemns unregulated sexuality, warning that 'fornication extends beyond the actual deed' — an observation with which Forster would have agreed, but from a different expositional viewpoint. Rather than analyse the benefits, or otherwise, which accrue from what he has observed, Borenius can only foresee disaster from unregulated sex. His answer to his own fears is to prescribe a further criminalisation, for 'until all sexual irregularities and not some of them are penal the Church will never reconquer England' (M, 222). Needless perhaps to add, 'Mr Borenius assumed that love between two men must be ignoble' (M, 223). This moralising outlook is the one which Clive, who earlier was scathing in his criticism of it with Maurice, is condemned by his class position to uphold, and, as a local magistrate, he will continue to sentence any working-class 'invert' brought before him, whereas Maurice, because of his class affinity, may well go free (M, 241).

The treatment of physical love in the novel was severely criticised by Forster's friend Lytton Strachey, who found 'the whole conception of male copulation in the book rather diseased — in fact morbid and unnatural' (P. Gardner, 431). Examples to substantiate such criticism may perhaps be found in Maurice's confused belief that his embrace of Clive has produced his hysterical collapse (M, 98), and in such gloomy observations as 'pleasuring the body... had confirmed his spirit in its perversion' (M, 199). Strachey also highlighted the narrator's negative attitude towards masturbation; one example being the passage where 'in his despair' Maurice 'turned to the practices he had abandoned as a boy, and found they did bring him a degraded kind of peace' (M, 149). Strachey had no doubt that the origin of this attitude lay in Forster himself, and confronted him with the accusation that it was sometimes difficult to distinguish his views from Maurice's (P. Gardner, 430). Clearly Forster had failed in his aim to make Maurice differ substantially from himself, for apart from his character's sporting prowess, few real differences exist.

Shortly after completing *Maurice* Forster wrote to Forrest Reid admitting that he did at one time feel that male love should not involve the physical, adding that now he felt quite differently (Furbank 2, 14). And in a later letter to Siegfried Sassoon, Forster acknowledged the difficulty he had had in the novel in writing about sex, and consequently revised his work accordingly, observing that 'Nothing is more obdurate to artistic treatment than the carnal, but it has to be got in I'm sure: everything has got to be got in' (Lago and Furbank 1, 316) — deliberate ambiguity was intended here, it would seem.

Forster's difficulty with the 'carnal' clearly relates to the fact that when he wrote *Maurice* in 1913, at the age of thirty-five, he had very little sexual experience of any kind to draw upon. A further three years were to pass before he achieved what he felt to be his first full sexual encounter when he had sex with a soldier on the beach during his war service at Alexandria. In a letter of 16 October 1916 to his friend Florence Barger concerning the incident Forster wrote that he had 'parted with respectability'.* His unease with the experience was acknowledged, and he confessed that he had realised by it how he was 'tethered to the life of the spirit — tethered by habit, not by free will or aspiration' and, noting his own inexperience, felt that 'the step would not have left me with these feelings had I taken it at the usual age' (Lago and Furbank 1, 243). It was only shortly afterwards that Forster felt he did achieve a relationship which could compare to that between Maurice and Alec, when he met his Egyptian friend Mohammed el Adl. Again he confided to Florence Barger, 'I wish I was writing the latter half of *Maurice* now. I know so much more' (Lago and Furbank 1, 274). Despite his later revisions of the text, Forster refrained from saying much about physical lovemaking between males, despite his accruing personal experience of it.

Although Forster gives 1913 as the year in which he wrote *Maurice*, this date is disputed by his recent biographer Nicola Beauman. She asserts that the characters of Maurice and Clive were not simply based on those of Forster and Meredith. Her argument is that Forster based them, in part, on Ernest Merz and Max Garnett. Beauman relates that after dining with Malcolm Darling on 8 July 1909, 'Morgan and Merz had walked a little alone' before parting. The following day Merz was found dead, having hanged himself (Beauman 1993, 226). Beauman asserts that Forster, who was apparently the last person to speak to Merz before his death, was profoundly shaken by the event. She maintains

---

* According to Beauman, 'semi-respectability seems to have meant mutual masturbation and loss of respectability fellatio'. Buggery did not seem to figure in his sex life at this time (Beauman 1993, 299-300).

that Merz was homosexual and suggests that Forster may have inadvertently contributed to his death. She proposes two possible ways in which he could have been involved. Firstly, she says, Merz may have asked Forster to be his 'special friend', and Forster had 'almost impatiently as was sometimes his way, rejected him'. Or, secondly, she suggests, perhaps 'Morgan had made a remark or an allusion that made Merz realise his true inclinations were now unconcealable,' and that 'it may have been Morgan's intuition that toppled Merz over into suicide.' She also speculates on two other possible causes of the suicide: perhaps 'he was accosted by a male prostitute and succumbed', or perhaps he was being blackmailed. Whatever the reason, 'Unable to live with himself, Merz drank whisky... and then found a rope' (Beauman 1993, 229-30). Beauman asserts that Forster could not forget he had been the last person to see Merz alive:

> He [Forster] also, even more importantly, identified with Merz, not merely because superficially they were alike but because their situation was indeed so similar... no one would ever know this, but Morgan was guilt-stricken, miserable and confused. The only remedy, the only form of exorcism, that he knew was a novel. And so *Maurice* was born.... It was the image of the hanging Merz that inspired his fifth novel (Beauman 1993, 230-1).

By allowing his male lovers to find happiness, Forster would thus be 'making amends to Merz' as well as making a 'Carpenteresque plea for sexual tolerance' and exploring the 'concept of the pastoral' and 'corollary values such as love, sensitivity, kindness and spiritual freedom which, in society as most of us know it, come second, Morgan felt, to conventional, suburban behaviour' (233).

Beauman then dates the writing of the novel to 1910, arguing that Forster went to Harrogate with his mother in July of that year and during that stay made the short visit to Carpenter at Millthorpe; it was on his return from this trip that the idea for *Maurice* occurred. She presents evidence to support this suggestion from various sources; the main source being the original draft of Forster's Terminal note to the novel, where the opening sentence read '*Maurice* "dates from 1910",' and at the 'end of the third paragraph Morgan wrote that "it was finished in 1912".' She finds this re-dating of the novel important, for its 'coming only a year after Merz's death, shows this event as well as the visit to Millthorpe as being the point of inspiration'. She also notes that a privately printed edition of Merz's letters came out in 1910 and 'they echo throughout the novel so much that it is clear that Morgan had it beside him as he wrote' (234). She follows the histories of both Merz and Max Garnett and notes biographical similarities betweem them and Maurice and Clive in the novel. The actual sexual orientation of Garnett is not certain. However, he was engaged to be married shortly before Merz's death, and Beauman hints that this may have led Merz to contemplate suicide, just as in *Maurice* Clive's engagment leads Maurice to despair and thoughts of suicide (M, 125). Interestingly Forster did speculate in his Terminal note that the novel might have proved acceptable to the public if he had ended it 'unhappily, with a lad dangling from a noose or with a suicide pact' (M, 236). Beauman also suggests that Forster may have held back from publishing the novel so as to spare the feelings of the Merz family (236-7).

Beauman's argument is quite persuasive, with regard to her suggesting 1910 as the date of the novel's origin. What she has not accounted for though is why Forster should have recorded in his diary entry of 31 December 1913 the note 'Maurice born on Sept. 13th' (Herz and Martin, 206), indicating that he had begun the novel on that day. Presumably this entry was made on or about that date and it would therefore considerably predate his Terminal note. It is difficult also to see how Merz's misery specifically contributed to the novel. Surely Forster just drew on his own sadness in describing that of Maurice, for he himself had contemplated suicide when his own love, Meredith, had become engaged in 1906 (Furbank 1, 141). Beaumont's view of the novel's happy ending as, amongst other things, 'making amends to Merz' is plausible, but there seems also a strong element of wish-fulfilment in Maurice's union with Alec, Forster clearly feeling the need for such a lover in his own life. It is difficult to evaluate her statement that Merz's letters echo throughout the novel. She herself does not provide evidence of any specific textual links betwewen them, nor examples to back up her assertion that 'it is clear that Morgan had it [the book of Merz's letters] beside him as he wrote.'

Alec's profession has generated discussion, for, despite Forster's assertion that his gamekeeper 'was senior in date to the prickly gamekeepers of D. H. Lawrence' (M, 238), parallels have been drawn between him and Mellors in *Lady Chatterley's Lover*. Dixie King, in her essay contrasting the two novels, finds the parallels between them striking:

> both novels take as their theme forbidden sexuality (homosexual
> in the one and female in the other); in both books, the full sexual
> initiation of the protagonists is strongly associated with wild
> woods which surround or lie adjacent to old, rotting mansions
> which are clearly symbols of stifled sexuality; the plots in both
> turn on the naive, frustrated loyalty of the protagonist to a
> bloodless, soulless lover...; and in both books, a very romantically
> conceived character, the gamekeeper — virile, primitive, yet
> wonderfully intelligent and sensitive — plays the critical role in
> the sexual initiation of the protagonist (King, 68).

King also quotes from V. S. Pritchett's early review of *Maurice*, where he notes that Forster's book is the male version of Lawrence's novel with 'the same

preoccupation with snobbery and class-consciousness, the same allegory of
the stagnant condition of English life' (69). King also notes parallels between
A Room with a View and Lawrence's *The White Peacock*, suggesting, along with
other critics cited in her article, that Lawrence appropriated thematic material
from Forster, transforming and developing it in his own work. Her case for such
a linkage is strong and persuasively argued. However she too easily rejects the
notion that 'some of these intersections in setting, plot, characterization, and
the dynamics of character relationships have more to do with the cultural and
literary milieu Forster and Lawrence shared than with any link established or
suggested between the two writers' (80). That Forster knew Lawrence and visited him is well known, as are certain details of their relationship. However the
information that is available is not exhaustive; in particular, it is not known if
Forster had allowed D. H. Lawrence to read *Maurice*, or if he even mentioned
it to him. What is established is the fact that both writers were familiar with,
and influenced by, the works of Walt Whitman and Edward Carpenter. Some
thematic parallels in their work could easily therefore be linked to their shared
reading. Whilst Forster, like Lawrence, seems to praise the physicality of working-class sexuality, he, unlike Lawrence, does not invariably accompany this
with an attack on bourgeois society itself. After the First World War criticism of
those parts of the establishment which were deemed to have sent others to their
deaths was not uncommon. Instead of getting rid of this part of society, Forster
proposed that the various social classes unite and progress together towards the
future as a wholly new society, envisaged along the lines proposed by Carpenter.
Lawrence, however, sees bourgeois society, exemplified by the impotent Lord
Chatterley, as a kind of dead wood to be cut away before the growth of a new
and more productive society can become a possibility.

King lists various parallels between the character of Maurice and that of
Connie Chatterley, asserting:

> for many reasons, because she voices [a] sexually naive and
> ambivalent perspective... because she is made the conduit for
> homoerotic descriptions of beautiful men — from Michaelis and
> Mellors to Daniele... and because she serves as a functional
> analogue to Maurice himself, Connie must be recognized as an
> ambiguously functioning vehicle for both explicit erotic and
> encoded homoerotic literature (King, 82).

From this observation it would seem that not only did Lawrence and Forster
share thematic material, but also literary strategies for expressing their own per-
ceptions and opinions within their fictional writings. The extent of Lawrence's
own homosexuality, however, remains a point of debate between academic critics, though almost all acknowledge the presence of homoeroticism in his
writings.

George Steiner, in his own early review of *Maurice*, tentatively suggested that Forster may have given Alec his profession after he had seen Lawrence's work, and poses the question, 'is Scudder's profession a stroke of feline malice, (not wholly uncharacteristic of Forster's late years), a wink to the informed reader that Lawrence's heterosexual posturing might be suspect?' (P. Gardner, 479).

The end of *Maurice* appears to have almost always attracted criticism. Forster noted that as far as he was concerned, 'A happy ending was imperative. I shouldn't have bothered to write otherwise', and that he was determined that 'in fiction anyway two men should fall in love and remain in it for the ever and ever that fiction allows' (M, 236). Before him, of course, he did have a sort of model in the relationship between the upper-class Carpenter and his proletarian lover Merrill. This couple, whilst not quite living in a greenwood exile, nevertheless shared a home in a countryside retreat in the sort of 'pastoral' characterised by 'love', 'sensitivity', 'kindness' and 'spiritual freedom' which Beauman had noted in the bond between Maurice and Alec. Forster however, in a letter to E. J. Dent of 6 March 1915, felt that there were no models upon which to base the future of his lovers; the literature of ancient Greece, with its reputed emphasis on paederasty, had seemingly no similar model for adult male love. Forster wrote:

> I... do feel that I have created something absolutely new, even to
> the Greeks. Whitman nearly anticipated me but he didn't really
> know what he was after, or only half knew — shirked, even to
> himself, the statement (Lago and Furbank 1, 222).

Lytton Strachey, on whom the character of Risley was based, was also highly critical of the novel's ending. In a letter to Forster of 12 March 1915 he commented that he felt the attraction of Maurice and Alec to have been based primarily on 'lust and sentiment' adding that he 'should have prophesied a rupture after six months — chiefly as a result of lack of common interests owing to class differences' (P. Gardner, 430). It was perhaps his criticism and the comments of friends who 'united in finding it preposterous' (Furbank 2, 15), which led Forster to curtail his rural fantasy by excising a later chapter, in which Kitty encounters the lovers labouring humbly together in the forest as woodcutters (M, 239).

As the novel progressed through its many revisions, so did Forster's thoughts on its ending. In a letter to Isherwood in 1938 he even stated that he had sometimes thought of Alec marrying and felt they would (like their spiritual predecessors in the Theban Band perhaps) have served together in the Great War (Lago and Furbank 2, 158). Further criticism by O. W. Neighbour produced a revision in 1959. The original ending to the novel came as Maurice watched Alec's boat depart for the Argentine and had noted that he was not aboard. Maurice then turned 'his face towards England in a brave blur of exalted hope'. Neighbour questioned how the two men could actually find each other after that, hence Forster added 'a passage in which Maurice is brought safely to Alec's arms' (Furbank 2, 304).

Critical dissatisfaction, however, did not end there, for on its first publication in 1971 the novel's romantic ending generated further adverse comment. Many critics decried its unreal dénouement. C. P. Snow noted 'the ecstatic ending... rings artistically quite wrong, as a wish fulfilment' (P. Gardner, 435) and Julian Mitchell cuttingly dismissed it as 'woman's magazine' and decided that the epilogue had been 'wisely repressed' fearing it would have proved little more than 'a Home Counties version of *The Song of the Loon*' (P. Gardner, 439-40).

Whilst Forster's writing is not, in general, quite so poor as the 'woman's magazine' remark implies, there are certainly passages (chapter 43 of *Maurice* in particular) where Forster appears to be writing the kind of romantic fiction which is produced primarily for women readers. Parallels are apparent with some of the characteristics of the Harlequin romantic novels identified by Ann Barr Snitow. Of the Harlequin series, Snitow writes:

> Since all action in the novels is described from the female point
> of view, the reader identifies with the heroine's efforts to decode
> the erratic gestures of 'dark, tall and gravely handsome' men.... In
> a sense the usual relationship is reversed: woman is subject, man,
> object. There are more descriptions of his body than of hers.... He
> is the unknowable other, a sexual icon whose magic is maleness
> (M. Eagleton, 134).

In *Maurice*, the protagonist's character is clearly 'passive' in relation to that of his dark lover Alec. And Forster's narrators frequently adopt a conventionally 'female point of view' in their descriptions of male figures. Examples of this can be seen in the descriptions of Gino in *Where Angels Fear to Tread*, and Gerald in *The Longest Journey*. Often the narrator and a 'passive' male protagonist, such as Philip Herriton and Rickie Elliot, are involved in 'efforts to decode the erratic gestures' of certain other, attractive males. Alec Scudder, Gino, Gerald and Stephen Wonham could each be described as 'a sexual icon whose magic is maleness'. In this the 'passive' male protagonists and narrators could be said to mirror Forster's own sexual situation, and his own desire to be loved by a strong young man of the lower classes. Likewise, Forster's homosexual readers could readily identify, by the 'private road', with those 'efforts to decode' erratic, masculine gestures.

Janice A. Radway, in her study of women readers of romantic fiction in the American community of Smithton, noted that 'escape' was overwhelmingly cited by the readers as the main reason for their choice of such fiction. Those readers used the word escape, both literally and figuratively:

> On the one hand, they value their romances highly because the act
> of reading them literally draws the women away from their present

surroundings.... On the other hand, the Smithton readers are
quite willing to acknowledge that the romances which so
preoccupy them are little more than fantasies or fairy tales that
always end happily (M. Eagleton, 129-30).

Maurice can be viewed in this context. It works as an 'escape' for like-
minded readers for it presents a utopian pastoral vision of what cross-class male
love could be, far removed from the 'present surroundings' of its first, and mod-
ern-day, gay readers. Literally it actually presents an 'escape', for Maurice and
Alec's love can only function, and their full happiness be realised, in a setting
removed from contemporary society, both urban and rural. Is the novel also
'escapist'? It could be argued that by indicating that male love may only find
fulfilment outside of 'normal' society, that such a romance merely confirms
homosexual men in their status as victims, that is, by inferring that only an
escape, running away, can lead to happiness. Forster, however, does not go that
far. He sees his contemporary society as unable to provide a 'home' for the
lovers. Their rural pastoral, however, is not only a retreat, but a promise of what,
should the British nation be transformed along Carpenteresque lines, could
reproduce itself throughout the whole of society. Instead of a love apart, it could,
if imitated, tend towards the realisation of that 'adhesiveness' commended by
Whitman. And, after all, Forster does not present the idea that homosexual love
is in itself at fault, nor even that it mirrors social inequalities, merely that existing social conditions, which repress it, are the cause of its suffering. The novel
itself is dedicated 'To a Happier Year',* indicating Forster's belief that total retreat is not always necessary to realise this dream of love, and, he emphasises
Maurice and Alec's exile is one 'they gladly embrace' (M, 236).

Radway also notes about her women readers 'that despite their disap-
pointments, they feel refreshed and strengthened by their vicarious participation
in a fantasy relationship where the heroine is frequently treated as they themselves would most like to be loved' (130). Such feelings of being 'refreshed and
strengthened' would seem to have been experienced by Forster himself once
he had written *Maurice*. Indeed a number of the novel's earliest readers were,
like Forster, essentially bourgeois men who liked to meet working-class youths
(Dickinson, T. E. Lawrence, Christopher Isherwood amongst others) and to
whom his fantasy would have appealed.

It is perhaps this element of class which most dates the novel. Class barriers had been significantly weakened by 1971. In a society which aimed to be
classless, idealisation of the working class as sex objects seemed dated and the
specific desire for working-class youths as partners, by those who were not
themselves working-class, was associated often with an ageing, bourgeois elite.
When *Maurice* was finally published, it attracted not only a general readership, but also a readership amongst homosexuals of varying class backgrounds.

---

* cf. The ending of *A Passage to India* which likewise looks forward to a future time when friendships
shall flourish unhindered.

A knowledge of the Greek classics was not seen as being as important as in Forster's day, and so his references to Plato and the love praised in his *Symposium* seem alien to many present-day gay readers.

Heterosexual romances, such as those of *Wuthering Heights* or *Pride and Prejudice*, do not seem to date quite so readily, for the conventions within which the actions of those novels take place are long-established and recognised even within today's society. Homosexual love does not enjoy such deep-rooted conventions. Indeed it is seen in Forster's writings as being all the better for its freedom from these. After all, in Maurice and Clive's love, 'No tradition over-awed the boys. No convention settled what was poetic, what absurd' (M, 83). For the general reader, *Maurice* requires to be understood much more within its historical context, whereas for Emily Bronte's or Jane Austen's novels, often the reader will not feel the necessity for such a contextual framework. The reason for this being quite simply that the general conventions in society are fundamentally heterosexual, and, by the usual processes of social conditioning, are passed on to all. Conventions attaching to homosexuality must be learnt later on in life, once one has found an appropriate teacher, or some other source of knowledge.

The world in which *Maurice* was first published also saw the rise of the Gay Liberation Front in the aftermath of the Stonewall riots in New York in 1969. And in England and Wales (only later in Scotland and Northern Ireland) sexual activity between male adult homosexuals had been partly decriminalised. So, inevitably, the novel could only be viewed as historical, and compromised, as Forster admitted, by having, for some at least, only 'a period interest' (M, 239).

Forster, however, felt that it was not only in 'its endless anachronisms — its half-sovereign tips, pianola records, norfolk jackets', etc, that the novel dated, but also 'for a more vital reason: it belongs to an England where it was still possible to get lost'. 'There is no forest or fell to escape to today,' he noted (M, 240).

THE 'UNCOMPLETABLE' AND
THE 'UNPUBLISHABLE'

Following the success of *Howards End*, Forster's publisher and his readership awaited a worthy successor, and in late 1911 the writer began the first draft of 'Arctic Summer' (AS, xi). The first part of the work proved relatively easy to undertake, even though Forster felt the need to revise radically these original fragments early the following year. The revision led to a new opening segment, known as the 'Radipole Version', but the whole project was abandoned later that year, and was superceded in 1913 by work on *Maurice*. Some further revision may have been made after *Maurice* was completed, but there is no clear evidence of this.

'Arctic Summer' deals with the March and Whitby families , and the March family reappear as characters, with different first names and with children, in 'Entrance to an Unwritten Novel', a short work published in 1948, which was subsequently to become a homoerotic short story 'The Other Boat', completed in 1957–58. It is not clear what, if any, rewriting Forster undertook on the fragments of 'Arctic Summer' after 1913, but the first five chapters of the work were given a public reading on 10 June 1951, in an event that formed part of the Aldeburgh Festival. The reading came about because of the writer's friendship with Benjamin Britten and Peter Pears; and Chapter 1 of the work was published in 1963 as part of *Tribute to Benjamin Britten on his Fiftieth Birthday*, edited by Anthony Gishford.

'Arctic Summer' deals with the developing friendship between two men. Clesant March, single, athletic, a mountaineer, a military man from a military family, not unintelligent, but certainly non-intellectual, and Martin Whitby, married with a three-year-old son, artistic, sensitive, a socialist from a Quaker manufacturing family, though a sceptic after his mother's death, who works as a clerk in the Treasury.

Their relationship, being that between an outdoor strongman and a married aesthete, seems at first to recall that of Gerald Dawes and Rickie Elliot in *The Longest Journey*. Clesant though is less boorish than Gerald, and Martin less inhibited than Rickie, and with a marriage that seems to be working less destructively. Nonetheless the opposition of rugged military male adored by another, sensitive, male seems to hold here. And, as with Rickie Elliot, it is difficult not to see aspects of Forster's own character in that of Martin Whitby.

The incomplete novel opens at the railway station in Basle. English tourists are crowding each other in a desperate bid to get one of the limited number of seats on a train to Italy. Martin appeals to the 'gentlemanliness' of his fellow travellers, trying to avoid a crush, but ends up being pushed before the wheels of the train. His danger is short-lived for Clesant, 'a warrior', then a stranger to him, responds to his appeal by pulling him away from the train. Though glad to be rescued, Martin is greatly deflated to find that his warrior is nothing more than 'a fair-haired ordinary public school type' (AS, 121); he had hoped to find a personal saviour, not a man who seemingly would have done the same for anybody else.

After their encounter Martin becomes restless, though he is not sure why. They soon meet again on the train and Martin is anxious to show Clesant the beauties of Italy. Unlike Rickie Elliot, Martin is not shy in his dealings with the material world, for, to him, 'the physical joined with the spiritual into one glory' (AS, 130). The narrator tells us that Martin had had difficulties and temptations in the past, and that he 'nearly became a bad citizen', but not how bad exactly. When beauty came into his adolescence, the 'wonder of life' dazzled him and he saw nothing else, for 'the world appeared as a sort of gymnasium in which fine fellows develop their muscles and swing about from rope to rope' (AS, 131). Whatever the temptations such a scene had engendered, he had overcome them when he 'took himself firmly in hand' (AS, 131). After resolving his difficulties, he found an 'orderly love' for he 'was one of the happy men upon whom Nature plays no tricks. He only loved where he had liked' (AS, 132). The phrase about Nature and her tricks clearly points to Martin's earlier difficulties being sexual, for in early and mid-twentieth century Britain 'men upon whom Nature had played a trick' was a slang phrase used to refer to homosexuals.* By taking himself 'firmly in hand', that is, by masturbation, Martin had managed to sublimate his desires, and settled down, not uncomfortably, into a 'not adventurous' love with Venetia.

The meeting between him and Clesant unsettles this apparent order in his life; clearly his earlier difficult desires had not quite been doused by marriage. Clesant had planned to see the frescoes of Tramonta with Martin and his wife, but due to a disagreement between them, he does not join the party. At Tramonta, Martin sees in a fresco a figure of a soldier who resembles his new friend exactly. Whilst Venetia speculates on heredity, Martin feels 'it touched him strangely', and finds it all 'very moving', and as he sketches the scene he senses that 'Another hand might have guided his pencil' (AS 148).

Returning from Tramonta to Milan, his emotional turmoil increases. Both Martin and his wife think the unease due to worry over his work, but his mother-in-law Lady Borlase knows better, and correctly diagnoses his problem: 'He'd be happier if there was another man', specifing a gentleman, not a social inferior (AS, 155).

But because of a quarrel with Clesant, made worse by his wife's rudeness — Martin warning her that if you wish to influence someone 'there must be affection' (AS, 152) — the friends seem set to be permanently estranged. Martin

---

* cf. the 1961 film *Victim*, where Henry, the hairdresser, speaking of his homosexuality says, 'Nature played me a dirty trick'; in an much earlier film, *Wanderer of the West* (1927), the clerk Clarence was 'one of Nature's mistakes in a country where men were men'.

does strike up a further friendship in Milan, not with the sort of gentleman his mother-in-law had commended but with one of those types of working-class males whom Forster had praised in an excised passage from *Where Angels Fear to Tread* (WAFT, 158). This is Aristide, a lame chauffeur, whom Martin takes to a cinema. When the building catches fire, Martin proves ill-equiped to rescue Aristide — so unlike his saviour Clesant, he muses, who had rescued him at the railway station.

At that point in the story Forster ended the 1951 revisions, the problem, he told his readers, was that he had not really worked out what was going to happen in the relationship between the two men. Martin and Clesant were to be brought together in England, in an attempt to prevent Clesant's brother, Lance, from being sent down from the Cambridge college where Martin's father-in-law just happened to be Master. But beyond that stage where could their relationship go? Forster feared that the 'novel might have ended with the two companions in defeat', adding that 'such an ending does not interest me' (AS, 162).

The remaining fragments of the work begin to tell the story of Lance's downfall at college, and of Clesant and Martin's joint effort to prevent this. When Clesant discovers that his brother is to be sent down for taking to 'filth' and going with women (AS, 191), the vehemence of his denunciation leads to Lance shooting himself. Having failed as Lance's protectors, there is nothing to indicate how their relationship could proceed further. Martin is not so dissatisfied by marriage as to wish to leave Venetia, and a ménage à trois as proposed in 'Ralph and Tony' would perhaps have proved unacceptable to a later, more sexually sophisticated, public; which left Forster recognising that there was nowhere to take this story. Shortly after abandoning 'Arctic Summer' however, he found a new way of developing relationships between men in *Maurice*, though the way to that discovery had been prepared earlier in his 'unpublishable' stories on homoerotic themes.

It is not clear exactly when Forster began writing what he termed his 'unpublishable' stories. In his diary entry of 8 April 1922 he suggests this was about fifteen years earlier, that is, in 1907, though he acknowledges that he is not certain about the date (LTC, xii). His biographer P. N. Furbank, however, dates the genesis of the earliest stories to 1911 (Lago and Furbank 1, 317). At whatever date they were commenced, and the titles and precise contents of those initial stories are not known, there is agreement that 'The Life to Come', written in 1922, is the earliest surviving example, and that 'Little Imber' was the last of such stories, being completed in November 1961 (Stape 158), though one story, 'The Torque' was revised as late as 1962 (Stape 159). Despite the loss of the earlier tales, and some later ones, these 'unpublishable' writings were occasional modes of creative self-expression for Forster for at least fifty years; and some of them provided him with a sense of creative freedom he was not to experience with his publishable works. Only much later in his life did Forster write of homosexuality in a work intended for publication, when, partnered by Eric Crozier, he adapted Herman Melville's work to prepare the libretto for Benjamin Britten's opera *Billy Budd*, which was premiered in 1951.

Regrettably only a fraction of Forster's private works appear to have survived. Many an 'unpublishable' tale was the victim of its creator's occasional bout of literary culling, termed a 'smut-scratch' by the writer himself (Parker, 422). Such 'scratches' were executed mainly in 1922 and periodically thereafter, finishing perhaps in 1958 (Stape,156), but possibly continuing right up to Forster's death in 1970. Furbank notes however that Forster occasionally lamented his burning of the earlier stories (Furbank 2, 138). Despite his ruthless handling, and perhaps this was the reason why he was so exacting with them, they were to him important elements of his oeuvre and, he maintained, any failure to take proper cognisance of them would seriously detract from any critical summation of his achievements as a writer. In a letter to T. E. Lawrence on 9 August 1927, Forster noted that Virginia Woolf's recent article on his work had failed likewise to sum him up, and that her attempt to do so had been flawed from the beginning, for she had not been aware of his private literary achievements (Lago and Furbank 2, 80).

During the writing of *Howards End*, Forster had been acutely conscious of the need to exercise greater control over his material, especially his use of words, aware that he was 'writing for an audience' which he had to please (HE, xii). This public readership was a very different audience to the private one that first read *Maurice* and his unpublishable stories. Writing to G. L. Dickinson in May 1917, Forster noted that the gulf between 'private' and 'public' had in the previous three years grown dizzying, and that thanks to scientific organisation more and more of men's energy was diverted to the public side. Perhaps it was his belief in this rather adverse social development, as well as the subject-matter of his stories, which would account for his withdrawal into a private world, with a private audience, in which to create his fictional works. Forster's letter shows how his creative crisis, his lack of any desire to produce 'public' fictions, mirrored his general feeling that the 'public' sphere of English life was working towards the extinction of those private personal values, of 'sweetness and nobility... in intercourse between individuals', which Forster himself, and his writings, had commended (Lago and Furbank 1 251). 'Public' writings like the 'public' world seemed to demand artistic stances which were significantly antithetical to individual perspectives. And 'scientific organisation', Forster had noted in his diary entry of 27 January 1908, seemed only to promise tyranny:

> Science, instead of freeing man — the Greeks had nearly freed him
> by right feeling — is enslaving him to machines.... Man may get a
> new and perhaps a greater soul for the new conditions. But such a
> soul as mine will be crushed out (HE, xi).

Set against this background, Forster's private fiction can be viewed as a deliberate retreat to a private world, in which artistic creation could progress unhindered, and unsurveyed by a public world which seemed to have little time for 'sentiment'; a world apart from a 'scientific' atmosphere, in which his love for his fellow men was condemned as a sign of mental disorder.

Forster's need to adopt a public silence, especially over matters of homo-sexuality, was learnt at a young age. When he was about eleven years old he met a middle-aged man whilst walking on the downs near to his school. The man induced Forster to masturbate him. Forster wrote to his mother about the inci-dent, and her subsequent response — and his school's — to this 'dreadful' and 'fearful thing' led Forster to realise the value of saying no more of the matter. Significantly this silence found expression in the diary he kept at school. Record-ing the incident he wrote simply: '<<<Nothing>>>'. Furbank adds to this entry that the word was 'to remind himself there had been something' (Furbank 1, 37-8). Homosexuality was deemed not only an unspeakable vice, but also to Forster an unwritable one as well, at least in the public domain, and initially, it would seem from his diary entry, in the private domain also.

Forster later discovered in 1919 that he was not the only English man of letters engaged in privately writing 'unpublishable' fiction on homoerotic themes, for Siegfried Sassoon then began to show him similar writings of his own (Furbank 2, 56). In return for this favour Forster lent him a manuscript of *Maurice*. Forster's initial regard for his 'unpublishable' works is clear from a letter written to Sassoon on 11 October 1920 in which he thanked him for having returned the manuscript and added that he could lend him some short stories one day, if he wished, which were 'less reputable' than his novel (Lago and Furbank 1, 316).

Nothing of the original stories lent to Sassoon apparently remains, for according to P. N. Furbank they were amongst those destroyed by Forster him-self in 1922 (Lago and Furbank 1, 317), although it is thought that Forster attempted to recreate the lost works from memory in later years. In a diary entry of 8 April 1922 Forster records his destruction of them and gives his reasons for doing so:

> Have this moment burnt my indecent writings or as many as the
> fire will take. Not a moral repentance, but the belief that they
> clogged me artistically. They were written not to express myself but
> to excite myself, and when first — 15 years back? — I began them,
> I had a feeling that I was doing something positively dangerous to
> my career as a novelist. I am not ashamed of them.... It is just that
> they were a wrong channel for my pen (LTC, xii).

Why Forster felt they would be 'positively dangerous' is not clear. Perhaps he simply dreaded the consequences of their being revealed to the public? Per-haps he feared that the police might view them as 'obscene' and begin asking awkward questions about his private life? As the subject of homosexual love was so very dear to his heart it is not clear how they could have 'clogged' him artis-tically — unless he feared that once he had developed the ability to express his truer sentiments in literature then a return to the publishable conventional novel would be all the more difficult if not impossible? Perhaps he feared that future publishable fiction would contain elements which might reveal him to his readers, especially in the post-First World War period when the insights of Freudian psychology were becoming more well-known. His literary sterility, at least with regard to his inability to produce publishable fictions, had provoked in him a sense of crisis, though he continued to produce articles and reviews which did prove both successful and publishable.

Whatever the reason, and despite his eschewing of such stories, three months later he noted in a letter to Florence Barger that he was at work on 'The Life to Come' — a story on a homosexual theme which he described as 'violent and wholly unpublishable' (LTC, xii).

Whereas its indecent predecessors had been viewed by him as having 'clogged' him artistically, 'The Life to Come' was a story Forster always treasured, and producing it proved a liberating experience, as he readily acknowledged in a letter to Sassoon of 21 July 1923. Sassoon had read, and clearly liked, the story and Forster, in reply, averred that he too thought it good, and wondered: 'Why can't I always be writing things like this — it is the only freedom' (Lago and Furbank 2, 43). Forster also showed the story to T. E. Lawrence, who liked it, and to Goldsworthy Lowes Dickinson, who did not. Lawrence thought it one of the funniest things he'd ever come across, and, suprisingly, inclined to consider it 'quite fit to publish' (Lago and Furbank 2, 56).* Together with Sassoon, and shortly afterwards J. R. Ackerley, they seem to have been the main audience for his private work at this time, though in later years many more selected friends were to be allowed access to it by Forster.

In discussing Forster's destruction of these stories, Oliver Stallybrass notes that 'though the 1922 holocaust may conceivably have been a necessary price for the completion of *A Passage to India*, thereafter there was no dilemma: as far as fiction went, it was unpublishable "sexy stories" (Forster's own phrase) or nothing' (LTC, xiv).

Another private tale, 'Dr Woolacott', this time with a homosexual ghost, was completed in May 1927 and subsequently shown to friends (Stape, 96). T. E. Lawrence was enthusiastic and Forster made amendments to the work in response to suggestions from him. As with 'The Life to Come', writing 'Dr Woolacott' was to give Forster a creative lift. In a letter to Lawrence on 17 November 1927 he enthused that the story was the best thing he had done and quite unlike any other writer's work:

> The story makes me happy. It gives bodily ecstacy [sic] outside
> time and place. I shall never be able to give it again, but once is

---

* It may well be his correspondence with T. E. Lawrence which first alerted the world to the existence of some of Forster's unpublishable writings. Lawrence died in 1935, and in 1938 a collection of his letters, edited by David Garnett, was published. Garnett included a letter of 8 September 1927, written to Forster, which referred to an unpublished 'long novel' [*Maurice*], a short story which 'isn't publishable' ['The Life to Come'?], and another story which 'wouldn't do for general circulation' ['Dr Woolacott'?] (248).

something.... I have gone through the story today in my mind, with the knowledge you have read it, and this hardens (got it!) me (Lago and Furbank 2, 81).

In the succeeding years of his life Forster added to and subtracted from his unpublishable short stories, and, as with *Maurice*, it was only after his death that they were collected together and published in 1972 under the title of *The Life to Come and Other Stories*, though some Forster stories without a homoerotic theme also appear in that collection. One further fragment of a homoerotic story given the editorial name of 'Stonebreaking' and the almost complete 'Little Imber' appeared with other uncompleted works in 1980 in *Arctic Summer and Other Fiction*.

Unlike his published novels, the short stories do not bear the signs of any significant influence by the ideas of Edward Carpenter. Perhaps those stories which Forster had destroyed in 1922 had done so, but certainly by 1929, if not earlier, Carpenter's work had lost much of its influence on him. In an entry in his Commonplace Book in 1929, Forster recorded his reassessment of the work of the man he had once 'approached... as one approaches a saviour' (M, 235):

Edward Carpenter.... Astonishing how he drains away. Poems I actually copied out for myself a few years back now seem thin whistling rhetoric. I know that the spirit is there but it has got into the wrong skin. Gerald Heard summed him up the other day at my request, and most devastatingly: 'An echo. Walt Whitman was the first who blew through that hollowed reed. Morris, J. A. Symonds — there you have the whole. He knew nothing, he couldn't think. 'Civilisation, its Cause and Cure'* — how can you conceive such a book having a huge circulation? He knew nothing about civilisation. He was always a clergyman... and he was always finding mystic reasons for doing what he wanted e. g.** I suppose there was something there, but as soon as one touches it, it's gone. Slow but steady decline of power' (CB, 52-3).

Whilst the 'unpublishable' stories all have a homoerotic theme, homosexual activity as such is only obliquely referred to in some, such as that between Denis and the statue in 'The Classical Annex' and between Clesant and the ghost in 'Dr Woolacott', and where it is described, as in 'Arthur Snatchfold' or in 'The Torque', for example, it is only fleetingly so in a few lines, though quite directly.

---

* Carpenter's book *Civilisation, its Cause and Cure*, a collection of essays, was first published in 1889, and went through sixteen editions before a final set of essays appeared in 1921 (Carpenter 1984, 50).
** Philip Gardner, editor of the *Commonplace Book*, notes 'There is a blank in the original after "e g". It perhaps represents "being a homosexual"' (CB, 275).

A further unifying motif in the tales is not merely their homoeroticism, but the fact that when homosexual relationships do occur, they always involve two protagonists of quite varying class, racial or social backgrounds: in 'Arthur Snatchfold' the upper-class Sir Richard Conway unites with Arthur the milk-man; in 'The Life to Come' an Indian chief loves the English missionary, Pinmay; Earnest, an elementary schoolteacher, has sex with Tiny, a rough, uneducated sailor in 'The Obelisk'; in 'The Torque', Marcian, an inhabitant of an early Christian, post-Roman world, delights in sex with the Goth, Euric; and similarly in 'The Other Boat' white English Lionel enjoys sex with the dark Indian, known by the name of Cocoanut. Unlike representations in the con-ventional heterosexual fiction of his time, nowhere in these stories do persons of the same racial or class backgrounds unite.

Forster in later life acknowledged the criticism of friends that his unpublishable stories were often too thematically repetitive. In a conversation with P. N. Furbank in 1957, subsequently recorded in Furbank's diary, Forster confided that 'people found his indecent stories monotonous: they ran to type. Whenever the same tall athletic figure came on the scene, eroticism started. This was limiting' (Furbank 2, 302). Forster's response to this was to produce a story which treated the subject of love very differently than hitherto he had done. His penultimate unpublishable story, 'The Other Boat', written in 1958, was consciously created with a theme than ran counter to much of his other work, both published and unpublished, when he presented a pair of lovers whose love for each other would not save them, but ensure their mutual destruction.

'The Life to Come', the earliest of Forster's 'indecent' stories that survive, deals with themes familiar from Forster's published work. The Indian chief Vithobai's sincere plea for spiritual love to be united with physical love is contrasted with the hypocritical, repressed sexuality of Pinmay, a Christian missionary. The theme recalls the similar conflict between Mr Emerson's claim 'that love is of the body' (RV, 202) and Cecil Vyse's sexually repressed medievalism in *A Room with a View*. Both Vithobai and Pinmay claim to speak of love, but only Vithobai acknowledges its sensual aspect.

In this story, as in other fiction by Forster, both published and private, an erotic encounter between two men, here Vithobai and Pinmay, occurs in a woodland setting, whose trees keep an 'unspeakable secret' (LTC, 66) — a secret, no doubt, concerning that 'love which dare not speak its name'. Vithobai repeatedly urges Pinmay to come with him 'into the last forest before it is cut down... and all may end well' (75), but his plea is rejected by the missionary, whose repressive religion has been instrumental in bringing about the destruction of the forest, by preparing the way for its exploitation by colonists. Significantly, as in other works by Forster, marriage is a prelude to the destruction of male bonds, for Pinmay marries a medical missionary, whose brother had a mining concession above Vithobai's village. It is the demand for timber for his mines which leads to the ruin of the forest (73-4), and to the love which prospered there.

It is perhaps this theme linking colonial exploitation and the destruction of the possibilities for male love which elucidates Forster's assertion that he wrote 'The Life to Come' 'in indignation' — Furbank explaining that: 'he [Forster] meant, partly, in indignation against British imperialism'. Forster had written the story shortly after the death of his Egyptian lover, Mohammed el Adl, and the writer believed that his friend's earlier imprisonment and mistreatment by the British authorities in Egypt had contributed to the deterioration of his health, and subsequent death from tuberculosis in early May 1922 — 'The Life to Come' being completed in early July of the same year (Furbank 2, 115 and 103) (Stape 79-80). Furbank adds that Forster's 'indignation' was also directed in part against himself, 'at some suspected over-cautiousness', and that, despite its being 'eloquent' and 'over-romantic', the story 'always meant a lot to him' (Furbank 2, 115).

Mohammed's death severely distressed Forster, and in the latter part of 1922 he began to write a long letter addressed to his dead friend. In his grief, he added 'another chapter' to 'The Life to Come', subsequently describing the addition in a letter of 21 July 1923 to Siegfried Sassoon:

> I tried another chapter, it is true, in the forests of the Underworld 'where all the trees that have been cut down on earth take root again and grow for ever' and the hut has been rebuilt on an enormous scale. The dead come crashing through the foliage in an infernal embrace. Pinmay prays to his God who appears on high through a rift in the leaves and pities him but can do nothing. 'It is very unfortunate,' says God: 'if he had died first you would have taken him to your heaven, but he has taken you to his instead. I am very sorry, oh good and faithful servant, but I cannot do anything'. The leaves close, and Pinmay enters Eternity as a slave while Vithobai reigns with his peers. (LTC, 237; Lago and Furbank 2, 43)

The rebirth of the forests and the hut in the Underworld, where the dead appear 'in an infernal embrace', underscores the link between imperial exploitation and the suppression of homosexual feeling, and point towards a future where friends may unite across racial divides. That all the trees which have been cut down take 'root again and grow for ever', symbolises the restoration of all those male loves which, like that of Maurice and Alec in *Maurice*, had flourished in the hidden world of the forests. This mystical restoration of lost loves recalls the final scenes of Krishna worship in *A Passage to India* (PTI, 294), where 'all men loved each other'. Given Forster's 'indignation' with the imperial authorities in Egypt, it is easy to see why he proposed a future life for the Indian chief in which the formerly exploited native can forever exploit his former colonial master, who enters into 'Eternity as a slave'.

The sick young squire Clesant at the centre of the story 'Dr Woolacott' (written in 1927), suffers from a 'functional' problem — 'Nothing organic' —which began with his heart: 'my heart makes my nerves go wrong, my nerves my digestion, then my head aches, so I can't sleep, which affects my heart' (LTC, 84). That his illness stems from his heart recalls Rickie Elliot's similar affliction in *The Longest Journey* (LJ, 23). In that novel Rickie's disability is linked to his homosexuality, both being viewed as hereditarily acquired conditions. Clesant's analysis of his problem as 'functional' rather than organic recalls the language utilised by Krafft-Ebing, in his description of what he termed 'congenital homo-sexuality'. Mental disorder was also to the fore:

> 4 Neuroses (hysteria, neurasthenia, epileptoid states, etc.) co-exist. Almost always the existence of temporary or lasting neurasthenia may be proved. As a rule, this is constitutional, having its root in congenital conditions. It is awakened and maintained by masturbation or enforced abstinence (Krafft-Ebing, 225).

The precise nature of Clesant's ill health, if ill he be, is in doubt, for it is Dr Woolacott himself who has defined the young man's supposed illness. Clesant's own definition of his condition utilises the medical model of a disease, described in a vocabulary taken from his doctor, who seemingly took it from Krafft-Ebing. Clesant's listlessness and fatigue, his anxiety, his headaches and ennui could be viewed as symptomatic of neurasthenia. The fact that Dr Woolacott recommended that he 'musn't be intimate with people' (LTC, 88), together with the whole tenor of the story, suggests that the doctor views Clesant's condition as having a sexual origin. Krafft-Ebing, as quoted above, notes such an aetiology arising from 'congenital homo-sexuality', especially when awakened and maintained by... enforced abstinence'. Clesant's 'condition' is clearly being exacerbated by his doctor's advice to avoid intimacy with others, to practise, that is, an 'enforced abstinence'; and, incredibly, both Dr Woolacott and Krafft-Ebing see 'abstinence' as both the cause of, and the only treatment for, a neurasthenia induced by 'congenital homo-sexuality'. Clesant's internalisation of the medical ideology which oppresses him is made plain by his ghostly visitor who tells him 'it's not your own thought you're thinking: Woolacott stuck it ready diseased into your mind' (LTC, 90).

The young ghost who calls is like other redemptive male characters in Forster's work, in that he is strong, handsome and from a lower social class than Clesant. The young man was formerly a soldier, and had studied agriculture at college; a 'muscular and intelligent farm-hand' (94), he found his studies 'too scientific' and had subsequently determined to 'get down into the manure' and 'feel people instead of thinking about them' (88). As a soldier in France he had been freer than at home in England, and fears to meet anyone other than the young squire in case 'they've heard of something I did out in France', something he cannot speak about, but which we can surmise may be connected to his homosexuality (92). He too had received treatment from Dr Woolacott, and had died, it is implied, as a result of it.

Clesant used to play a violin, but his doctor advises he avoid music. There is clearly a link between his playing the violin and his life, his 'abstinence' from playing being associated with 'abstinence' from intimacy. The reference recalls Mr Emerson's dictum, borrowed from the writer Samuel Butler, and used by Forster in *A Room with a View*, that 'Life… is a public performance on the violin, in which you must learn the instrument as you go along' (RV, 201). By not playing the violin, Clesant is not living, having 'barricaded himself in the circle of his thoughts' (85).

During Clesant's encounter with the ghostly young man, the other members of the household hear the sound of a violin. Eager to prevent what they perceive as Clesant's inappropriate playing, they rush to his room. Clesant, fearful of their possible condemnation, decides 'He must betray his friend…' (92); words which are clearly meant to be damning by Forster who placed such a high regard on friendship, and who later declared, in 'What I Believe', that he would rather betray his country than his friend (TCD, 76).

As Clesant does betray his friend, 'He [Clesant] groaned, shrieked, but love died last;' and 'he fell back into the apparatus of decay' (93), that is, into Woolacott's deathly ideology of 'abstinence'. This ideology is the 'disease' which tells Clesant that his error was 'intimacy', and which urges him to deny the reality of his young ghostly friend: 'He does not exist. He is an illusion, whom you created in the garden because you wanted to feel you were attractive…. He never sat down on the sofa by your side and made love. You handed a pencil, but he never took it, you fell into his arms, but they were not there, it has all been a daydream of the kind forbidden… your muscular and intelligent farm-hand, your saviour from Wolverhampton in his Sunday suit — was he there?' (94). When Clesant affirms the reality of his love, his 'disease' then dies away, the 'nightmare passed, he felt better', his 'disease' groans feebly, 'Then silence' (94). He calls to his ghostly lover to 'pour life into me and I shall live as before when our bodies touched' (95), and realises, 'Ah, that was the word — love — why they pursued me… love was the word they cannot endure' (95), realising at last that he had been persecuted for wishing to act on forbidden desires. His phantom lover then joins him, to be with him for ever, free of Dr Woolacott, 'life's universal lord', and 'his army' (95). No *Maurice*-like escape into the greenwood awaits these lovers, for Clesant's friend has already expired under Woolacott's treatment, and so Clesant may only join in him in his grave. His death is prefigured in an earlier passage which describes the mysterious violin music heard by the young squire's household, yet 'no one could find out where it was':

Playing all sorts of music, gay, grave and passionate. But never completing a theme. Always breaking off. A beautiful instrument. Yet so unsatisfying… leaving the hearers much sadder than if it had never performed. What was the use (someone asked) of music like that? Better silence absolute than this aimless disturbance of our peace (LTC, 93).

Accepting Mr Emerson's linkage between playing the violin and life, it is perhaps easier to understand Clesant's acceptance of death, for 'Better silence absolute than this aimless disturbance of our peace'. Were Clesant's lover not already dead, of course, and the squire's death not seen as a prelude to their reunion beyond the grave, this passage could lend the author to accusations of recommending suicide as an escape from homophobic intolerance.

In his essay on 'Dr Woolacott', James S. Malek noted that to many of his critics this story is regarded as 'Forster's most negative assessment of homosexuality or as an expression of his guilt and regret at being homosexual', for they had made the error of viewing homosexuality, not homophobia, as the source of Clesant's disease (Malek, 319). Malek, refuting such mistaken critics, asserts also that 'Whether real or imaginary, the farm-worker functions as a symbol, not a character, in the story; he is the lust for life, in this case homosexual, that delivers Clesant from death-in-life' (Malek, 319).

The negative views of those critics refuted by Malek are in sharp contrast to Forster's own assertion contained in a letter to T. E. Lawrence that 'Dr Woolacott' was 'the best thing I've done' (Lago and Furbank 2, 81). Lawrence's letter to Forster shows that he regarded the story as essentially favourable to his own sexuality:

> There is a strange cleansing beauty about the whole piece of
> writing. So passionate, of course: so indecent people might say: but
> I must confess that it has made me change my point of view. I had
> not before believed that such a thing could be presented — and so
> credited. I suppose you will not print it? Not that it anywhere says
> too much: but it shows far more than it says: and these things are
> mysteries. The Turks, as you probably know (or have guessed,
> through the reticences of the Seven Pillars) did it to me, by force:
> and since then I have gone about whimpering to myself, unclean,
> unclean. Perhaps there is another side, your side, to the story. I
> couldn't ever do it, I believe: the impulse strong enough to make
> me touch another creature has not yet been born in me: but
> perhaps in surrender to such a figure as your Death there might be
> a greater realization — and thereby a more final destruction — of
> the body than any loneliness can reach (Lawrence 1992, 360).

Lawrence's letter shows that the story had been interpreted by one of its earliest readers as positive in its presentation of homosexuality. Lawrence's care-fully phrased reference to the Turks hints at their gang rape of him during the First World War when he was held in their captivity.* Lawrence, aware of his own homosexuality but fearful of expressing it, like many other victims of

---

* The incident occurred in November 1917 at Deraa, a halt on the railway line between Damascus and Amman. See H. Montgomery Hyde's life of Lawrence, *Solitary in the Ranks* (39).

sexual violence regarded himself as 'unclean'. As he acknowledges in this letter, 'Perhaps there is another side, your side, to the story.' Forster's other 'side' being clearly seen as supporting acceptance of the physical expression of one's homosexuality. Furbank notes that Lawrence's feeling for the story became, for Forster, a permanent bond between them (Furbank 2, 150).

'Dr Woolacott' therefore is a story which aims to attack the disease theory of homosexuality promoted by the science of Forster's day, and can clearly be viewed as his response to the threat this destructive ideological use of science posed to both the writer and to his homosexual friends. Such a response was in line with Forster's fears that, under a tyrannical use of science, a soul like his would be crushed out.

The character of Arthur Snatchfold, in the story which bears his name, is sentimentally idealised. A young working-class milkman, the milk being suggestive perhaps of semen, he is strong, able and very willing. The narrator's description of him is revealing, for it links his attractiveness to his class origins, and the similarity of language used to describe Arthur to that Forster applied to the Indian punkah-wallah in *A Passage to India* (PTI, 207) implies that lower-class Briton and Indian occupy similar positions as sex objects for the bourgeois white male:

> Seen at close quarters he [Arthur] was very coarse, very much of
> the people and of the thick-fingered earth; a hundred years ago his
> type was trodden into the mud, now it burst and flowered and
> didn't care a damn (LTC, 102).

This young god makes himself sexually available to the upper-class, elderly bisexual Sir Richard Conway, for, after all, Conway muses, 'There was probably nothing the lad wouldn't consent to if properly handled, partly out of mischief, partly to oblige' (102); such comments echo similar ones found in works of heterosexual pornography, where often the female protagonists are presented as willing 'to oblige'. As frequently happens in Forster's work, a wood provides a place for men to meet — Arthur later observing that it was a pity they did not meet the previous day for they could have met 'where I have my swim' and 'You could 'elped me strip' (104), perhaps bathing in another of Forster's 'Sacred Lakes'. The older man sets out to seduce Arthur, and soon, after a gentle massaging of his forearm, Arthur is 'amused', 'charmed', 'hooked', 'a touch would land him' (103).* After sex Conway discards the young milkman, as 'the sensation for which he had planned so cleverly was over. It was part of the past. It had fallen like a flower upon similar flowers' (103). Afterwards, Conway 'guessed that he [Arthur] was vain, the better sort often are'

---

* cf. 'Stonebreaking', the fragment of a homoerotic story where a young road-labourer is likewise caressed by an upper-class male down from London (AS, 250-1).

(103), and offers him money. Arthur refuses, though Conway tries to insist: 'it might come in useful. To take out your girl, say...' (104); the reference to a girlfriend highlighting the fact that, for Conway, as for Forster, their preferred male lovers were those ostensibly heterosexual young men who became available.* Forster's friend G. L. Dickinson, in his autobiography, noted what he saw as a decided preference amongst the homosexual men he knew for heterosexual partners when he wrote that 'a homosexual man is often attracted only to those who are "normal"', and that for this reason, 'on the physical side... the passion is constantly unsatisfied' (Dickinson 1973, 11).

Significantly, nowhere in 'Arthur Snatchfold' does Forster speculate that money might have influenced the young man's conduct — it is specifically kept out of the discussion by Arthur's swift refusal of the cash, before he finally does take it. Perhaps the reason for this is so obvious that such discussion would seem out of place in a short piece of erotic fiction; perhaps also it was Forster's desire to avoid any speculation on what might have motivated some of his own working-class lovers.**

To Conway the affair is a trifle and 'It was so pleasant to have been completely right over a stranger, even down to little details like the texture of the skin. It flattered his vanity. It increased his sense of power' (105). Later, however, Arthur is arrested, having been seen with Conway. Due to the stupidity of a local policeman only the young milkman is detained. There is clear evidence against him, for he was seen by the constable, there was 'abundant evidence of a medical character' and 'also there was the money on him, which clinched his guilt' (110). Arthur is sent to prison, but refuses to name his 'friend', Conway. His elderly lover considers handing himself over to the police, but realises it would do no good 'and he would not save his saviour'; as Conway recalls, 'It had all seemed so trivial,' but for Arthur, 'his lover', it was a disaster (112). 'Arthur Snatchfold' dates from 1928 and was written during a period of Forster's life in which, primarily through the mediation of J. R. Ackerley, he came into contact with a number of young working-class men, both homosexual and heterosexual. Sexually this appears to have been Forster's most active period, Furbank averring that Forster found physical sex easier 'with people outside his own social class' (in Page, 44). In this regard, however, Forster was not unlike other upper-class male homosexuals of the period who also preferred young

---

* All of the men for whom Foster held his strongest feelings, H. O. Meredith, Syed Ross Masood, Mohammed el Adl and Bob Buckingham, were eventually married. Forster claimed not to have had sex with either Masood or Buckingham; in Buckingham's case, however, this is now thought to have been a deliberately misleading remark by the writer. (See Belshaw, 159-61 and Beaumann 1993, 349-50.)

** cf. Forster's offering Mohammed el Adl money in the early part of their relationship, which was refused (Furbank 2, 36 & 39). Furbank notes also 'It is noticeable that the offering and rejecting of money also figured in those two important incidents of Forster's early life, the occasion he was sexually molested as a schoolboy and his encounter with a lame shepherd-boy in Wiltshire' [See Furbank 1 37 & 116-7] (Furbank 2, 36).

working-class lovers.*

The words written by Forster in 1935 that he wanted 'to love a strong young man of the lower classes and be loved by him and even hurt by him' (LTC, xiv) have often been quoted to illustrate his preferences. One of the many dangers sometimes involved in the pursuit of 'rough trade', that is black-mail, was acknowledged by Forster in *Maurice*, where Maurice fears Alec might try to blackmail him (M, 210). And Forster himself is believed to have been the victim of a blackmail attempt in November 1928, J. H. Stape suggesting that the experience may have provided part of the inspiration for 'Arthur Snatchfold' (Stape, 100).

In her recent biography of Forster, Nicola Beauman speculates as to why middle-class homosexual men should so often seem to have preferred working-class partners, and sometimes still do so today. She argues that those who take lovers of the same sex have 'to create otherness, the other: class, and an unordered relationship, are the obvious means' (Beauman 1993, 302). Beauman's point however has limited validity for it does not deal with the general preference of working-class homosexual men for men from their own class rather than from another. It seems right to say of Forster, however, that he wanted the roughness, virility and indifference to bourgeois values which he found in his working-class lovers and which he himself lacked. In 1926, Forster, through Ackerley, met a young working-class man referred to as Arthur B——, and their 'acquaintance turned into an affair'. Forster's reaction to this Arthur mirrors Conway's initial response to Arthur Snatchfold:

> Arthur was affectionate and made Forster laugh, and that was as
> far as matters went, emotionally. Forster generalized to himself:
> 'Coarseness and tenderness have kissed one another, but
> imaginative passion, love, doesn't exist with the lower classes. Lust
> & goodwill — is any thing more wanted?' (Furbank 2, 137)

Later that same year Forster met Harry Daley, again through an introduc-tion by Ackerley. Daley, a working-class police officer, became Forster's lover and through him the writer met a great number of working-class men, policemen, criminals and 'It was all an education to him in working-class life' with Daley chattering, 'as he constantly did, about life on the Hammersmith Streets' (Furbank 2, 142). They frequently went swimming together at the local baths, as well as making trips to the theatre (Furbank in Daley, xi-xii). Eventually Forster got to know Daley's family, often chatting to Daley's mother, and would 'bring her

---

*The relationship between Conway and Arthur Snatchfold mirrors aspects of Forster's own sexual life, for the majority of his known sexual partners came from social backgrounds very different to his own. Indeed Peter F. Alexander, in his biography of William Plomer, a close acquaintance of Forster's, notes that one of the curious features of English homosexuals of the upper class of this period was that as a general rule they did not regard each other as potential lovers. He quotes Stephen Spender's observation that such a homosexual relationship 'would have been almost impossible between two Englishmen of our class' (Alexander 180).

presents of vegetables', and when she fell seriously ill, Forster gladly paid for her to have a necessary operation (Furbank 2, 143). Clearly during this period, between 1926 and 1928, Forster changed his opinion on the lower classes. He moved from seeing his working-class lovers like Arthur B— as devoid of 'imaginative passion' and 'love' which 'doesn't exist with the lower classes' towards a very different perspective on working-class life. This shift in Forster's perspective is echoed in Conway's move from seeing his relationship with Arthur initially as something 'trivial and crude' (104) towards his later realisation that it had been much more, and that the working-class milkman, 'his saviour', had showed himself to be the nobler lover; Conway recognising 'that little things can turn into great ones' (112).

According to Nicola Beauman, 'all Morgan's lovers were bisexual' and their families were important to him, 'as if he were trying, domestically, to turn the lover into the brother he had always longed for' (Beauman 1993, 319). Perhaps Forster, who later declared that he should like to 'lie in Stephen's arms' (Furbank 2 319), hoped through his contact with these young men to achieve that relationship which Rickie Elliot had hoped to realise with his half-brother Stephen Wonham in *The Longest Journey*. Jeffrey Weeks, in his study of male prostitution in the nineteenth and early twentieth centuries, notes:

> Despite the wide social range of the subculture, from pauper to peer, it was the ideology of the upper classes that seems to have dominated, probably because there was a much more clearly defined homosexual identity amongst men of the middle and upper middle class and because these men had a greater opportunity, through money and mobility, to make frequent homosexual contacts (Weeks 1991, 202-3).

This point would appear to be supported by the wealth of material from homosexual writers such as J. A. Symonds, F. W. Rolfe, Forster himself, T. E. Lawrence, the Uranian poets and many others. For much of what we know of homosexual life of the period is a one-sided account, provided in the main by those middle- and upper-class men with a reasonably firm sense of their own sexual identity, and with enough money and/or education and leisure to realise and act upon their desires and, subsequently, to record them. The views of their working-class lovers has never really been fully articulated. Harry Daley refused to write about his liaison with Forster in his memoir *This Small Cloud*, though Patrick Belshaw, in *A Kind of Private Magic*, gave an account of his uncle, Charles Lovett, and his friend Ted Shread, who were both working-class homosexuals intimately known to Forster and his friend (and, later, executor) the sociologist W.J.H.Sprott.

'The Obelisk', completed in 1939, is clearly, as Norman Page writes, 'the extended literary equivalent of a Donald McGill postcard'; Page also notes that the story's sea-side setting and its characters conform to the 'cheeky postcard' genre (Page, 50). Earnest and Hilda, the married couple in the tale, resemble the caricatures presented in McGill's postcards: the schoolmaster, Earnest, was 'very, very small', his wife, Hilda, 'was larger herself: tall enough to make them look funny as they walked down the esplanade' (LTC, 113). The two sailors Tiny and Stanhope likewise epitomise similar postcard characters who, whilst on shore leave, are on the lookout for a good time. The phallic significance of the obelisk is quite obvious, intentionally so claims Page, who sees the story, in part, as 'sniping at the excesses of Freudian criticism and the quest of literary symbolism... [and] That the most explicit allusions to the symbolism of the obelisk should be uttered by the stupidest member of the party may be all part of the joke' (Page, 51). In accordance with its origins in seaside postcard humour, the story is replete with music hall double-entendres (such as those employed at that time by Max Miller and George Formby, for example), especially in the scene where Tiny says that he hoped Stan [Stanhope] had showed Hilda the obelisk: 'Ope you showed it 'er properly while you was about it, Stan. Don't do to keep a thing like that all to yourself, you know.... Anyone ever seed a bigger one? ... Stands up, don't it? ... No wonder they call that a needle, for wouldn't that just prick' (126).

Judith S. Herz observes that in 'The Obelisk', the double-plot, which she asserts is present throughout most of Forster's fictional writing, 'is visible in its most schematic form':

> There the resolution of the double structure takes the form of a
> good joke consummately well timed and delivered. In that story
> the two 'romances' are literally played out together. The wife's story
> (the heterosexual romance) and the husband's story (the
> homosexual romance) contain the same characters, setting, events
> and words. But the stories absolutely oppose each other and,
> because the wife's story finally includes the husband's (she realizes
> what must have happened; he does not), the comic punch line
> turns on itself and both wife and reader are left with an awareness
> that the laughter cannot quite displace (Herz, 52).

The double-plot, in this private piece of writing, is to the fore, unlike those in his publishable fiction, where the homosexual romance is carefully presented as subordinate to the surface 'heterosexual' plot.

'What Does It Matter? A Morality' was written sometime in the 1930s, and is a jokey fantasy morality tale set in the fictional, Ruritanian-like kingdom of Pottibakia. When it becomes known that the bisexual President of the country has had sex with a policeman, Mirko, a scandal is set to ensue. In an effort to forstall this, and the machinations of his rival, Count Waghaghren, the President himself decides to announce to the nation the details of his sexual encounters

with the policeman and with two women, declaring, 'What does it matter?'
(LTC, 142-3), and eventually succeeds in convincing the Pottibakian people of
his view. Initially the President sets up a 'Ministry of Morals' (143) headed by
the Count, whose moralistic zeal in his new office leads to a civil war. On losing
the war, the Count regains his old office, now renamed 'the Lunatic Asylum',
of which he is the sole inmate (145). The story ultimately transposes a different
morality from that of the conventional one Forster knew in England, where
sexual repression seemed, on the surface, to be the rule, bluntly substituting
England's 'thou shalt not' with the crude assertion of a Pottibakian proverb that
'Poking doesn't count' (140), a phrase which can be neatly transposed to refer
to the President's rival, by stating 'the count does not poke'. Despite its fantasy
setting, the story does not foresee a simple transition from sexual witchhunt to
sexual freedom, for seemingly only the cataclysm of civil war could eventually
produce the desired result.

'The Classical Annex' (1930–31) likewise ridicules a prurient moralism, though
in this story such an outlook is mediated through the 'artistic' values of a group
of 'City Fathers' who run a provincial Municipal Museum. Set in Bigglesmouth,
a name which implies a seaside location, the museum in the story can be seen
as a civic manifestation of the sexual attitudes which go hand in hand with the
'cheeky postcard' values satirised, and subverted, in 'The Obelisk'. Earnest, the
schoolteacher in 'The Obelisk', would have been bound to uphold in public the
sex-negative views of the museum's Curator, whatever his own private thoughts
on the matter. And in both stories, beneath a surface veil of respectability, there
lurks a covert world of sexual exuberance.

Exemplifying the values of its governing body, the museum's collection of
classical artefacts is kept in what 'was by far the least attractive room in the
museum' (LTC, 147).* To the museum's Curator, the supposed unimportance
of these artefacts is epitomised by 'a worthless late Roman work.... [which]
represented an athlete or gladiator of the non-intellectual type' (147). The
Curator regards his son Dennis as much more personable than this 'classical
lout'. His denigration of the statue, clearly damns him in Forster's eyes. Such
disdain for classical art, especially for a work representing a sportsman, clearly
registers negatively in the writer, whose criteria for moral and physical excellence were exemplified by those values commended by the ancient Greeks.
When the statue begins to show signs of tumescence, the Curator flees in
terror.

Unknown to him, his son Dennis, with 'practically nothing on but his
football shorts' (149), has gone to the museum in search of his father, to tell
him 'They've won the match' (149). The young man becomes, in a sort of

* One possible source of inspiration for the story may have been Samuel Butler's experience at the
Museum of Natural History in Montreal, where a plaster cast of one of the most famous of all the
ancient Greek statues of an athlete, the Discobolus, had been banished to a back room. The Museum's
custodian explained they had hidden it because it was 'vulgar'. Butler refers to his disdain for such an
attitude in his satirical poem 'A Psalm of Montreal' (Raby 150-1).

paradic bathos, a victorious athlete returning from the scene of his triumph, such as the one celebrated in the museum's despised statue. Later, Dennis is found by his father back in the museum. Giggles and the cry of 'Aren't you awful?' (a phrase reminiscent of the 'postcard sexuality' of 'The Obelisk') are heard, followed by 'Gladiatorial feints, post-classical suctions', more giggling, and 'a ground-bass of grunts' (150), clearly suggestive of sexual intercourse. Upon the Curator's making of the sign of the cross, the museum lapses into silence, but not before Dennis has formed part of a new statue with the ancient Greek one.

The story ends by recording that 'in after years a Hellenistic group called The Wrestling Lesson became quite a feature at Bigglesmouth'; the success of the new statue, no doubt, also reflecting, both pictorially and by its popularity, the emergence of new appreciation of the classical arts in the town. Councillor Bodkin, whose name is clearly suggestive of 'prick', is left to make the final comment of the story, in words with an obvious double-entendre hinting at buggery: 'Look 'ow the elder brother's got the little chappie down. Look 'ow well the little chappie's taking it' (150).

'The Torque' (1958), an historical tale set in the early period of Christianity in Italy, concerns the differing views of sexuality represented by the repressed Perpetua, whose chastity is preserved by her religious fanaticism, and that of her bisexual brother Marcian, who ironically helped preserve her chastity by allowing an invading Goth, Euric, to bugger him instead of raping her. The story is a humorous reworking of a perennial Forster theme, that of sex-negative Christian fanaticism in opposition to a pagan celebration of sexuality. Naturally enough paganism and an exuberant bisexuality, exemplified by Marcian's exploits, triumph here over a sterile Christianity, promising 'bumper crops' in this 'charmed spot' (LTC, 165). That paganism and its attendant sexuality survived better in Italy than in the Sawstons and Tonbridges of England, is a familiar Forster theme, having been utilised in such publishable works as *Where Angels Fear to Tread* and *A Room with a View*.

'The Other Boat', completed during 1957–58, actually originated as an idea which occurred to Forster on his first sea voyage to India in 1912, when, together with G. L. Dickinson, he met the homosexual English soldier, Kenneth Searight, both later staying with him at Peshawar. On the same voyage out Forster also encountered 'a solitary Indian passenger'. At first he willingly conversed with the Indian; subsequently though, finding him tiresome, he dropped the acquaintance. Shortly afterwards the news went round the ship that the Indian had accused his cabin-mate of attempting to throw him overboard; very soon thereafter however, the two again became friends. Their speedy reunion clearly puzzled Forster, and forty years later he used the event (Furbank 1, 224), and some pages of an abandoned novel of his (Furbank and Lago 2, 165), as the basis of 'The Other Boat'. A fragment of the earlier work was published as 'Entrance to an Unwritten Novel' in *The Listener* in 1948 (Lago and Furbank

2, 265), but its further development along more explicitly homoerotic lines,
like that of nearly all of Forster's fiction after *A Passage to India*, proceeded in
secrecy, with a select audience in mind.

In a letter to P. N. Furbank of 4 September 1957, Forster clearly set out
the development of the plot:

> The movement, as you have seen, falls into (i) Profane love (ii) the
> long conversation culminating almost but not quite in (iii) a sort of
> Sacred Love — by the way all sensuousness, acceptable elsewhere,
> must be... removed here (iv) Mutual destruction (Lago and
> Furbank 2, 265).

In the first part of the tale, Lionel and Cocoanut meet in childhood, and
their playfulness together is in sharp contrast to the personal distance that is
expected from them in adulthood. Lionel has grown into a 'rising young officer',
'clean-cut, athletic, good-looking without being conspicuous'. He has 'thick fair-
ish hair, blue eyes, glowing cheeks and strong white teeth'; the 'springy gleaming
hairs' on his hands 'suggested virility', and 'he wore a mess uniform slightly too
small for him, which accentuated his physique' (171-2). Physically, then, he is
the ideal Forster 'type', a character who seems certain to be instrumental in the
'salvation' of another, usually male, character. He is racist, significantly in a letter
to his mother, referring to 'dagoes', 'a touch of the tarbrush', and the 'dusky
fraternity' (171), though the narrator later notes that 'his colour prejudices were
tribal rather than personal, and only worked when an observer was present'
(174). Lionel fears his mother's response to his developing intimacy with Cocoanut more than the reactions of his fellow whites on board, for she has a particular
hatred of Cocoanut in particular, believing him to have caused the death of her
youngest child soon after their parting on the first voyage (185).

Meeting again on a second voyage Cocoanut conspires to get closer to his,
now adult, childhood friend. Having bribed officials, he engineers that they
share a cabin together. His first move towards Lionel however is rebuffed (174).
Lionel, having made futile attempts to denounce Cocoanut to the Master at
Arms, and to move to another cabin, is forced to return to his would-be se-
ducer: 'Here was the worst thing in the world, the thing for which Tommies
got given the maximum, and here was he bottled up with it for a fortnight'
(175). Once the ship has left English waters, however, passed by Gibraltar and,
significantly, nears Italy, the situation swiftly alters:

> Resistance weakened under the balmier sky, curiosity increased....
> Lionel... permitted a slight, a very slight familiarity with his person.
> The ship did not sink nor did the heavens fall.... More happened
> off the coast of Sicily, more, much more at Port Said, and here in
> the Red Sea they slept together as a matter of course (LTC, 177).

The further he travels from England, the more Lionel feels free to love. This freedom seems also to apply to other passengers for Lady Manning, linked earlier to Lionel in a bridge game where she is his 'partner' (172), is later discovered in the cabin of the Second Engineer (180). Once the boat approaches India though, society reasserts its control over Lionel.

The early phase of his relationship with Cocoanut, where sex is permitted as long as no one can see him, corresponds to Forster's description of 'Profane love', though it is not without hints of 'Sacred love' as 'They lay entwined, Nordic warrior and subtle supple boy' (174). Cocoanut had longed for Lionel ever since their first meeting, he had 'embraced him in dreams', 'marked him down, spent money to catch him and lime him, and here he lay, caught, and did not know it' (174). He wishes Lionel to remain with him forever, unheedful of the difficulties ahead.

Subtly, their relationship alters; Cocoanut, the passive partner in their love-making, asserts control, the change being hinted at in the narrator's description of Lionel, as he hands a drink to Cocoanut, as 'Half Ganymede, half Goth'. Lionel is further referred to as 'a Viking at a Byzantine court, spoiled, adored and not yet bored', as Cocoanut pays his gambling debts and showers money on his friend. His life of 'luxury, gaiety, kindness, unusualness' has a 'delicacy that did not exclude brutal pleasure' and he delights as a 'brute' in 'carnality' (180). Eventually Lionel realises his situation, wondering even if he has become 'a male prostitute' (190). From here onwards, the story relates their 'mutual destruction'.

Lionel, returning to speak to his own white Anglo-Indian peers, significantly above deck, decides that he cannot give up his race, his class, his Army career, nor his fiancée, which the furtherance of his relationship with Cocoanut would inevitably demand. In three days the ship would land in Bombay, and the charmed world he had enjoyed with Cocoanut below deck would either have to evaporate or become known to all; he realises that 'He must keep with his own people, or he would perish' (195). The main factor in his urge to finish his affair with Cocoanut lies in his relationship with his mother:

> But behind Isabel, behind the Army, was another power, whom he
> could not consider calmly: his mother, blind-eyed in the midst of
> the enormous web she had spun — filaments drifting everywhere,
> strands catching. There was no reasoning with her or about her, she
> understood nothing and controlled everything.... she was outside
> carnality and incapable of pardoning it (193).

Her presence has influenced the whole course of his relationship with Cocoanut. Her hatred of him, as a 'silly idle useless unmanly little boy' (170), becomes expressed in a more deadly form through her son Lionel. She is also presented as the arbiter of racial relations involving her son, and the one who has ensured that he develop, along socially appropriate lines, as a man.

When Cocoanut tries to kiss Lioniel, he becomes enraged. The scar of a wound in his groin, which one of Cocoanut's 'fuzzy-wuzzy cousins' had caused and which had 'nearly unmanned' Lionel (179), now opens (195). Cocoanut had earlier observed that a 'dervish, a very holy man, had once told him that what nearly destroys may bring strength and can be summoned in the hour of revenge' (179). Lionel, his wound re-opened, draws on this strength to revenge himself on Cocoanut, who has 'unmanned' him. Lionel strangles him, and naked, 'with the seeds of love on him he dived into the sea' (196). Whatever heights their love, unfettered, might have been able to attain, it assures not their mutual salvation — only, as Forster observed, their 'mutual destruction'.

Returning to Forster's letter to Furbank of 4 September 1957, we see that he did not intend Cocoanut to be seen as having entrapped Lionel by himself; Lionel too was a hunter:

> L. [Lionel] is the (physical) hunter who takes a little time to get
> under way. C. [Cocoanut] is the (psychological) hunter who nearly
> gets his quarry at the end of the long conversation. Essentially they
> are both hunters. That is how they both get trapped.... L. is trapped
> by devices he doesn't recognise. At the same time, he wouldn't have
> been trapped if C. had been a dusky replica of Colonel Arbuthnot
> (Lago and Furbank 2, 265).

In a later letter to Furbank of 7 September 1957, Forster states that he had not intended the story to end in tragedy, but that tragedy was unavoidable for these lovers, who 'with their different sorts of strength and weakness were likely to destroy one another. No wonder they both felt afraid near the end' (Lago and Furbank 2, 266).

On 16 July 1958, Forster wrote to Furbank that 'a little of him [Mohammed el Adl] reemerged in Cocoa' (Lago and Furbank 2, 271), and the story presents an alternative picture to that of Forster and Mohammed, of a cross-racial homosexual love which fails to resist the pressures of a racist imperialism. Forster and Mohammed had freely entered into a relationship, each accepting its sexual component. Lionel's contact with Cocoanut by contrast is subject to Lionel's own self-hatred, reinforced by his peers, and presented by Forster as originating with his mother. His dependence on society's affirmation of his behaviour contrasts with Cocoanut's disdain for convention. Hence Lionel's terror at his discovery that their cabin door had been left deliberately unlocked by Cocoanut during their love-making (189). Mid-way on their sea journey society could be almost forgotten, but once the ship approached India, Lionel is forced either to choose to re-embrace society's values, or to abandon such rules and live at the whim of Cocoanut. Neither character being strong enough to live entirely outside of social convention, nor able to live covertly within it, they are set on a course of mutual destruction. Lionel's anger and hatred is first directed at himself for having allowed himself to enjoy sex with Cocoanut, but subsequently is turned on his lover in a deadly mixture of homophobic and racist violence, which destroys them both.

Forster's collection of essays inspired by the city of Alexandria, *Pharos and Pharillon*, 'represented [to him] a kind of tribute to Mohammed, and he gave the book a dedication... [in Greek] (To Hermes, leader of souls) which alluded cryptically to him'. Furbank asserts that 'This concept of Hermes was a cherished private cult of Forster's symbolising the aid that one soul can give another. It had first been inspired, it may be guessed, by the Greek sculpture in the British Museum of a beautiful Hermes escorting Alcestis to the underworld' (Furbank 2, 109). The theme of lovers aiding each other was a dear one to Forster, but in 'The Other Boat' he chose to reverse it, showing love as destructive.

Furbank had in 1959 typed the final drafts of 'The Other Boat' for Forster and in his own diary he recorded the reason the writer had given for the downbeat ending of the story. Forster had thought the tragic theme of 'The Other Boat', that of 'two people made to destroy each other', was more interesting than the theme of salvation he had often used before; the rescuer from 'otherwhere', the generic Alec (Alec Scudder in *Maurice*) that, Forster declared, was a fake. People, he affirmed could help one another, but they were 'not decisive for each other like that' (Furbank 2, 303).

Forster's theme of the mutual salvation of true lovers, which had inspired much of his work since its very beginning with Sidney and Edgar in 'Nottingham Lace', thus gives way to a much darker theme of mutual destruction in one of his final pieces of fiction. Formerly his fictional lovers had endeavoured to 'save' each other, but in 'The Other Boat', 'salvation' and 'the rescuer from "otherwhere", the generic Alec. That was a fake.' Despite the grimness of 'The Other Boat', its theme, that homosexual love could be mutually self-destructive, was to Forster, perhaps, as unpublishable as a work in which homosexual love was openly celebrated.

A PASSAGE TO INDIA

> we shall drive every blasted Englishman into the sea, and then'...
> 'and then,' he concluded, half kissing him, 'you and I shall be
> friends.' 'Why can't we be friends now?' said the other, holding
> him affectionately. 'It's what I want. It's what you want' (PTI,
> 312).

A Passage to India closes the with call of an Englishman, Fielding, for his
Indian friend, Aziz, to join him in realising the full extent of their friendship.
The intimacy and yearning which these romantic words convey, and the apparent hopelessness of Aziz and Fielding's earlier intimacies, surely signify that
this novel provides something more than Nirad C. Chaudhuri's summation of
the novel as 'a verdict on British India' (Rutherford, 69). The passion in those
words betokens more than a purely political analysis, certainly an analysis based
on personal feeling and experience. That it deals with more universal issues is
also evident as Lionel Trilling averred: 'Great as the problem of India is, Forster's
work is not about India alone; it is about all of human life' (Rutherford, 32).

It might be argued that the novel deals with 'all of human life', but it
would appear to have specifically identifiable origins in Forster's own life. 'All
of human life' or 'of universal interest' are phrases which can often provide a
potent smokescreen, hiding more localised issues and events. By obscuring
meanings and origins it can provide a 'mystery' or promote a 'muddle'; thus it
can so often obscure specificities — of class, race, gender — and, most impor-
tantly here, of sexual preference.

Forster's handling of Fielding and Aziz's friendship has much to do with
concealing its possible homoerotic origins. Drawing upon ancient Greek concepts, and on the biblical model of David and Jonathan, male friendships
could be described ennoblingly, for 'manly love' as a theme could still be presented to readers. With the more general spread of basically Freudian ideas
regarding human sexuality during the late 1920s and 1930s, however, such
seemingly innocent friendships could no longer escape unwelcome scrutiny.
Both Aziz and, later, Fielding marry and so it would have been assumed by
most readers that their friendship was chaste. That Fielding's wife is apparently dull and sparingly considered by the author, while Aziz's first wife is dead
and his second referred to, but not described, in a mere few lines of the text,
was enough to infer to the general reader that the protagonists were hetero-
sexually orientated. When we examine both the history of the writing of *A
Passage to India* and the final text, however, it proves impossible to avoid placing Forster's own sexuality at the centre of discussion of the novel, and

consequently the sexuality and relationship of both protagonists appear in a different light.

The genesis of the book can be dated back to 1906 when Forster became tutor to Syed Ross Masood, to whom 'and to the seventeen years of our friendship' he later dedicated the novel. Masood was heterosexual; the close relationship between the two men, as far as is known, never involved physical intimacy, but at the end of 1910 Forster declared to Masood his love for him, only 'to be repulsed by a gentle, "I know"' (AS, xxii). That the novel had its origins in this friendship was recorded by Forster in his essay on Masood included in *Two Cheers for Democracy*:

> My own debt to him is incalculable. He woke me up out of my
> suburban and academic life, showed me new horizons and a new
> civilization, and helped me towards the understanding of a
> continent. Until I met him, India was a vague jumble of rajahs,
> sahibs, babus and elephants, and I was not interested in such a
> jumble; who could be? He made everything real and exciting as
> soon as he began to talk, and seventeen years later when I wrote *A
> Passage to India* I dedicated it to him out of gratitude as well as
> out of love, for it would never have been written without him
> (TCD, 295).

Forster made three journeys to India during his life. His first trip lasted from October 1912 to April 1913, when he travelled to Bombay accompanied by friends including Goldsworthy Lowes Dickinson. On the voyage out he met Kenneth Searight,* a young officer in the Queen's Own Royal West Kent Regiment. Searight was writing his autobiography in verse in a style meant to imitate that of Byron. The work named *Paidikion* described various sexual encounters he had had with young men in Britain, in the army and in India. The setting of their meeting was later used by Forster in his 'unpublishable' story 'The Other Boat' and the encounter may have spurred Forster into writing about homosexuality himself, for shortly after on his return to England he began to write *Maurice*. Whilst in India, Forster and his friends stayed with Searight at Peshawar, boarding at the military barracks and dancing after dinner with soldiers of the regiment. Forster later recorded that it was on this evening he had first seen his friend, Dickinson, as 'a solid figure, who had his own place in the world, and held it firmly' (Furbank 1, 231-2).

His main purpose in that first journey, however, was to visit Masood, and

---

* Forster describes Searight in a letter to Florence Barger of October 1912, noting in particular that 'He is very intimate with natives, & might show me a lot' (Lago and Furbank 1, 140). Writing from Alexandria to Dickinson about Mohammed el Adl in June 1917, Forster alluded to his meetings with the young Egyptian rather guardedly, in a kind of private code, referring to it as more like an affair of Searight's than anything else he could indicate, adding: 'This will convey to you age, race, rank, though not precisely relationship' (Lago and Furbank 1, 253).

with introductions gained from him and from his contacts in England, Forster
visited a number of Indian states. His second visit from March 1921 to early
January 1922 was undertaken not only to see Masood again, but also to take
up an offer of employment: from March to October 1921 Forster worked as
private secretary to Sir Tukoji Rao Puar III, the Maharajah of Dewas State
Senior, later undertaking various private visits to Masood and to other Indian
and Anglo-Indian friends. A third visit was made in 1945 when Forster was
invited to attend a conference at Jaipur arranged by the international PEN
organisation.

He did not begin to write *A Passage to India* until July 1913, abandoning
the first manuscript in September of that year and spending the following ten
months in the writing of *Maurice*. Further spells of work on the novel were
undertaken between April and June 1914, but by the end of that year Forster
had written to his publisher, Edward Arnold, informing him that further work
had been abandoned because of the war (PTI, xii); and in his diary entry for
31 December 1914 he wrote that he would never complete another novel
(PTI, xii).

For the time being the manuscript remained discarded and Forster turned
to writing articles, essays and short stories. Apparently there was no further
work on the novel until 1922. At the end of March 1921 Forster travelled to
India to take up his post with the Maharajah, taking the manuscript of the
uncompleted novel with him, but he found it impossible to work on it whilst
actually in India, one of his distractions being his problematical relationship
with a catamite kindly provided by his employer.

On the return boat journey to England via the Suez Canal, Forster stopped
off in Egypt, travelling to Mansourah to visit his friend and former lover,
Mohammed el Adl. Their friendship and sexual intimacy had begun in 1916,
when Forster was 38 years of age and Mohammed about 17. Mohammed
worked as a tram conductor in Alexandria* where Forster had been working
for the Red Cross during the First World War. Despite the difference in their
ages, neither partner was particularly knowledgeable about physical intimacy,
and for Forster it was his first real experience of a sexual relationship, and one
of the best relationships he ever knew. Arriving at Mohammed's home, Forster
found his friend, now married and with a family, sick and dying from tuberculosis. He described the visit in a letter to Florence Barger of 28 January 1922
and recorded that though he felt his lover was rallying from this particular
attack, he knew that it was the last time he would see him alive (Lago and
Furbank 1, 21). Mohammed's subsequent death was to preoccupy Forster's

---

* During his stay at Alexandria, Forster wrote a guide to the city, *Alexandria: A History and a Guide*.
Lawrence Durrell, in his Introduction to a later edition of the book, wrote how he felt it was apparent
that Forster was 'deeply happy, perhaps, deeply in love', when he wrote the book 'for his joie de vivre
rings out in every affectionate line' (ix). In the guidebook Forster makes careful note of those tram
lines which a tourist would find useful, no doubt Mohammed made a modest contribution here.

thoughts throughout 1922 and in August of that year he began 'a long and impassioned "letter" or book addressed to him', in which he intended to describe every moment of their friendship; in his diary entries of this period Forster records that Mohammed featured prominently in his dreams (Furbank 2, 113-4). So throughout the later period of the writing of *A Passage to India* Forster was concerned with the nature of relationships between people of the East and of the West, and specifically of sexual relationships between men, his own intimacy with Mohammed (and also Masood and other Indians) providing some direction and inspiration to his writing. To date, Forster's 'letter or book' addressed to Mohammed remains unpublished, but we can see something of their life together expressed in a letter he wrote to his friend Florence Barger on 25 August 1917. Forster declared the relationship 'a triumph over nonsense and artificial difficulties', averring that there were many other such triumphs in the same spirit of which the wider world knows nothing. Whenever he was with Mohammed, Forster added, he saw beyond his own happiness and intimacy to that 'of 1000s of others' whose names he would never know, but who form 'a great unrecorded history' (Lago and Furbank 1, 268-9).

Two weeks after this letter, Forster was writing to Masood that Mohammed sometimes reminded him of him (Lago and Furbank 1, 269). Forster declared his relationship with Mohammed to be a triumph, for it cut across barriers of race, class and income, and to be trusted across those barriers 'is the greatest reward a man can receive' (Lago and Furbank 1, 263). It is significant that Forster links his relationship with Mohammed to other similar ones for, in a later letter to Florence Barger of 13 September 1917, he sees such relationships as indicative of a Carpenteresque view of human evolution, a view which informs the closing scenes of *A Passage to India*:

> And apart from the joy of all this [his union with Mohammed] I
> feel, more deeply, its solemnity, and think of what you once said
> that the   possibilities of human intercourse are only beginning. I
> hate faith as a creed — but when something happens that gives
> you faith you're very near heaven (Lago and Furbank 1, 271).

Returning from Egypt to Britain in February 1922 Forster was encouraged by Leonard Woolf to resume work on his 'Indian novel', which he did. Shortly afterwards, however, after failing to make much progress, Forster destroyed many of his earlier erotic writings, declaring that he felt that they had clogged him artistically (LTC, xii).

How exactly could such writings, then presumably finished and done with, have clogged Forster artistically? Why should he have felt when he began them   that he was doing something 'positively dangerous' to his career as a novelist? Possession of such 'pornography' would have proved dangerous if the police had been informed, but what kind of threat they were to him as a novelist is unclear. If they were a 'wrong channel for my pen', the apparently right channel was his then current project — the reworking and completing of his unfinished novel set in India. But often, in the classic pattern of displacement, what one seeks to repress is merely shifted elsewhere, especially if it relates to sexual desires. The repression of consciously expressed sexuality in Forster's writing merely paves the way for its covert presence in the text. And to hold the view that open expression is 'positively dangerous' adds to the passion of the denial mechanism; it simply fuels the development of literary stratagems of deception, here utilised perhaps unconsciously as well as consciously, which contain the very essence of that which it is desired to suppress.

Whatever Forster's intentions, within three months of his manuscript-burning he had written another indecent — 'violent and wholly unpublishable' — short story, 'The Life to Come', also set in India and describing a homosexual relationship between an English missionary and an Indian chief (LTC, xii). This work did not forestall progress on *A Passage to India*. Indeed, as will be discussed later, it is something of a companion piece to the novel.

By the latter part of 1923, having written* to Masood for information on court procedures in India (to use in his description of Aziz's trial) and on a certain group of transvestite male prostitutes he had heard about whilst in India, Forster was near to completing his novel. Masood failed to provide the legal information, though he had earlier promised details on both the Indian legal system and on the transvestite 'degenerates', who still carried on their profession in Hyderabad (PTI, xix).

The 'degenerates' referred to were 'hijras', defined by Serena Nanda as 'eunuch-transvestites' (Nanda, 18). A number of hijra sects were, and still are, devotees of the god Krishna. In many such sects, Krishna is seen as all male. The devotees, by directing their worship towards Radha, Krishna's consort, and, by assuming a female role, hope to become one of her companions and thereby approach the Godhead. Some sects devoted to Lord Krishna involved the male devotees wearing women's clothing, and they 'were supposed to permit the sexual act on their persons (playing the part of women) as an act of devotion' (Bullough 268).** Forster's attention was drawn to these sects as they were the socially unacceptable form of the acceptable Krishna worship he knew from the courts of the Maharajahs of Chhatarpur and Dewas Senior, and, as will be seen later, his knowledge of the practices that attend some forms of Krishna worship is evident throughout the novel.

Help with the final pages of *A Passage to India* was to come from Joe Randolph Ackerley, a close homosexual friend of Forster's, who was at that time employed by the same Maharajah of Chhatarpur whom Forster and

---

* Some of Forster's earlier correspondence with Masood, in 1916, was intercepted and examined by the wartime postal censor in Bombay, who judged Forster to be 'a decadent coward and apparently a sexual pervert'. It is not known if Forster ever became aware of this (HD, xl; Furbank 2, 28-9).
** Descriptions of hijra Krishna devotees may be found in Bandarkar 1, 22-4; Bullough, 267-8; Dynes 1, 591; Nanda 18-20; and Walker 1, 44. A more detailed description of hijras and their histories (many of them were, and are, *not* prostitutes) can be found in Zia Jaffrey's *The Invisibles: A Tale of the Eunuchs of India*.

Dickinson had visited in India in 1912. Forster recorded his debt to him in a letter of 29 January 1924, where he noted that Ackerley's letters were 'a god-send' to his 'etiolated novel', and that as soon as he had copied passages of them into the work, it had promptly become 'ripe' for publication (Lago and Furbank 2, 48). Forster was especially amused by what he called the 'crafty-ebbing' details of the Maharajah's private life which Ackerley had recounted (Parker 75).* Ackerley's own later published version of his sojourn at Chhatarpur, *Hindoo Holiday* (1932), provides a description of the court life at Mau, including a discreet account of the troupe of boy actors and catamites kept by the Maharajah.

In addition to Ackerley, a further three homosexual writers were acknowledged by Forster as providing him with varying degrees of inspiration. The first was his friend T. E. Lawrence, whose exploits, as recorded in his book *The Seven Pillars of Wisdom*, were said by the writer to be useful in completing his novel (Lago and Furbank 2, 2). Lawrence, like Forster, had personal experience of cross-racial male and homoerotic friendships, and his insights into such relationships, and on the Orient in general, would no doubt have proved invaluable.

The second writer whose influence Forster admitted was Marcel Proust. In his diary entry for 7 May 1922 he records that he had sat gloomily before his Indian novel all that morning, but that six days later he was making 'careful and uninspired additions... influenced by Proust' (PTI, xv), a writer whose influence he also acknowledged in a letter to J. R. Ackerley on 26 April 1922 (Lago and Furbank 2, 24). Precisely what additions were made is open to conjecture. Furbank suggests that the primary influence on Forster from Proust's work was its contribution to his increasing unease about orthodox fictional forms (Furbank 2, 106). The letter to Ackerley, however, indicates a different influence. There Forster quotes an idea from Proust that the souls of deceased loved ones, after having first transmigrated into lower animal forms, may, after having been recalled to mind by the lover, subsequently return to live with him or her in spirit. Forster expressed his personal scepticism at this notion, though given the numerous references to animals in *A Passage to India*, it is tempting to suggest that he made artistic use of the idea. Possibly the animals referred to are intended to recall the links through love between the living and the dead; and, given that shortly after writing to Ackerley, Forster was grieving for the death of Mohammed, perhaps to recall also those links between Forster and Mohammed and the thousands of others 'whose names I shall never learn'? The suggestion of the transmigration of souls into animal forms would neatly find an echo in the Hinduism which informs the novel.

Finally, of course, there the is title itself — *A Passage to India*. Forster took the title from Walt Whitman's poem 'Passage to India' only when he was about to finish the novel. In a letter to his publisher on 2 December 1923, he

---

* 'Crafty-ebbing' meaning sexual, the word being derived from the name of the famous German sexologist. Two of Ackerley's letters which survive can be found in Braybrooke, 6-13.

notes that he had first thought of using the title only one month earlier (PTI, xviii). Oliver Stallybrass in his Introduction to the Abinger edition of *A Passage to India* puts this forward as the main evidence against the theory that Forster built into the novel a number of detailed analogies with Whitman's poem (PTI, xviii). Certainly this does appear to disprove the idea of 'detailed analogies', but the borrowing of the title by Forster for his novel dealing so centrally with male friendships across racial, cultural, political and social boundaries points towards his having found some of his inspiration from a fellow homosexual writer who celebrated in verse both erotic male and universal bonding — especially when Whitman's words are utilised in a description of forbidden love in *The Longest Journey* and his influence, via Edward Carpenter, is so clear in *A Room with a View*. And it is quite possible that Forster drew some inspiration for his novel from the poem itself, even though it was only during the final stages of his work that he made the decision to borrow its title from Whitman.

The novel was eventually completed on 21 January 1924, with an emotional, and rather moving, use of a keepsake, as Forster recorded in his diary: 'Finished A Passage to India and mark the fact with Mohammed's pencil' (PTI, xix). Like the pencil, the novel acts as a reminder of things past. The writing of the book, which had originated in a one-sided, but from Forster's point of view, intense homoerotic attachment to the Indian, Masood, ended with an almost sacramental use of his souvenir of a physically active homosexual relationship with the low-class Egyptian, Mohammed. Both relationships involved a white middle-class male with a darker-skinned colonial subject; neither directly served as a model for the relationship between Fielding and Aziz but, as they were both so intensely felt by the author, they surely contributed to its conception. That Mohammed's pen should be so utilised at the novel's completion points to his presence in the work at some level and clearly in his examination of male friendship in *A Passage to India* Forster drew on his own experience of cross-racial friendships with both Masood and Mahommed.

Historically the East, generally, has provided Western writers with an escape from domestic social and sexual taboos; Eastern 'vice' often providing welcome relief from Western bourgeois virtue. Edward Said observes:

> the association is clearly made between the Orient and the
> freedom of licentious sex. We may as well recognize that for
> nineteenth-century Europe, with its increasing embourgeoisement
> sex had been institutionalized to a very considerable degree... the
> Orient was a place where one could look for sexual experience
> unobtainable in Europe. Virtually no European writer who wrote
> on or traveled to the Orient in the period after 1800 exempted
> himself or herself from this quest: ... In the twentieth century one
> thinks of Gide, Conrad, Maugham, and dozens of others. What
> they looked for... was a different type of   sexuality, perhaps more

libertine and less guilt-ridden... (Said, 190).

Forster, too, found many such sexual adventures in the Orient, in both Egypt and in India, as the account in his 'locked diary' of his relationship with the catamite Kanaya at the court of the Maharajah of Dewas State Senior particularly indicates (HD 3,10-324). It is difficult not to see this freedom as being very influential in Forster's view of India, especially when he speaks of 'the happiness...[and] the peacefulness which have made my own visits to the country so wonderful' (GLD, 141).

Forster found sexual excitement and friendship in India and, as a setting for his novel, it also offered him a certain creative freedom. The narrator depicts India as 'a frustration of reason and form' (PTI, 275), speaks of the Marabar Caves as having a reputation which 'does not depend upon human speech' (PTI, 117), where there is 'something unspeakable' (PTI, 116), and warns that 'in the tropics... the inarticulate world is closer at hand and readier to resume control as soon as men are tired' (PTI, 105). This fluidity is in sharp contrast to the world of Anglo-India where order, form, rank and convention were most rigidly adhered to. According to the Indian scholar Nirad C. Chaudhuri:

> English life in India, if it was to be kept sane and wholesome, had to run, like a train, on rails, and the two rails were patriotism and duty. To allow anybody to slip off that rigid track was to invite disaster as much in public as in private life (Chaudhuri, 137).

Divergence from conventional forms and ideas characterises not only the author but also the characters he creates. The four major protagonists of *A Passage to India*, Adela Quested, Mrs Moore, Fielding and Aziz, all testify to the inadequacy of patriarchal discourse in describing their experiences of life. Adela's first moment of revelation occurs early in the novel, when she realises exactly what dreariness would ensue should she become the wife of an Anglo-Indian magistrate (PTI, 41). Mrs Moore, however, has glimpsed a life 'between the acts' (PTI, 24), and shared that glimpse with Aziz in their encounter in a mosque. As in *Where Angels Fear to Tread* where Caroline Abbot becomes close to Gino (Philip's beloved), so here another English woman (Mrs Moore) becomes close to the foreign beloved (Aziz) of another English man (Fielding). Both women learn to appreciate qualities of the beloved known also to his lover. And in both novels Forster links such women to the divine; Caroline to the goddess Selene (WAFT, 147), while after her death Mrs Moore is deemed a goddess by Indian natives and is frequently linked in the text to spiritual matters. Similarly, her first introduction to the reader is set primarily in a religious building (the mosque where she encounters the Friend, Aziz).

Aziz, gazing at the structure by moonlight, becomes aware of an ambiguity between its outward form and structure and what it actually contains, for a 'contention of shadows' belies the rigid dualism symbolised by its frieze of black and white stone. He tries to 'symbolize the whole into some truth of religion or love', but it cannot satisfy his yearning. The marble stones, which purport to express the qualities of the divine in their ninety-nine names of God, are shown to be inadequate to such a task; the patriarchal god of ortho-dox Islam, unlike those of Hinduism, recognises no pluralistic discourses. Finding it inadequate to mirror his desire, Aziz disregards the conventionally sanctioned message of the structure, and gives it a meaning the original builder had never intended (PTI, 13-4). He achieves this by imagining what his own mosque, if ever built, should mean, for all who passed by it were to experience the happiness that he now felt. Near to the mosque will be found his tomb, covered with an inscription in Persian:

> Alas, without me for thousands of years
> The Rose will blossom and the Spring will bloom,
> But those who have secretly understood my heart —
> They will approach and visit the grave where I lie.

> He had seen the quatrain on the tomb of a Deccan king and
> regarded it as profound philosophy — he always held pathos to be
> profound. The secret understanding of the heart! He repeated the
> phrase with tears in his eyes... (PTI, 14).

'The secret understanding of the heart' is the key phrase, for this is what concerns Forster in the novel. He does not remove those things which obscure the 'secret', indeed a feature of his art is his skill in disguising it, but by look-ing closely at the final text and its earlier manuscript forms, it can be delineated. And in the poetry of its expression, its romance and delicacy and in its reli-gious profundity, 'the secret understanding of the heart' required an Oriental setting for its expression. If the novel had been set in the England of the nineteen-twenties, its poetry would have appeared grossly incongruous, such is the power of patriarchy here, but in India, pejoratively feminised in imperi-alist propaganda and ubiquitously romanticised in popular fiction, male hearts can express at least some of those intimacies which in Britain are more often met with violent aggression. Today, as in the nineteen-twenties, it is far easier to speak in India of 'manly love', without mentioning homosexuality, than it is in Britain.

Such an atmosphere no doubt contributes to Fielding's desire to go to the Orient; once there however it seems as if, in Anglo-India at least, the situation is far worse. Fielding noted how the gulf between himself and his countrymen widened distressingly when he went to India. And part of his estrangement appears linked to his inability to conform to gender stereotypes, which 'would have passed without comment in feminist England' but which did him great harm in Anglo-Indian society (PTI, 55-6).

On the surface at least, his friend Aziz conducts his life according to the social forms and customs of Indian Muslim society, and as a doctor employed by the Raj, he conforms outwardly, as far as he is able, to Anglo-Indian societal norms; but this compliance is on his own terms. Both men are sceptical of the validity of social conventions, though Fielding's dilemma is harder for him to bear, for he feels to maintain his integrity he should at least challenge them; Aziz however eludes much of their influence by his avoidance of open conflict. His own strict personal moral code, which maintains that neither God nor a friend should be deceived, proves sufficient to maintain his acquiescence to the demands of society.

This strict personal morality, however, is given no positive recognition when Aziz is placed on trial, indeed his refusal to do more than outwardly conform to Anglo-India's conventions is seen as proof of his perversity. The prosecutor McBride conducts the case against him by specifically pointing out Aziz's failure to conduct his life in full accordance with social norms. It is no accident that this condemnation of him can be read as if the accused were charged with other sexual 'crimes' of the period, in both India and in Britain, such as the 'crime' of homosexuality, and Forster would certainly be conscious of this. McBride's choice of language evokes some descriptions of homosexual 'pathology' found in unsympathetic works of medical literature during this period (and since):

> The prisoner is one of those individuals who have led a double life. I dare say his degeneracy gained upon him gradually. He has been very cunning at concealing, as is usual with the type, and pretending to be a respectable member of society, getting a Government position even (PTI, 213).

No doubt Forster would have agreed that the words might easily have been applied to himself, for he too led 'a double life' which he had been 'very cunning at concealing', and for many years had seemed to be 'a respectable member of society'.

McBride, bizarrely to most modern readers, commenced his attack on Aziz by contending that his behaviour was the inevitable outcome of the Indian climate, for, as his theory ran, all 'natives are criminals at heart, for the simple reason that they live south of latitude 30', and so could not be held fully responsible for their behaviour (PTI, 158). However, McBride's contention that climate can dictate behaviour did not seem quite so outrageous to the novel's first readers. The particulars of his theory seem to have been borrowed from a notion first proposed by the nineteenth-century orientalist Sir Richard Francis Burton. Writing in the 1880s about homosexuality, Burton proposed the existence of a Sotadic Zone in which 'the Vice [of buggery] is popular and endemic', claiming that the 'topographical details concerning pederasty' were 'geographical and climatic, not racial'. He further asserted that 'within the Sotadic Zone there is a blending of the masculine and feminine temperaments, a crasis which elsewhere occurs only sporadically' (Burton, 175-6). Burton, in locating the Zone, described it as 'bounded westwards by the northern shores of the Mediterranean (N. Lat. 43) and by the southern (N. Lat. 30)' and listed the countries affected, including parts of Northern India and what is now known as Pakistan (Burton, 175). Perhaps Forster, familiar with Burton's idea, deliberately presented McBride's theory as a kind of private joke. For, in McBride's version, climate influences the 'criminality' of those who live south of latitude 30, whereas in Burton, it affects those who live north of this latitude, in the area of the Mediterranean at least.

The theme of male love becomes quite evident in the drafts of *A Passage to India* where it is linked to the characters of Aziz and Fielding. In these early sketches for the novel, Ronny Heaslop speaks to Adela of 'queer things coming out' about Aziz's reputation (PTI-MS, 359), the narrator speaks of Aziz playing 'a queer game' (PTI-MS, 93), and Ronny also accuses Fielding of 'queer notions' (PTI-MS, 95). In the nineteen-twenties 'queer' was sometimes used, as today, to mean 'homosexual'. Forster discarded these lines in the final draft of the novel, though the word does still appear at other points in the version he presented to his publisher. He may well have made these excisions for purely artistic reasons as he revised the work, but other discarded parts of the manuscript, which hint further at homosexuality, were deliberately removed from the final, publishable, form of the novel.

The manuscript drafts reveal that originally the character of Aziz had 'broad shoulders and strong arms. He had fenced in Germany, loved riding, and did dumb bells every morning.... Indeed he made something of a cult of the body' (PTI-MS, 19). His physical presence is emphasised and masculinity and athleticism are here clearly linked to manly love. In the final published version of the novel both Fielding and Aziz are described as 'athletic' (PTI, 39 & 12), but it is only Aziz's sporting abilities which are shown. Utilising his gift for irony in the final version of the novel, Forster is careful not to oversubscribe to conventional gender stereotypes and he frequently employs a rather deflationary 'camp' style to make his point, as the following extract demonstrates. Fielding exhorts Aziz:

'Accept the consequences of your own actions like a man.' Aziz winked at him slowly and said: 'We are not in the law courts. There are many ways of being a man; mine is to express what is deepest in my heart.' 'To such a remark there is certainly no reply,' said Hamidullah, moved (PTI, 258).

Whilst it may be accepted that there are 'many ways to be a man', in Forster's novel — and in his work generally — it is clear that men deemed worthy of praise almost always possess strongly 'masculine' attributes. This bias of Forster's would account for the lack of any real sympathy being shown in the novel towards Nureddin, the effeminate grandson of the Nawab Bahadur, whose 'pretty lips' are noted by the narrator (PTI, 90); a similar process is at work in *Howards End* where Tibby's effeminacy is treated rather disparagingly.

One notable passage excised from the final version provides background detail to Fielding's character. Forster gave him a history of close friendships in England where he had friends of his 'own type' (PTI-MS, 464). An early draft also relates Fielding's former partnership with a soldier, whom he had served with in the armed forces. Fielding, like his friend, had been an army coach and the entire episode of their friendship recalls the notion of 'athletic love', a concept revived in Fielding's later encounter with Aziz. On leaving the forces the two army comrades had hired a house together on the edge of Dartmoor where they 'received backward youths < at fancy prices > (PTI-MS, 76).* This friendship, however, eventually terminated, for though 'pleasant enough for many years', when Fielding's partner subsequently married, 'the atmosphere < of precaution > that ensued proved too much' for him (PTI-MS, 76). Why exactly there was a need for precaution after his army friend had married is not explained in the drafts which survive, but one may surmise that the nature of their relationship was not one which they wished the partner's wife to be aware of. Eventually the friendship disintegrated. Fielding reacted strongly and 'a short disreputable < period >' ensued, which was followed by a 'period of "repentance"'... far more dangerous than the excesses that had induced it' (PTI-MS, 77). By that time his father had refused to continue to support him and so Fielding sought employment. After working at a provincial university, he eventually gained, through 'a friend in the India Office', his post as Principal at the College in Chandrapore (PTI-MS, 77).

It is interesting that Fielding should gain, through a friend, the post of College Principal, for Edward Carpenter, in his account of his travels in Ceylon and India, *From Adam's Peak to Elephanta*, had identified a Mohammedan Anglo-Oriental College as affording 'a striking example of a rapprochement taking place between the rulers and the ruled'. He noted the cordial feeling existing between the two in Aligurh (now usually spellt as Aligarh) and said it was due to that College being 'run by Englishmen whose instincts and convictions lie a little outside outside the Anglo-Indian groove'; and significantly, a number of those Englishmen had been educated at Cambridge (Carpenter 1910, 271). It was an earlier Principal of that same college at Aligarh, Theodore Morrison, who introduced Forster to the Maharajah of Chhatarpur, and in 1906 to Masood;** Forster visiting both the Maharajah and the college on his tour of India in 1912–13.

Carpenter's book may well have provided Forster with part of his inspiration for *A Passage to India*. Topics dealt with similarly by both writers include, for example, British colonial courts (83), a visit to a native's house which

---

* Given Forster's penchant for using words ambiguously, this phrase may also be read as implying that the youths were received in a backward manner by Fielding and his companion, that is, anally, and that the fancy prices were paid by the men not the youths.
** In 1929 Masood accepted the post of Vice-Chancellor of the College.

recalls Fielding's visit to Aziz (313), the difficulty, as Adela Quested notes in
the novel, of seeing the real India (263), and the problems faced by a young
Anglo-Indian official (recalling Ronny Heaslop's predicament) (267). One additional theme they share is that of the apparently insuperable gulf between
the British and the Indians, coupled with their desire to traverse that gap:

> The more one sees of the world the more one is impressed, I
> think, by the profundity and the impassability of the gulf of race-
> difference. Two races may touch, may mingle, may occupy for a
> time the same land; they may recognise each other's excellences,
> may admire and imitate each other; individuals may even cross
> the dividing line and be absorbed on either side; but ultimately
> the gulf reasserts itself.... There are a few souls, born travelers and
> such like, for whom race-barriers do not exist, and who are
> everywhere at home, but they are rare.... in India the barrier is
> plain enough to be seen — more than physical, more than
> intellectual, more than moral — a deepset ineradicable
> incompatibility (Carpenter 1910, 264).

Both Carpenter and Forster, in their travels and in their writings, explored the reality of those 'rare' individuals who had surmounted the barriers
between the races. With Masood and with Mohammed Forster attempted to
do just that. Only by occupying, perhaps simply in the imagination, an intermediate state outside the barriers could cross-race friendship hope to flourish.
And so in *A Passage to India* the main theme is male friendship between the
races, and 'friend' and 'beloved' become key terms in Forster's novel. To do
this he utilised concepts of friendship derived from Persian and Urdu poetry,
where the nature of the relationship between a human soul and God is expressed in terms of the relationship between the 'Lover' and the 'Beloved'. A
significant convention in such poetry is always to refer to the Beloved by the
use of a male pronoun — even should the Beloved be known to be female.

Forster interspersed these Oriental ideas with, what were to him, the
more familiar notions of ancient Greece, where the physical and spiritual are
intertwined. Here however, unlike in other novels such as *Maurice* and *The
Longest Journey*, he makes less use of ancient Greek models of male friendship;
instead he concentrates on the Greek ideal of physical male beauty, best exemplified in the perfect figure of a youthful athlete, which in *A Passage to India* is
personified by the punkah-wallah at Aziz's trial.

In addition to these sources, Forster also drew on the legends associated
with the god Krishna, and on the notion of 'bhakti' which he took from Hinduism. Forster pursued the theme of cross-race friendship between Fielding
and Aziz, seeing in it not only a purely private relationship between individuals, but speculating also on the possibility of it passing, in G. L. Dickinson's
phrase, 'beyond persons to objective ends, linking emotion to action' (Dickinson

1909, 179). By linking ancient Greece with the Islam of the poets, 'friendship' could also symbolise a union of East with West, and, through the legend of the loves of Lord Krishna, link the love of Forster and Mohammed El Adl to those of '1000s of others'.

David Lean's 1984 film version of *A Passage to India*, whilst visually alluring, has little of the homoerotic in it. Victor Banerjee as Aziz has a difficult job engaging James Fox's Fielding in any semblance of a genuine friendship. It is difficult to see this wooden, self-enclosed, somewhat cold, Fielding appealing to anybody, much less earning any of the plaudits acceded to him in the film by his students. So much in India has to do with the heart, yet Fox's Fielding has no heart, he could never establish any understanding with an Indian like Aziz. Head and shoulders above Lean's offering was the 1965 BBC presentation of Santha Rama Rau's play based on the novel, directed by Waris Hussein. Cyril Cusack's interpretation of Fielding in that production is a character of warmth, with whom rapport and intimacy may be possible. Hussein clearly demonstrates that he does understand the passion of the novel. When Michael Bates, as Godbole, sings of Krishna and the Milkmaids, he is accompanied by a visual montage of Indian faces; the last face being quite masculine but seemingly in feminine attire suggesting a hijra. Likewise the punkah-wallah: Lean has a crabby pensioner, but Hussein presents a youthful Apollo. In Hussein's masterpiece, when McBride asserts that the darker races are invariably attracted by the fairer, the punkah itself moves back to light up the punkah-wallah's face, subverting his words, as if to say, here is a representative of that darker race which many of the fair would wish to know. Hussein presents the heart of the novel, Lean but a lavish and expensive version of imperial angst.

Returning to the novel, *A Passage to India* begins and ends with a discussion on friendship, rather in the manner in which the subject of marriage is treated in many nineteenth- and early twentieth-century novels; Austen's *Pride and Prejudice* or Lawrence's *Women in Love*, for example. Chapter 1 of the final published version of *A Passage to India* sets the scene in Chandrapore, but it was not the first chapter to have been written. Chapter 2 contains a detailed discussion between Aziz and his companions on the nature of friendship and the possibility of Englishmen and Indian men becoming and remaining friends. There is also a discussion regarding friendship with English women, which the Indians do not see as possible in India, though later in the same chapter Aziz meets Mrs Moore for the first time. Stallybrass maintains that what is now chapter 2 of the novel was originally intended as the opening chapter, and that the present chapter 1 was only written after chapters 2 to 7 had been drafted (PTI-MS, 6). So it appears that friendship was intended to be the major theme from the very start of the book. It is also significant to note the care with which this theme and the characters of Aziz and Fielding are introduced, and to contrast this with the rather brusque introduction, in chapter 3, of Adela Quested and Ronny Heaslop, indicating the narrator's apparent lack of interest in the romantic involvement of the heterosexual couple (PTI, 19).

This heterosexual love interest is disposed of about two-thirds of the way through the novel, leaving the remaining third to deal with the wider implications of personal friendships. Not all commentators, however, have seen the importance of this however. In a letter to James R. McConkey of 21 September 1957, Forster noted that one or two critics had told him that nothing in *A Passage to India* has any importance after the trial scene: 'One can but bow and smile a little wanly,' Forster observed (Lago and Furbank 2, 267).

Returning to chapter 2, we find Hamidullah's wife enquiring of Aziz why, after the death of his wife, he refuses to remarry. She asks plaintively, what would become of all their daughters if men refused to marry them, a question which so distresses Aziz that Hamidullah has to use 'soothing words' (PTI, 9) to calm him down. Later, he reveals that no woman could take the place of his first wife, declaring that 'a friend would come nearer to her than another woman' (PTI, 49). Pacified by his friend, Aziz then responds, but not directly, to the issue raised by Hamidullah Begum. He does this by beginning to recite poems by Hafiz, Ghalib, Hali and Iqbal, in Persian, Urdu and in Arabic, which are greeted with delight by his friends (PTI, 9-10)

The poems recited by Aziz are significant, being a coded reply to Hamidullah Begum, and hinting at reasons for choosing not to remarry. Tariq Rahman points out some of the significant features of the works, linking them with Forster's friend Masood:

> The four poets quoted, Hafiz, Ghalib, Hali and Iqbal combine Masood's love for classical love-poetry and new Muslim revivalist poetry. Hafiz ...is one of the greatest of the Persian love poets of mysticism. In his poetry God is the ultimate beloved and the soul calls to the beloved to absorb it in itself. The imagery is very often of adolescent boys as the cup-bearers and wine as the symbol of divine love. On a secular plane the poetry is some of the tenderest and most exquisite expressions of ephebophilia. The same can be said of the poetry of...Ghalib ...Hali and Iqbal are the revivalists though in love poetry their images too are ephebophilic (Rahman 1984, 51-2).

An interest in Persian poetry becomes a euphemism for other interests in the novel, and this shared enthusiasm between Aziz and Fielding becomes a key feature in their relationship. Persian poetry in the form of the *Rubaiyat* of Omar Kahyyam is mentioned frequently in Forster's work. For example, a copy of it is to be found in Rickie Elliot's room at Cambridge in *The Longest Journey* (LJ, 9), and in 'Nottingham Lace' Edgar's interest is aroused by the discovery that Sidney had heard of Omar (AS, 19). The edition of the poetry referred to, in all cases, is almost certainly the version of Omar Khayyam's poems produced in translation in 1859 by Edward Fitzgerald.

In a letter to William Plomer of 20 November 1963, Forster commented on Plomer's then recently written article on Fitzgerald. Forster observed that he could see many of his own tendencies in Fitzgerald, but that fortunately his had been blessed (Lago and Furbank 2, 287). Plomer's article had implied that Fitzgerald was homosexual and had referred to his disastrous marriage (Plomer 97-8) and an equally disastrous male friendship (99-100); Forster whilst sharing Fitzgerald's sexuality had, unlike him, been blessed by successful male friendships.

Plomer's essay provides more pointers to Forster's interest in Fitzgerald, an interest which Edward Carpenter had earlier taken when he included a section on him in his *Anthology of Friendship: Ioläus*. Carpenter noted that Fitzgerald had said of himself that 'My friendships are more like loves,' and he quotes from Arthur Christopher Benson, (the brother of E. F. Benson of *Mapp and Lucia* fame), whose biography of Fitzgerald had appeared in 1905, that 'He seems to have been one of those whose best friendships are reserved for men' (Carpenter 1929, 222-3; A. C. Benson, 172).

Carpenter went on to quote further from Benson in describing Fitzgerald's friendship with Posh,* an East Coast fisherman, which had lasted over many years:

> In the same year [1864] came another great friendship. He made the acquaintance of a stalwart sailor named Joseph Fletcher, commonly called Posh. It was at Lowestoft that he was found, where Fitzgerald used, as he wrote in 1850, 'to wander about the shore at night longing for some fellow to accost me who might give some promise of filling up a very vacant place in my heart' (Carpenter 1929 223-4; A. C. Benson, 48).

It may well be that through his acquaintances at Cambridge, or in his own reading of Fitzgerald's work, Forster came to realise, as with the work of A. E. Housman, that he and the writer shared a similar desire for male friendships, especially for those which cut across class boundaries. Forster could also have read about Fitzgerald's implied homosexuality in Havelock Ellis's book *Sexual Inversion* which discussed the subject (Ellis 1, 50). Forster corresponded

---

* Fitzgerald's own description of Posh is striking, for in many respects it describes Forster's own ideal 'friend', as exemplified by the character Stephen Wonham, in *The Longest Journey*:
  Posh was, in Fitzgerald's own words, 'a man of the finest Saxon type, with a complexion, vif, mâle et flamboyant, blue eyes, a nose less than Roman, more than Greek, and strictly auburn hair that woman might sigh to possess'. He was too, according to Fitz, 'a man of simplicity of soul, justice of thought, tenderness of nature, a gentleman of Nature's grandest type'. Fitz became deeply devoted to this big-handed, soft-hearted, grave fellow, then 24 years of age (Carpenter 1929, 224; A. C. Benson, 48-9).
  The young man's nickname of 'Posh' bears a noticeable resemblance to Stephen Wonham's nickname, 'Podge'. Forster's friend T. E. Lawrence had a 'special friend', E. S. Palmer, a fellow private in the Tank Corps, whose nickname also was 'Posh' (Lawrence 1992, 263).

with A. C. Benson in 1910, after Benson had written to him with his, and his mother's, opinions of *Howards End*. In a letter to Benson of 13 December 1910, Forster mentioned that he hoped to visit him when next in Cambridge* (Lago and Furbank 1, 119). No doubt, in his personal contact with Benson, Forster acquired a great deal of unpublished — and, perhaps at that time, unpublishable — information about Fitzgerald.

Robert Bernard Martin in his study of Fitzgerald, *With Friends Possessed*, intriguingly notes that what he left out of his translation tells us 'a great deal more than he intended' (16) and that in the *Rubaiyat* Fitzgerald had specifically decided to obscure the gender of the beloved in the poems, 'leaving the sex an open question' (208). Plomer's article,** reprinted in his *Electric Delights*, drew links between a famous section of the *Rubaiyat* and its author's fondness for the company of working-class males:

> 'I am happiest going in my little boat round the coast to
> Aldeburgh, with some bottled porter and some bread and cheese,
> and some good rough soul who works the boat and chews his
> tobacco in peace.' [Plomer, having quoted the above extract from
> Fitzgerald adds:] This seems almost like a paraphrase of the most
> hackneyed quatrain in the Rubaiyat: all we have to do is to
> substitute a mast for the bough, and a bottle of porter for the jug
> of wine, and add a little cheese to the bread; and the enigmatic
> 'thou', singing in the wilderness, is seen to be a congenially rough
> soul chewing tobacco in the North Sea (Plomer, 92).

Returning to *A Passage to India*, when Aziz and Fielding first meet, Persian poetry and the meeting of friends are linked. The mention of 'Persian poetry' functions like the mention of the word 'friend' or 'soldier' in Forster's work, discreetly addressing those astute and sympathetic readers who could recognise its encoded homoerotic subtext. Speaking of Persian poetry also func-

---

* In 1886, a novel, *The Memoirs of Arthur Hamilton*, written by Benson appeared under the pseudonym of Christopher Carr. Part of this novel, dealing with the protagonist, Arthur's relationship with a fellow male student whilst at Cambridge University is reprinted in Brian Reade's *Sexual Heretics* (199-203). In 1914 Benson became Master of Magdalene College, Cambridge.

** In 1963 *Tribute to Benjamin Britten on his Fiftieth Birthday* was published, edited by Anthony Gishford. In his Foreword to the book, Gishford recorded that he had asked 'those of Mr Britten's friends and collaborators who we thought would like to join in such a gift' to contribute 'something that they themselves liked and that they thought would give the recipient pleasure' (11). Amongst the contributions included in the work, Plomer submitted his article on Fitzgerald, and Forster the first chapter of 'Arctic Summer'. Also printed was a description of travels in the East by Ludwig, Prince of Hesse and the Rhine which included an account of his visit to the Theosophical Society in Madras where, in describing a performance of Indian dance, he observed: 'It seems that in these eastern countries, differences of sex, (among dancers at least), have become rather indistinct. A kind of bisexual dance-being has emerged' (63). Part of the performance included a re-enactment of the story of Krishna and Radha, where the abandoned Radha 'calls with her hands: Come! Come!' to her beloved (64).

tions as a 'password' in Fielding's relationship with Aziz, the mention of the subject alerting each one to a secret desire of the other. When Aziz meets Fielding he specifically mentions that the latter's 'warm heart' had aroused his curiosity, and that he had fantasised about meeting him, for he was also known as 'a celebrated student of Persian poetry' (PTI, 57).

Aziz had longed to meet a like-minded person. His yearning recalls a similar desire of Forster himself, and Fitzgerald's 'longing for some fellow... who might give some promise of filling up a very vacant place in my heart'. Even before the meeting, Aziz had had a premonition of its success, and that the one serious gap in his life was going to be 'filled' by their relationship (PTI, 54).

Aziz and Fielding's friendship soon becomes intimate, with a commitment from both that promises to endure until death. Aziz's expectations of friendship are very high for he takes as his ideal the Emperor Babur, who never in his whole life betrayed a friend (PTI, 135). Through the tribulations of the Quested affair, their fidelity to each other is proven, for 'All that existed, in that terrible time, was affection' (PTI, 223). And later, on the night of Aziz's acquittal, as the friends lie gazing at the starlit sky, Aziz urges that they dream plans for their future together (PTI, 238). This homoerotic idyll is short-lived. Their friendship is not immune to all changes of circumstance, and despite their desire to negate them, racial differences remain. And later, when Fielding marries, a further rift is created between them, just as the marriage of his army friend had ended an earlier relationship in England.

Neither Fielding's wife nor Aziz's appear to be closely involved with their husband's friend. In an early manuscript draft, Aziz does not marry for the second time, having a concubine rather than a wife (PTI-MS, 521). It is possible that Forster originally intended to end the novel with a triangular relationship involving Fielding, his wife Stella Moore, and Aziz. Evidence to support such a suggestion is to be found amongst the manuscript drafts of the novel, where one of the sheets, written in Forster's own hand, contains the final paragraphs of D. H. Lawrence's *Women in Love* (sheet B15v PTI-MS, 580). In those final sentences Rupert Birkin, speaking to Ursula Brangwen, proposes just such a relationship:

> 'You are enough for me, as far as a woman is concerned. You are all women to me. But I wanted a man friend, as eternal as you and I are eternal.' (541)

Ursula believes that such a love is impossible to realise:

> 'You can't have two kinds of love. Why should you!'
> 'It seems as if I can't,' he said. 'Yet I wanted it.'
> 'You can't have it, because it's false, impossible,' she said.
> 'I don't believe that,' he answered. (541)

Forster's novel may well have begun as an effort to show that it was possible to have two kinds of love; he had hinted at such a possibility in the
triangle of characters at the close of *Where Angels Fear to Tread*, and in 'Ralph
and Tony'. However the published text does not disclose that possibility, nor
even the desirability of maintaining two different and equal loves. Interestingly, like Forster in his writings, prior to publication Lawrence also excised a
part of *Women in Love* which had dealt with homosexual desire; in his suppressed Prologue to the novel he revealed that 'it was for men that [Birkin] felt
the hot, flushing, roused attraction which a man is supposed to feel for the
other sex' (Cooke, 57). At the end of the final published version of the novel,
Birkin is dissatisfied that he does not have a male partner to relate to in addition to Ursula; by contrast, in *A Passage to India*, Forster seems quite happy to
end the novel by concentrating on a male couple.

But what of Stella? We do not know why she should choose to marry
Fielding. She is blamed for causing the two boats to capsize on the sacred tank
at Mau, by her lurching from her husband towards Aziz. Did she in other
ways capsize their relationship? What exactly was her role to be in this triangle? The only really significant fact about Stella is that she is the daughter of
Mrs Moore, who had earlier formed part of a loving triangle with Fielding and
Aziz. Does she merely replace her mother in a triangle, which Mrs Moore's
other children, Ronny and Ralph, in a 'publishable' novel, cannot? Forster
denies Stella a voice and so it is her husband who tells us what effect Mau had
had upon her, for there she 'found something soothing, some solution of her
queer troubles' (PTI, 309). Whether her 'queer troubles' refers to problems
with her 'queer' husband and his friend is open to speculation; Stella cannot
tell us, nor from behind the purdah do we ever hear one word from Aziz's
second wife.

Whatever Forster's original intention, the final published draft of *A Passage to India* clearly concentrates on the relationship between two men. Whether
or not D. H. Lawrence knew that Forster had looked carefully at the end of
one of his novels during his writing of *A Passage to India*, is not known. Forster
did send him a copy of the novel, which seemed to displease Lawrence, who
wrote back criticising Forster for hingeing the book on 'a very unsatisfactory
friendship between two men' (Furbank 2, 124).

Lawrence, like Forster, was influenced by the work of Walt Whitman but
their views on the role of marriage in a triangular affair differ. Lawrence's
position has been summarised by the critic George H. Ford:

> For having sung of the 'love between comrades' Whitman is
> highly praised by Lawrence as one who made pioneering efforts
> on behalf of a great cause. Such a love, provided that it never acts
> 'to destroy marriage', is recommended as healthy and life-giving. If
> it becomes an alternative to married love instead of a supplement,

it is, on the contrary, deathly (Cooke, 181).

Forster would not have seen the love of comrades as 'deathly', nor would he have chosen as a partner for one of his fictional male lovers quite such an aggressive and rapacious man as Gerald Crich, to whom Birkin is attracted in *Women in Love* (though Forster might perhaps have felt a certain frisson of pleasure, given his excitement over Gino in *Where Angels Fear to Tread*). Whether 'love between comrades' is deathly to a married love or not is debatable, but Forster seems to have little interest in showing how it can supplement a marriage, nor how manly love itself can be supplemented by marriage. The two loves are presented as separate areas of life.

As in other Forster novels women are frequently shown to interrupt relations between men, rather than to promote them. Adela Quested causes Aziz to be arrested and placed on trial, and is the source of the major estrangement between him and Fielding; only Mrs Moore is a force for good. However she has little social power, only in the 'twilight of the double vision', as a 'withered priestess' (PTI, 197-8) is she acknowledged as potent. Perhaps it is no accident that in this role she is most appealing to Aziz, whose earliest commendation is that she is an 'Oriental' (PTI, 17), nor that she comes to be worshipped by other Indians as a goddess. Her stereotypically feminine powers are only appreciated by what, according to imperialist rhetoric, is an effeminised race. She later finds a special place in the Krishna festival at Mau. It is worth noting, perhaps, that intimate friendship is possible with Mrs Moore, now elderly and — by implication at least — no longer sexually active, but not with the women whom the friends have married. Marriage destroyed Fielding's relationship with the army coach and it seriously disrupts his friendship with Aziz, although much of Aziz's anger arises from his mistaken belief that Fielding has betrayed him by marrying Adela. In Forster's novel, then, can it be bisexuality which is seen as the real threat to male love?

If most of the references to friendship in the novel use sources drawn from Oriental poetry, Forster does not wholly put aside his passion for ancient Greece. He does not draw solely on its models for friendships, preferring rather to utilise similar Indian concepts, but he does find inspiration in one of Greece's models of male perfection, the god Apollo. And it is not by accident that he chose a god who had a special relationship towards homosexual love. As Robert Graves notes, Apollo was the first Greek god to woo one of his own sex (R. Graves, 1 78), and Carpenter points out:

> Apollo... was a strange blend of masculine and feminine
> attributes.... He was the patron of song and music. He was also,
> in some ways, the representative divinity of the Uranian [that is,
> homosexual] love, for he was the special god of the Dorian
> Greeks, among whom comradeship became an institution
> (Carpenter 1984, 256).

Apollo was regarded as the god of the sun, and it is in relation to this aspect of him that some of the references in the novel are made. The Indian sun, whose nature takes up the whole of chapter 10, is a fierce and cruel force, yet its Apollonian links are established in the narrator's observation that the sun was 'not the unattainable Friend' (PTI, 106). On the morning of the doomed visit to the Marabar Caves, it fails to rise as expected, as though prefiguring those trials through which Aziz and Fielding's relationship must go. The language used to describe the failure of its appearance clearly has a textual eroticism:

> Colour throbbed and mounted behind a pattern of trees, grew in
> intensity, was yet brighter, incredibly brighter, strained from
> without against the globe of the air. They awaited the miracle. But
> at the supreme moment, when night should have died and day
> lived, nothing occured.... Why when the chamber was prepared,
> did the bridegroom not enter with trumpets and shawms, as
> humanity expects? The sun rose without splendour. He was
> presently observed trailing yellowish behind the trees, or against
> insipid sky, and touching the bodies already at work in the fields
> (PTI, 129).

'[T]ouching the bodies already at work in the fields' — the last comment is significant, for it foreshadows the god's reappearance later in the novel in the forms of the punkah-wallah and 'the Indian body again triumphant', the low-caste labourers appearing to assume aspects of the Apollonian godhead. In a letter to Mary Aylward of 30 October 1912, on his first visit to India, Forster described a meeting with some Indian villagers, in which he had compared them to ancient Greek statues and supposed they were the equivalent of a yokel on Salisbury Plain (Lago and Furbank 1, 142); rather like Stephen Wonham from *The Longest Journey*, no doubt.

The Olympic athletes of ancient Greece competed in the games held in honour of Apollo, and their physical perfection, which palely mirrors that of the god himself, finds an echo in *A Passage to India* in the beauty of certain low-caste Indian men, the punkah-wallah in particular:

> the man who pulled the punkah. Almost naked, and splendidly
> formed, he sat on a raised platform near the back.... He had the
> strength and beauty that sometimes come to flower in Indians of
> low birth. When that strange race nears the dust and is
> condemned   as untouchable, then nature remembers the physical
> perfection that   she accomplished elsewhere, and throws out a
> god — not many, but one here and there, to prove to society how
> little its categories impress her... he stood out as divine, yet he was

of the city, and its garbage had nourished him, he would end on its rubbish heaps...he seemed apart from human destinies, a male Fate, a winnower of souls (PTI, 207).

'Strength', 'beauty' and 'physical perfection' combined, these are attributes of of a young Greek god. In India, Krishna has similar aspects, but Krishna is not 'a male Fate'. This divine untouchable has more in common with Apollo and the values of the Hellenic world than those of his native land. Above the farce of the trial, unimpressed by society's little categories — of gender, sex, race, nationality, class or caste — he remains unmoved. The 'sun rose without splendour', for its Apollonian splendour has been transferred to the beautiful pariah youth, and, like the contemporary devotees of Apollo's love, he is a social outcast.* Forster's entry in his Indian Journal of 25 March 1913 describes his visit to an Indian courtroom, where a punkah boy, seated at end of table, had 'the impassivity of Atropos' (HD, 22). Stallybrass uses this entry to link the punkah-wallah in the novel to the ancient Greek mythological female figure of Atropos, hence Forster's stressing that his Fate was male. The name of Atropos means, significantly, 'irresistible'** and she 'was one of the three Moirai, daughters of Zeus and Themis, and dispensers of Fate' (PTI, 362). Her other two sisters are Clotho and Lachesis. Robert Graves in *The Greek Myths* notes that of these three Fates, Atropos, though the smallest in stature, is yet the most terrible. According to Graves:

> Zeus, who weighs the lives of men and informs the Fates of his decisions can, it is said, change his mind and intervene to save whom he pleases, when the thread of life, spun on Clotho's spindle, and measured by the rod of Lachesis, is about to be snipped by Atropos's shears (R. Graves 1, 48).

In the trial scene Aziz's fate literally hangs in the balance, but his escape has already been secured, for his 'Fate' has been replaced by the youthful punkah-wallah, an embodiment of the beauty of Apollo, the god most favourable to male love. In this act of rescue, the Apollonian envoy recalls the god's earlier

* The importance of this character in the novel was highlighted by Forster himself. In a letter of 10 January 1961 to Santha Rama Rau, who had written a play based on *A Passage to India*, and which was shortly to be presented at the Ambassador Theatre, Forster wrote of his great disappointment that due to technical resons there was to be no punkah-wallah in the third act of the drama. In a later letter to her of 23 October 1961, Forster discussed how the trial scene could be presented, and the technical reasons overcome, asserting that 'MOST IMPORTANT OF ALL the nude beautiful punkah wallah' [the capital letters are Forster's own].... He can easily be contrived.... Will you please impress this on all whom it may concern' (Lago and Furbank 2, 280-1). Rau had clearly understood Forster's regard for the character, for in her play, she devotes half of her introductory stage directions to Act Three, the trial scene, to the punkah-wallah, 'a very young and extraordinary beautiful INDIAN SERVANT' (Rau, 93-4); he is also the subject of the final stage direction as the curtain falls at the close of the play (123).
** 'Irresistable', the word Mr Beebe applied to George Emerson in an early draft of *A Room With a View* (Lucy 108). See above, p.111.

deliverance of a friend from the Fates, for, as Graves explains, 'some say that
Apollo once mischievously made them drunk in order to save his friend Admetus
from death' (R. Graves 1, 48). As Apollo rescued his own friend, so the god's
representative intervenes to save, for Fielding, his friend Aziz. In the story of
Admetus, his later deliverance from death is ultimately secured by his wife,
Alcestis, who sacrifices herself on his behalf (R. Graves 1, 224). An echo of
this is, perhaps, to be found in Adela Quested's 'sacrifice' on behalf of Aziz.
Adela, by her truthful witness at Aziz's trial, saves him, but takes his place as
the object of Anglo-Indian derision, just as Alcestis offers to rescue her husband from the underworld by taking his place amongst the dead.

Later, towards the end of the novel, Apollo is seen in another incarnation
at the high point of the Krishna festivities at Mau. Here he appears as the man
whose duty it is to throw the image of the god's birthplace into the sacred tank
of the temple: 'He was naked, broad-shouldered, thin-waisted — the Indian
body again triumphant — and it was his hereditary office to close the gates of
salvation' (PTI, 304).

The phrase, 'the Indian body again triumphant', seems to confirm the
connection with the punkah-wallah, and his crucial role in the Krishna rituals
shows his links with the divine. And he is present in the water when 'the
unattainable', the God who cannot be apprehended, 'not now, not here', is
thrown away (PTI, 304).

Just as in Persian poetry and often in the homoerotic poetry of ancient
Greece, the love which is inspired by Apollo, the pure love of the Friend, of
the Beloved is as unattainable as the divinity itself, whose divine love the love
of friends palely prefigures. 'Not now, not here', writes Forster in the final
published text, but in an earlier draft he wrote, 'not here, where the earth says
"be different" from the start of time' (PTI-MS, 562). Forster makes it clear
that it is the conditions here on earth which prevent the attainment of the
Friend. And if the god 'was an emblem of that', of that unattainable love, it is
easier to see why Forster uses a religious myth, that of Krishna and the Milkmaids, to speculate on a future utopian state in which the unattainable may
finally be realised, for in *A Passage to India* Forster examines not only the
personal joys to be gained from friendship, but also looks at the possibility of
such friendships transforming present-day social arrangements. He seems to
be exploring imaginatively his earlier thoughts that the love which he and
Mohammed el Adl had shared was in some way related to the love of thousands of others who had likewise crossed the barrier of race.

There are three main places in *A Passage to India* where Forster points towards
the potential for male love and friendship to link human beings in a new and
more fulfilling social organisation, free of the racial, class and gender divisions
which characterise present-day social arrangements.

The first setting where utopian dreams arise is in the mosque, where Aziz
meets Mrs Moore. In a later conversation with her he significantly refers to it
as 'our mosque' (PTI, 134). Aziz recreates the building in his dreams as a

suitable habitat for himself, his family and his friend Fielding. Indeed the vision is prompted by his love for him, for 'they were friends, brothers... they trusted one another, affection had triumphed for once in a way'. This, of course, is a personal utopia, or perhaps, more correctly, an Arcadian refuge, one which depicts an escape from the world, not one which sees human nature as capable of transformation, 'a region where joy had no enemies' and 'bloomed harmoniously in an eternal garden' (PTI, 113).

The same Arcadian desires figure in the second location of Forster's utopian hopes. Symbolically situated between the European colony and the Indian part of the city, the maidan at Chandrapore is the location of a polo game* involving an English soldier, Aziz and some of his Indian friends. This scene of male athleticism recalls the bathing scene in *A Room with a View*, the cricket game in *Maurice* and other sporting scenes in Forster's work, and like them links male comradeship and physicality. Even the language which Forster uses to describe the game is innocently homoerotic. Riding into the middle of the maidan, Aziz began to knock a ball about, before a stray shot meets with a soldier, a subaltern, who was also practising his game:

> The newcomer had some notion of what to do, but his horse had none, and forces were equal. Concentrated on the ball, they somehow became fond of one another, and smiled when they drew rein to rest. Aziz liked soldiers — they either accepted you or swore at you... (PTI, 51).

In an earlier manuscript draft Forster added that soldiers 'either clasped you to their hearts or kicked you' (PTI-MS, 69), but — like that by the Sacred Lake in *A Room with a View* — this collective male joy is short-lived for a wider world will not allow its continuance:

> They reined up again, the fire of good fellowship in their eyes. But it cooled with their bodies, for athletics can only raise a temporary glow. Nationality was returning, but before it could exert its poison they parted, saluting each other. 'If only they were all like that,' each thought (PTI, 51-2).

Referring again to Forster's manuscript drafts, we see that initially it was not only nationality which poisoned 'good fellowship'. Forster appears to have originally intended to make the point that physical and emotional male intimacy was subject to attack from other quarters; and significantly, perhaps, he

---

* Ronald Hyam in *Empire and Sexuality* notes the comments of John Masters, a long-time resident during the early part of this century in India under the British Raj: 'In India there was always an unnatural tension... and every man who pursued the physical aim of sexual relief was in danger of developing a cynical hardness and lack of sympathy.... Of those who tried sublimation, some chased polo balls...' (Hyam, 122).

includes Mrs Moore in the idyll. Continuing the last quotation from the final published text, given above, an earlier manuscript draft reads:

> before … \ it could poison the meeting / the subaltern <cried>
> said Well so long, and «, idealising <the> one another, » « they
> parted <for ever> » rode away. 'Unlike the rest' thought Aziz, as
> he knocked the ball about \ alone /. 'For an Englishman of that
> <sort> \ type / I could die.' <He remembered Mrs Moore> Twice
> in a few   days he had slipped the \ grim / sentries \, and found
> friendliness   behind them / … slipping by the solemn guards who
> forbid us joy (PTI-MS, 70).*

Outside the patriarchal order, 'Between the acts', past the '\ grim / sentries' and 'solemn guards', Aziz could find his friend — 'For an Englishman of that <sort> \ type / I could die.' Here Forster speaks of the possibility of a transformed world where friends may meet and joy is not forbidden, and in the scene at the temple at Mau, the reunion of friends is seen as the instrument by which the world will be transformed. Unfortunately, after the arrest of Aziz the poison of nationality soon regains its strength, and the subaltern, who had joined in the polo match, calls for educated Indians to be stamped on and sides with Major Callendar in his attempts to bully Fielding at the club (PTI, 177-180). Aziz continues to dream about a universal brotherhood and he tries to express his idea of it, 'but as soon as it was put into prose it became untrue' (PTI, 136).

The third and final setting of Forster's utopian project is at the temple at Mau, but its importance is prefigured by Godbole's poetry, with his hymn to Krishna expressing desire for a personal union with the god and linking the concept to universal and divine love. Godbole places himself in the position of a *gopi* or milkmaid, and calls upon Krishna to multiply himself into a hundred Krishnas, and send one to him and one to each of his hundred companions (PTI, 72). Each devotee would then have a personal contact with the god, and, through his own Krishna, contact with those others who worship the same deity. Forster takes this myth of Krishna, and as will be seen below, embellishes it with ideas derived from ancient Greece to provide a vision of

---

* cf. the scene on the maidan involving soldiers, and Aziz's idea of universal brotherhood, with Forster's letter to G. L. Dickinson of 28 July 1916, where he describes a group of hundreds of young soldiers bathing by the sea at Montazah in Egypt. This scene also is clearly homoerotic: 'They go about bare chested and bare legged, the blue of their linen shorts and the pale mauve of their shirts accenting the brown splendour of their bodies; and down by the sea… many of them spend half their days naked and unrebuked…. It is so beautiful that I cannot believe it has not been planned, but can't think by whom nor for whom except me. It makes me very happy yet very sad — they came from the unspeakable, all these young gods, and in a fortnight at the latest they return to it: … I come away from that place each time thinking 'Why not more of this? Why not? What would it injure? Why not a world like this — … It's evidently not to be in our day, nor while nationality lives, but I can't believe it Utopian, for each human being has in him the germs of such a world' (Lago and Furbank 1, 237).

social transformation.

Both Carpenter in *From Adam's Peak to Elephanta*, and G. L. Dickinson in his account of his Oriental travels in *Appearances*, made numerous, usually favourable, comparisons between religious practices in India and those of ancient Greece, pointing out possible contacts between the two in a now forgotten past. Carpenter even quotes from a Mrs Speir, who in her book *Life in Ancient India* noted the proposition, made by the ancient Greek writer Megasthenes, 'that Siva worship was derived from Bacchus or Dionysos, and carried to the East in the traditionary expedition which Bacchus made in company with Hercules' (Carpenter 1910, 126). When Forster came to India he did so prepared to identify the links between ancient Greek religion and contemporaly Hinduism.

To understand more specifically how Greek and Persian concepts of love and friendship became linked by Forster to the legends of the Indian god Krishna, reference needs to be made to the friendship between the writer and Vishwanath Singh Bahadur, the Maharajah of Chhatarpur, who also was homosexual.

During his first visit to India in 1912, Forster, accompanied by G. L. Dickinson, stayed with the Maharajah. Dickinson's description of the Maharajah does not make him sound appealing:

> he was a homosexual, in a curious (or not curious) way which
> combined what would be called perverted sexuality with
> philosophic and religious curiosity and learning. He was an ugly
> little man, who dressed in white drawers, slippers and a very
> vulgar yellow ulster. He took us drives in his car, the long trains of
> bullocks leaping wildly into the ditch as he passed, absorbed in
> questions about Plato or Herbert Spencer (Dickinson 1973, 179).

Whatever his views on the ruler, Dickinson thought his palace at Mau the most beautiful and appealing place he had ever seen (Dickinson, 1973). And in letters home to his mother Forster described the Maharajah's kingdom as a paradise (Lago and Furbank 1 162), later dubbing the British Political Agent resident at Chhatarpur the 'serpent' in that paradise (Lago and Furbank 1, 170). Forster had numerous conversations with the Maharajah concerning male homosexual love, ancient Greece, and their philosophical connections with love of the divine. It was these conversations which seem first to have alerted Forster yet further to the links which could be made between the gods of Hinduism and those of ancient Greece. Forster, unaccompanied, paid a second visit to Chhatarpur in September 1921 (Furbank 2, 93).

In *Hindoo Holiday*, J. R. Ackerley described his time at the Maharajah's court, when in October 1923, on Forster's recommendation, he became the Rajah's Private Secretary (Furbank 2, 117). In his book, 'Chhatarpur' becomes 'Chhokrapur', and he records his employer's obsession with ancient Greece.

The Rajah kept a Greek toga and, when friendly visitors from England came to stay would wear it and talk of Classical Greece; and his friends would clap their hands and say 'The Greeks have been born again in Chhokrapur' (Ackerley 1932, 36). The Rajah also made clear his desires: 'Goodness, wisdom, and beauty — that is what the Greeks worshipped, and that is what I want... a good, wise, and beautiful friend' (34). He kept a troupe of young male dancers who privately performed for him and his guests,* and, significantly, during Forster's stay at his palace he saw enacted a play based on the story of the birth of Krishna, the event which is celebrated in the temple at the close of *A Passage to India*. Naturally both Dickinson, the Greek scholar, and Forster were questioned by the Rajah in his search for a friend (GLD, 139):

> 'Oh when will Krishna come and be my friend.... If the soul has walked with the Gods, and if the Beloved on earth is a staircase by which we can climb to Heaven again, then will you tell me who has put the barriers in the way?' (Furbank 1, 235-6)

Forster could have told him of the nature and origin of some of the barriers, especially about those which had caused him to burn some of his own writings and to suppress others, but his reply to the Maharajah on this occasion is not recorded. However in describing the event in his biography of Dickinson, Forster records that he 'found these questions grotesque, but Dickinson attuned them to his own Platonism, and there was instant sympathy' (GLD, 139).

The Maharajah had a second, ruined, palace in the middle of a lake, which he offered to both Forster and, later, to Dickinson (Furbank 1, 236). Furbank records that the location was of special significance for the Rajah for it was there that 'he hoped to meet Krishna, the divine friend' (Furbank 1, 236). The location of this ruined palace is significant, for it was in a place called Mau (Furbank 2 94), the same name which Forster gives to site of the Krishna rituals in 'Temple', the final part of *A Passage to India*. The description of Mau given by Forster in his Indian Journal entry of 3 December 1912 (HD, 156-7) clearly recalls the setting of the Maharajah's palace at the close of the novel. In Forster's story, however, Mau is not a ruined palace but the living centre of Krishna worship and, symbolically, the celebrations held there are to greet the arrival of the newly-(re)born Krishna. It is clearly a fitting location for the reunion of Fielding and Aziz, and, as Fielding tells his friend, 'What I want to discover is its spiritual side, if it has one' (PTI 309).

On his second visit to India, during a stay with the Maharajah of Dewas

---

* G. L. Dickinson's account of one of their performances in his *Appearances* (20-3), specifically links the dances in honour of Lord Krishna to those of ancient Greece: 'For the first time I seemed to catch a glimpse of what the tragic dance of the Greeks might be like. The rhythms were not unlike those of Greek choruses, the motions corresponded strictly to the rhythms, and all was attuned to a high religious mood. In such dancing the flesh becomes spirit, the body a transparent emblem of the soul' (Dickinson 1914, 22).

State Senior, Forster obtained more information on Krishna and imagined scenes of divine sportiveness:

> 'He [Krishna], the one deity of all sacrifices, exhibiting the gaiety of lads, while the celestial world looked on' ... and when he is tired he 'goes beneath a tree and rests on beds of tender leaves, with his head cushioned on a herdsboy's thigh'. (HD, 73)

He also acquired more information on the story of Krishna and the milkmaids, referred to in Godbole's song, later describing his vision of the central scene of the legend:

> I saw the milkmaids, all wanting to dance with Krishna, and Krishna, to oblige them, multiplying himself, so that each milkmaid thought that she had him for her individual partner. (HD, 239)

The main emphasis in the worship of Krishna is *bhakti*, defined as the 'Love of God; single-minded devotion to one's Chosen Ideal (Sri Ramakrishna, 1031). Godbole, as is to be expected from a Hindu brahmin pandit, provides the link between *bhakti* and resistance to the destructiveness of nationalism. Most of Aziz's later poetic writings celebrate Indian nationalist sentiment and advocate political action in support of its aims. Forster's aim however, like Godbole's, is to show the limitations and dangers of nationalism, and to dream of replacing it by a universal comradeship. One of Aziz's poems, which differs from the rest, especially attracts Godbole's attention by its appeal to internationality, which he finds indicative of *bhakti* (PTI, 284).

The story of the multiplied Krishna repeatedly provides the subject matter for Godbole's songs inviting the god to come, and this supplication is linked thematically with Aziz's Persian poetry. When Aziz quotes from a poem of Ghalib's, Krishna is also invoked:

> Less explicit than the call to Krishna, it [the poem] voiced our loneliness nevertheless, our isolation, our need for the Friend who never comes yet is not entirely disproved. (PTI, 97)

G. L. Dickinson, who accompanied Forster on his 1912–13 journey to India, visited on that trip the ashram near Calcutta that had been home to the Indian sage Sri Ramakrishna (1836–1886).* Reading through the teachings

---

* Christopher Isherwood, novelist and friend of Forster, was to become a devotee himself of the teachings of Sri Ramakrishna and in 1965 he published a biography of the guru, *Ramakrishna and his Disciples*. Isherwood did attempt in his letters during the Second World War to explain his beliefs to Forster, but his response was discouraging, Forster saying that he couldn't imagine the belief that God could help him (Furbank 2, 237).

of Ramakrishna, Dickinson had been impressed, pondering 'Was this Athens or India?', and was 'this all-comprehensive Hinduism, this universal toleration, this refusal to recognise ultimate antagonisms... after all, the truest and profoundest vision?' (Dickinson 1914, 36). Ramakrishna had preached the virtue of *bhakti*, its practitioner being called a *bhakta*, and had explained the path of *bhakti* to a devotee as follows:

A BRAHMO DEVOTEE: 'Sir, has God forms or has He none?'
MASTER: 'No one can say with finality that God is only 'this'
and nothing else. He is formless, and again He has forms. For the
bhakta He assumes forms.... The bhakta feels that he is one entity
and the world another. Therefore God reveals Himself to him as a
Person.... Think of Brahman, Existence-Knowledge-Bliss
Absolute, as a shoreless ocean. Through the cooling influence, as
it were, of the bhakta's love, the water has frozen at places into
blocks of ice. In other words, God now and then assumes various
forms for his Lovers and reveals Himself to them as a Person. But
with the rising of the sun of Knowledge, the blocks melt. (Sri
Ramakrishna, 148)

To Dickinson, Ramakrishna's teachings were in part restatements of similar ideas he had gathered from Plato. In *Plato and his Dialogues*, Dickinson noted that the true purpose of male love was 'to lead the soul of the lovers to the higher life' and quoted Plato's words, 'that it is not easy to find a better assistant than Love in seeking to communicate immortality to our natures' (Dickinson 1944 210; 227). The *bhakta*, like the follower of Plato and the pairs of male lovers he described, needed to find a physical image of Love, before they were to move to the next stage of Love of the Divine for itself alone.

At Ramakrishna's ashram, as a spiritual exercise known as 'the discipline of madhur bhava', a male devotee would regard himself as a woman 'in order to develop the most intense form of love for Sri Krishna, the only purusha, or man in the universe' (Sri Ramakrishna, 23). Sri Ramakrishna himself would dress in a woman's costume (Bullough, 268; Isherwood 1965, 111-5) and would worship God as his beloved Krishna, looking upon himself as one of the God's handmaidens. The ritual would culminate with the devotees calling for Krishna, after which they 'felt a surge of divine emotion and danced around the Master. He too danced in an ecstasy of joy', and by doing so he was continuing a religious practice with a centuries-long history in India (Sri Ramakrishna, 445-8). As both Dickinson and Forster would have known, the Greek Aphrodite (Aphrodite Urania, the goddess of the 'Uranians') 'was worshipped by men habited as women' (Carpenter 1984, 257); the practice may have had a special resonance for Dickinson for he felt he possessed 'a woman's soul shut up in a man's body' (Dickinson 1973, 111).

Christopher Isherwood in his book on Ramakrishna explains that '*madhur bhava*' is a method of overcoming the illusion of sex-distinction by revealing that these distinctions are not absolute (Isherwood 1965, 112). Isherwood also noted that devotees were taught to meditate on the relationship between Krishna and the milkmaid, Radha, a relationship, that is, between a God and his lover, rather than the relationship of a husband and wife, 'because, it is said, one must have the reckless love and disregard for public opinion which is felt by a paramour and his mistress; married people are careful of the rules of respectability and their behaviour is more circumspect'. The relationship however is not thought of as sexual for it is deemed to 'far transcend even the thought of sex' (74).

Such sincerely held beliefs were the acceptable public aspect of transvestism in the worship of Krishna, unlike the unacceptable aspect found in the *hijra* prostitutes, about whom Forster had solicited information from Masood prior to his completion of *A Passage to India*. It is these aspects of Krishna worship referred to in the novel which not only inform the scenes in the temple at Mau, but significantly are also enacted, in private, by the male troupe of actors kept by the Maharajah there. These dancers are clearly based on those kept by the Maharajah of Chhatarpur, and described by Forster in his letters to his mother (Lago and Furbank 1, 165-6 and 171), by Dickinson (Dickinson 1914, 20-3) and later by Ackerley (1932, 39-51). What had been, in 1912, an essentially private vision, to be shared only with a few like-minded friends at the court of Chhatarpur, becomes in Forster's novel the public enactment of his private dream in the temple at Mau.* For there, too, when Krishna danced 'all became one' (PTI, 294).

The closing section of the novel begins with Godbole's summons to Tukaram, a Marathi saint and poet, a paragon of *bhakti*, and beloved friend of the seventeenth-century Marathi ruler Sivaji (PTI, 274). Forster, in *The Hill of Devi*, described Sivaji as a great warrior belonging to a low caste, who like the other devotees of Krishna, believed 'in bhakti, in our union with the Divine through love' (HD, 71). Sivaji's friend, from an even lower caste than he, the poet-saint Tukaram, worshipped God in the figure of the merciful Vithoba of Pandharpur, whose name recalls that of Vithobai, the homosexual chieftain in Forster's 'unpublishable' short story 'The Life to Come'. And according to the historian, Ramakrishna Gopal Bhandarkar, 'Vithoba', and 'Vitthala', are local names at Pandharpur for the god Krishna (Bhandarkar, 127). Dilip Chitre, in a recent collection of the poems of Tukaram, reveals that both names are derived from the name 'Vitthal', and that Vithabai (with an 'a' instead of Forster's 'o'), means 'Lady Vitthal', a feminised form of the masculine proper noun (Chitre, 226). Clearly, Forster's textual playfulness — if not 'campness'

---

* One of the friends to accompany Forster to India in 1912 was Robert Calverley Trevelyan (1872–1951). Trevelyan became enthusiastic about the Red Temple at Brindaban, the legendary site of Krishna's dance with the Gopis. Brindaban, and Gokul, the site of Krishna's birth 'haunted' him, and 'after seeing a mystery play at Chhatarpur' was inspired to write his play *The Pearl-Tree*, which was later turned into an opera by Edgar Bainton (Trevelyan 449).

here — encodes Vithobai's sexual passivity in his name. Chitre confirms that for Tukaram, 'Vitthal and Krishna are synonymous' (219), and he provides a description of the statue of Vitthal at Pandharpur. Reading the description it is easy to see why this manifestation of the god had aroused Forster's interest, and why Tukaram's Krishna should be specifically invoked by Godbole:

> In brief, Vitthal's image at Pandharpur is a male figure, stone-black in colour, and standing erect on a raised slab known as 'the Brick'; arms akimbo and hands on hips, the figure is perfectly symmetrical; in terms of proportions, it is a stocky figure of medium build... the image is adorned with sweet basil beads turned into a necklace; the left hand holds a sea-conch and the right hand holds the stalk of a lotus... the cloth that covers the loins is skin-tight and the shape of the genitals shows through the garment; (Chitre, 226-7)

In *A Passage to India* the link is forged between the love of the friends Sivaji and Tukaram, and their union through *bhakti* with Krishna; the emphasis here being on the relationships and iconography which inform the vision of universality at the height of the temple ceremony. Krishna is regarded as the eighth incarnation of Vishnu (Knappert, 270). Edward Carpenter associated Vishnu with Evolution, being in his words 'the process by which the inner spirit unfolds and generates the universe of sensible forms', which was accompanied by a devolved form of the godhead, 'the form of humanity', represented by Siva 'as a complete full length human being conjoining the two sexes in one person' (Carpenter 1910, 307-8). The incarnation of Vishnu whose birth is celebrated at Mau is not only that of Krishna, but an incarnation which represents evolution in 'the universe of sensible forms', leading ultimately to the birth of a new human being 'cojoining the sexes in one person'; and at this festival of friends, 'all men loved each other' (PTI, 294).

Godbole dances in the temple at the height of the Krishna rituals and becomes possessed by the spirit of the God. Loving all of creation he sees visions of Mrs Moore (herself now transformed into the goddess 'Esmiss, Esmoor' by the Indian peasantry), and of a wasp. His concept of the divine knows no barriers, he even admits to the presence of God this 'little, little wasp' (PTI, 281), which Mr Sorley, the modern young Christian missionary, had previously declared unsuitable for admission to heaven (PTI, 32). Godbole declares that the heaven of Krishna knows none of the barriers erected by Christians, and one can call to mind here so many groups whom Christian

---

* In Forster's short story 'Mr Andrews', after his death the protagonist goes to Heaven, where he notices, amongst all the places reserved for various religious groups, that 'There was even an intermediate state for those who wished it' (CS, 185). 'Intermediate' was of course Carpenter's word for homosexual. Forster's publishers had qualms about printing the story, believing some would deem it blasphemous (Lago and Furbank 1, 116 n6).

theologians have declared to be unsuitable for admission to heaven; unlike conventional Christianity, Hinduism allows its male lovers into paradise.* Forster noted the inclusiveness of Krishna worship in his Indian Journal entry of 9 January 1913: 'Krishna worship admits all types and no doubt same is true of Siva though his symbol [the lingam] suggests only one' (HD, 176).

Returning to the discussion of Proust's influence on Forster in writing this novel, where the writer spoke of the souls of lovers being transmigrated into animals after death, perhaps the wasp in the vision at the temple is there to recall a lost love, a Friend now returned to his lover in the presence of the god, perhaps even for Forster a Mohammed restored?

Godbole's invocation to the god to 'Come, come, come, come' (PTI, 281), has a parallel in the plaint of Vithobai, the Indian chieftain, in 'The Life to Come', which was written whilst Forster was working on *A Passage to India*. The story deals with the homosexual relationship between the Indian and a young Protestant missionary. After a night of shared sexual intimacy, the missionary, in a fit of self-righteousness, turns from his former friend. To the chieftain, during their night of love, God had come, and he patiently waits for God to come again, that is, for the young missionary to sleep with him once more. It is not difficult to link Vithobai's call to his male lover to come, to that of Godbole's call to Krishna to multiply himself into a hundred Krishnas and to send one to him. And both works make use of the refrain, 'God is Love'.

At the high point of the Krishna ritual, when the model of the god's birthplace is thrown into the sacred tank, so too are Fielding, Aziz, Ralph and Stella thrown into the water as their boats collide. Having discovered that his friend is innocent of the duplicity and betrayal he had earlier believed him to have perpetrated, Aziz begins his friendship with Fielding anew.

Forster felt such breaks to be beneficial in a friendship, as his letter to Malcolm Darling of 15 September 1924 indicates. There he speaks initially of his old university days at King's College, Cambridge, before turning to his novel:

> ... I have acquired a feeling that people must go away from each
> other (spiritually) every now and then, and improve themselves if
> the relationship is to develop or even endure. *A Passage to India*
> describes such a going away — preparatory to the next advance,
> which I am not capable of describing. It seems to me that
> individuals progress alternately by loneliness and intimacy, and
> that legend of the multiplied Krishna... serves as a symbol of a
> state where the two might be combined. (Lago and Furbank 2,
> 63)

Aziz and Fielding are reconciled, but not re-united. Nevertheless a start towards that union, the 'next advance' which Forster declares himself 'not capable of describing', is made, perhaps the evolution of 'the universe of sen-

sible forms' which Carpenter had recognised? As usual the movement by Aziz
begins with his use of Persian poetry:

> When he had finished, the mirror of the scenery was shattered,
> the
> meadow disintegrated into butterflies. A poem about Mecca —
> the
> Caaba of Union — the thorn-bushes where pilgrims die before
> they have seen the Friend — they flitted next; he thought of his
> wife and then the whole semi-mystic, semi-sensuous overturn, so
> characteristic of his spiritual life, came to an end like a landslip
> and rested in its due place, and he found himself riding in the
> jungle with his dear Cyril. (PTI, 310)

It is immediately noticeable that Fielding is no longer referred to by his
surname, then a common way for a male to address another, for Aziz reverts to
his earlier, intimate but short-lived way of referring to him by his first name,
Cyril, or rather, more intimately here as 'dear Cyril'.

In his notes to the Everyman edition of the novel Forster revealed that
the poem referred to in the passage came from the Masnavi of the Sufi poet
Jalaluddin Rumi. Tariq Rahman defined it as an example of the genre of Ghazal
poetry, seeing it as a poem of union, termed 'Visal' (Rahman 1988 110), and
June Perry Levine specifically identified the poem as 'The Call of the Beloved'.
As is common to the Ghazal genre, desire for union with the Friend is linked
to desire for union with God ('the Caaba of Union').

When Krishna's shrine was open, the friends had reunited, but as the
festivities were drawing to a close, this magical period was too, for 'The divisions of daily life were returning, the shrine had almost shut' (PTI 311). Finally,
however, Aziz and Fielding part, they cannot yet attain the highest union of
friendship, too many barriers, '\ grim / sentries' and 'solemn guards' lie in their
way — '"No not yet," and the sky said, "No, not there"' (PTI, 312).

At first glance the novel appears to end on a negative note, and this is the
judgement of Tariq Rahman who writes that 'A Passage to India is, in the final
analysis, the story of a blighted homosexual love-affair' (Rahman 1984, 53).
This view, however, ignores the possible development of the relationship at
some future date for, as Forster's letter earlier indicated, separation is part of
the necessary progress of a relationship, and there is yet to come a further
stage, which, as a writer, he felt incapable of describing. Aziz himself avers
that once the struggle for Indian nationalism has finished, 'you [Fielding] and
I shall be friends' (PTI, 312). 'No not yet' and 'No, not there' implicitly point
toward the possible existence of a time and a place in the future, which will see
the final union of the lovers. The words echo those given earlier in the description of the ceremony at Mau, where the narrator speaks of 'a passage not easy,
not now, not here, not to be apprehended except when it is unattainable; the

God to be thrown was an emblem of that' (PTI, 304). So if the 'God to be thrown is an emblem' of the 'unattainable' — the future hope of a better time and place — what does this God represent? At the close of the novel, the horses, the earth, the temples, the sky, and a long list of other objects seem to want to divide Fielding from Aziz, significantly though, the sun is excluded from this list, for representing Apollo, he would not wish the friends to part. In the ceremony described at the temple two 'gods' are present. The 'Indian body again triumphant', that is the Apollo of the Dorian Greeks, 'the representative divinity of the Uranian love', and Krishna, who is linked to Vitthal, Vithabai, and to the friendship and *bhakti* of Tukaram and Sivaji; in short the two deities invoked represent western and eastern utopian visions of the collective spiritual union of individual friendships, and they are the 'next advance', Vishnu's evolution, which Forster, unlike Carpenter, confessed he could not describe.

The Indian critic J Birje-Patil discusses the close of the novel with reference to *Maurice*, seeing links between the yearning for a better world which informs both novels:

> Would it be far-fetched to imagine that Krishna's Brindaban
> garden where, according to the legend, he lived in a state of
> pastoral polygamy, served as a 'substitute greenwood'? The Alecs
> and Maurices were expelled from their greenwood in England and
> they found in Dewas a place of refuge which lacked some features
> of the original yet satisfied their basic needs. When, overcome by
> his sense of isolation, Maurice calls Alec, the word that leaps out
> is Godbole's 'come'. 'Whom had he called? He had been thinking
> of nothing and the word had leapt out... He wasn't alone'. [M
> 163] (Das and Beer 107)

Birje-Patil's theory is persuasive, but it could be argued that Edenic Mau* and the court at Chhatarpur, rather than Dewas, seemed to Forster to offer the ideal Indian greenwood, for it was there rather than at Dewas that male love was accorded its due recognition, and where Krishna was due to come and be a Friend.

Birje-Patil is correct to note that Hinduism could be seen to offer Forster, and those like him, 'a spiritual order that would accommodate his uranian impulses', a validation of feeling which contemporary Christianity would never provide. In particular, he notes that the story of Krishna and the Milkmaids also offered 'a subtle combination of the religious and erotic which would certainly fascinate someone in search of an order which would allow rationali-

* It is perhaps more than a coincidence that 'Mau' forms the first three letterse of Maurice; 'rice' is traditionally thrown at Indian and some European weddings, and hence suggestive of permanent union. What better name than Maurice therefore for Forster to give to a character who does realise his Utopian dream?

sation of impulses whose very existence was an affront to the social order he had inherited' (106-7).

G. L. Dickinson in his essay 'Religion and Immortality', which first appeared in 1911, pointed out that Christianity 'cannot serve as an expression of our emotional attachment to the world', and that for such expression 'we have to turn elsewhere, and construct for ourselves, if we can, new myths' (Dickinson 1948 165). Dickinson, like Forster after him, then goes on in this essay to use Walt Whitman's poem 'Passage to India' in his quest to elucidate the meaning of immortality (202-3), before speaking of the survival of the self after death, and of the hope that if we have formed in this life 'a beautiful relation, it will not perish at death, but be perpetuated... in some future life' (204-5). Having discarded his Christian beliefs many years before, Forster attempts in *A Passage to India* to follow Dickinson's injunction to find new myths* to express our emotional attachment to the world, and, in his continuing grief at Mohammed's death, to suggest, artistically at least, the continuance of a 'beautiful relation' after death.

History attests to the interrelationship of sexuality and religion, and Brian Reade in his Introduction to *Sexual Heretics* discusses the specific relationship between spiritual feeling and homosexual emotion as expressed in the poems of Gerard Manley Hopkins (1844–89). Reade views certain poems, notably 'The Bugler's First Communion', as evidence of a link between homosexual emotional crises and religious emotional crises generally, during the late Victorian and Edwardian periods in Britain:**

> The poems... indicate what links arise, or may have arisen then, between homosexual emotional crises and religious emotional crises. It is not hard to see how the difficulty of gratifying erotic emotions on one plane — the difficulty of *l'amour de l'impossible* — led by imaginative extensions to a vanishing point of safety in 'God'. For the 'love of God', a predominantly Christian conception, can only be communicated in figures of speech inspired originally by erotic sensations; and this spiritual love on the part of men for a masculine force can thus be rendered backwards into homosexual emotion which has taken refuge in the clouds of intellect. (Reade, 12)

Utilising Reade's analysis, Forster, whilst having no belief in a Christian god, could be seen to have created, artistically, a pagan heaven which would provide a setting for the reconciliation, and resolution, of sexual and religious feeling. If 'God si [sic] Love', then Krishna's Brindaban could promise a spir-

---

* In 'Passage to India' Whitman also called for the myths of India to be used to reveal the life of the spirit to the Western World (ll,16-29).

** A. C. Benson underwent a similar crisis as an undergraduate at Cambridge following a difficult relationship with a younger man (Masters, 76-8).

itual home for that homosexual love which, in conventional Christianity, condemns a 'sodomite' to hell. And in two of his short stories, 'The Point of It' and 'Mr Andrews', both dating from around 1911, Forster had already presented an afterlife in which male friendships had triumphed. In 'The Point of It', the protagonist Michael is literally rescued from hell by the re-appearance of his friend Harold. And in 'Mr Andrews', the protagonist meets a Turk in a heaven where 'No aspiration of humanity was unfulfilled' (CS, 185). Whilst Forster in his maturity could not be regarded as a believer in any religion, nevertheless homosexuality and religion were clearly linked in the early part of his life, for he counted his emancipation from Christianity as the first grand discovery of his youth, and the realisation of his sexual love for H. O. Meredith as the second (Furbank 1, 98).

Despite Stallybrass's scepticism about the idea that close parallels exist between Forster's novel and Whitman's poem, some do seem valid. In Whitman's poem, his vision of the meeting of East and West through technological advances, when 'All affection shall be fully responded to, the secret shall be told,' and 'All these separations and gaps shall be taken up and hook'd and linked together' (ll 108-9) is obviously echoed in the final scene at Mau, when in the dance of Krishna and the milkmaids, 'all became one'. The festival in the temple where 'all men loved each other' recalls Whitman's notions of 'adhesiveness' and 'comradeship'. Further parallels are also obvious. When Whitman presents a vision of the soul's final resting-place, 'the aim attain'd', his male lovers, like those of Forster's, unite before a God:

Reckoning ahead O soul, when thou, the time achieved,
The seas all cross'd, weather'd the capes, the voyage done,
Surrounded, copest, frontest God, yieldest, the aim attain'd
As fill'd with friendship, love complete, the Elder Brother found,
The Younger melts in fondness in his arms. (ll, 219-23)

Despite the evidence scattered throughout the text pointing towards male love, criticism of Forster's novel has invariably centred on his denunciation of the British Raj (even though he was just as scathing about Indian society in the novel and in his supplementary writings). Consequently 'the secret understanding of the heart' remained obscure to all but those readers attuned to the writer's coded style. His vision in the final part of *A Passage to India* celebrates a collaboration, not in the actual writing of the novel, but in its inspiration, which artistically unites Forster's friends and those writers who appealed to him. This vision of male love promising to transcend a world which seemed set to destroy it, is informed by his friends — Mahommed, Masood, Carpenter, Dickinson, T. E. Lawrence, D. H. Lawrence, Ackerley, the Maharajahs of Chhatarpur and of Dewas Senior — and by writers from both East and West — Whitman, Proust, Tukaram and the Oriental poets quoted by Aziz — all united in a commendation of the spirit of *bhakti*, under the gaze of an 'Apollo—

Krishna', who represents the more progressive elements of Western and Oriental religion.

Clearly such a massive project required an all-encompassing vision, and it is a tribute to Forster's genius that he could attempt it, and succeed, in a novel intended for open publication. Forster, however, would perhaps have cut this rather grand notion down to size with a suitable, deflationary camp remark, like the one he made to Duncan Grant in 1922. Whilst Forster was working on *A Passage to India*, Grant asked him about the novel. Forster replied, cryptically, the book 'was to have a great central nave, a succession of side-chapels and a lady chapel at the end' (Furbank 2, 109).* Perhaps this was meant to be a chapel to Vithobai or, recalling *The Longest Journey*, a chapel to the Cnidian Demeter?

---

* cf. Forster's description of Mau in his Indian Journal of 1912-13: 'Mau is on a Lake, beyond which is a hill and tombs. One — 200 years old — is called the "Queen's". "She was a nymph, and used to walk on the top of water-lilies". Here H H [the Maharajah of Chhatarpur] would meet Krishna, and is never happy on account of this loneliness.... And it is true he desires the impossible. Yet how unassuageable his sorrow, because it is a poet's and includes ours. Egoism without imagination is the vilest, with it the highest. — We drove back starlit' (HD, 156-7).

CONCLUSION

Forster's homosexuality was clearly the major factor in his personal and creative life. Numerous themes in his work echo the concerns and influences of fellow homosexual artists of the period, as can be seen, for example, in his references to Italy, ancient Greece, bathing, and Persian poetry. In many other aspects of his writing, too, he was clearly drawing upon material familiar to a contemporary, educated, bourgeois, homosexual subculture. Forster was quite aware how much his being sexually different from the majority had affected his social and creative existence, noting bitterly in 1963, towards the end of his life: 'I am almost 85 how annoyed I am with Society for wasting my time by making homosexuality criminal. The subterfuges, the self-consciousness that might have been avoided' (AS, xxx). His struggle with homophobic social attitudes had been a feature of his entire life, and, not suprisingly perhaps, such negative attitudes were also to influence his reputation and the standing of his works long after his death.

In 1932, when Forster was engaged in composing his biography of G. L. Dickinson, he had to guide him his subject's autobiographical manuscript, in which he detailed his homosexual experiences. Forster chose to leave out those frank confessions in his own final text, feeling inevitably 'condemned to omissions'. However he made it clear to his own friend, Joe Ackerley, that he desired a full biography of himself to be produced after his death, one where everything should be told (Furbank 2, 177). Despite Furbank's own later caveats about the use of biography to find 'explanations' of Forster's novels, and the criticism of those who seemed to suggest that homosexuality had only a peripheral inference on the manifestation of Forster's genius, the invaluable biographical details which Furbank collected have revealed much about the sources of Forster's inspiration, and about the writer's treatment of the material he took from his life as a homosexual man in a very hostile world. Forster would have approved of Furbank's candour. And being aware, as the writer was, of 'the sexual bias in literary criticism' (AS xvi), he would not have suprised that the revelation of his sexual orientation had led some critics to re-assess the merits of his works rather negatively.

To some Forster scholars, homosexuality is a topic which perhaps ought not to be pursued, for as noted in the Introduction to this work, there has been a fear that to concentrate on this issue will somehow diminish the standing of the writer. Regrettably these fears did not prove ill-founded, at least in the 1970s when the pressure to downplay his homosexuality, following the generally negative criticism which greeted the publication of *Maurice*, seemed strong.

Monique Wittig contends that a text by a minority writer only works if it succeeds in making the minority point of view universal. The fear amongst some Forster critics seems to be that the writer's work is inevitably diminished by referring to his homosexuality, for, by doing so, his oeuvre's much asserted 'universality' would be jeopardised. If Forster studies venture too far out of the closet, and stray into the area of gay studies, or even further into 'queer studies', the implication is that his reputation would diminish.

One critic writing shortly after Forster's death even seemed to warn that the achievement of gay civil rights would seriously affect the quality of a homosexual writer's work. Jeffrey Meyers asserted in 1977: 'When the laws of obscenity were changed and homosexuality became legal, apologies seemed inappropriate, the theme [of homosexuality] surfaced defiantly and sexual acts were grossly described', and the 'emancipation of the homosexual has led, paradoxically, to the decline of his art' (Myers, 3).

The damage critics have been willing to inflict on Forster's reputation, armed with the club of his homosexuality with which to beat the author, continued through into the 1980s. Joseph Epstein asserted that the chief impulse behind his novels 'with their paeans and pleas for the life of the instincts, was itself homosexual' (Epstein, 18). His point of course, is valid, but he adds to this observation a crude, derogatory dismissal of Forster's work, declaring that in 'a curious way the effect of this is to render E. M. Forster's novels obsolete, and in a way that art of the first magnitude never becomes' (Epstein, 18). The message from Epstein is clear, homosexual art is second best, and homosexuals creatively inferior, only the inspired art of heterosexuals can lay claim to 'the first magnitude'.

The fact that a new generation of gay men and women in Western societies were openly declaring their sexuality on a scale not known before, and were demanding civil rights, seemed to provide a marked contrast to the comparatively quiet protest of the sufferings of Maurice, who, whilst himself condemning society, saw change only as a very distant prospect, and escape into the greenwood with Alec as the only answer to its oppressiveness. It could be that the contrast between the vocal gay reformers and the rather measured plea for tolerance in Forster's work led some critics, who admired his gentle, encoded approach, to lecture against the adoption of a gay critical stance in examining the work of the writer. Such a critical position infers that a gay person fights only for 'gay' causes (as if such causes can be separated from other social struggles), and reduces everything to a perspective based solely on sexual orientation. In reality, however, such a view is simply heterosexist prejudice projected onto gay men and lesbians generally, for more usually it is others in society, ostensibly heterosexual, who are incapable of viewing gay people as anything other than a race apart. The present writer's aim, in concentrating on Forster's sexuality, has not been to feed such prejudice, but to open up discussion of the issue by refusing to accept that the subject should remain a marginalised issue in Forster studies. It is a quarter of a century since *Maurice* was first published; the information that Forster was homosexual and much explicit biographical detail has been in the public domain all that time, yet his works remain highly regarded. 'One little, little wasp' of gay criticism will hardly transform his reputation, and a thorough examination of the effect his sexuality had on his work is clearly long overdue.

The primary objection to the approach adopted in this work is that by arguing that Forster's sexuality is central to the understanding of his writing, somehow the universality of his work (and by implication its power and applicability) will be diminished. This argument is mistaken. All written work is produced by a person with a sexual identity (even if this identity is one which purports to hold itself aloof from all sexuality), in a particular social, economic, political and historical environment. Heterosexuality, in none of its variant forms, can lay a greater claim to universality than can homosexuality, for all sexualities are contingent. There are multiple sexual identities, none of which are consistently stable, yet it is possible generally to map these changes within a writer and to speculate on their effects. To do so effectively, and without prejudice, there is a need to accept Margaret Schlegel's assertion in *Howards End* that 'people are far more different than is pretended' and such difference is 'part of the battle against sameness. Differences — eternal differences, planted by God in a single family, so that there may always be colour; sorrow perhaps, but colour in the daily gray' (HE, 335-6). Forster, for whom Margaret speaks, was clearly well aware of the specifities (cultural, racial, socio-economic, psycho-sexual, for example) of subjectivities and of identities, as his work amply demonstrates. He recognised that no one is a universal type, and that, consequently, no one is a universal writer.

BIBLIOGRAPHY

WORKS BY E. M. FORSTER

SECTION ONE
All editions are 'London: Edward Arnold, Abinger edition'

Where Angels Fear To Tread, 1975
The Lucy Novels, 1977
The Longest Journey, 1984
A Room With A View, 1977
Howards End, 1973
The Manuscripts of Howards End, 1973
A Passage to India, 1978
The Manuscripts of A Passage to India, 1978
The Hill of Devi and Other Indian Writings, 1983
The Life to Come and Other Stories, 1972
Arctic Summer and Other Fiction, 1980
Goldworthy Lowes Dickinson and Related Writings, 1973
Aspects of the Novel and Related Writings, 1974

SECTION TWO
The following are also 'London: Edward Arnold',
but do not form part of the Abinger edition

Goldsworthy Lowes Dickinson, 1938
Abinger Harvest, 1942
Maurice, 1971
Marianne Thornton (1797–1887): A Domestic Biography, 1956

SECTION THREE
Miscellaneous publishers

The Celestial Omnibus and Other Stories, London: Sidgwick & Jackson, 1924.
The Eternal Moment and Other Stories, London: Sidgwick & Jackson, 1928.
Collected Short Stories of E. M. Forster, London: Sidgwick and Jackson, 1947.
Pharos and Pharillon, London: The Hogarth Press, 1961.
England's Pleasant Land, London: The Hogarth Press, 1940.
Two Cheers For Democracy, Harmondsworth: Penguin, 1972.
Commonplace Book, Aldershot: Wildwood House Ltd, 1988.
Alexandria: A History and a Guide, London: Michael Haag Ltd, 1982.

SECTION FOUR
Articles and Letters

'Society and the Homosexual: A Magistrate's Figures', in *The New Statesman and Nation*, 31 October 1953.
Letter on 'Vice Prosecutions' in *The Spectator*, 17 January 1958.
Letter on 'Wolfenden Report' in *The Times*, 9 May 1958.

SECONDARY SOURCES

Abrams, M. H., *A Glossary of Literary Terms*, New York: Holt, Rinehart and Winston Inc, 1985.
Ackerley, J. R., *Hindoo Holiday*, London: Chatto and Windus, 1932.
           My Sister and Myself; The Diaries of J R Ackerley, edited by Francis King, Oxford: Oxford
           University Press, 1990.
           E. M. Forster: A Portrait, London: Ian McKelvie, 1970.
Alexander, P. F., *William Plomer: A Biography*, Oxford: Oxford University Press, 1990.
d'Arch Smith, T., *Love in Earnest*, London: Routledge & Kegan Paul, 1970.
Aristophanes, *The Archanians: The Clouds: Lysistrata,* translated by A. H. Sommerstein,
           Harmondsworth: Penguin, 1979.
Ashby, M., *Forster Country*, Stevenage: Flaunden Press, 1991.
Auden, W. H., and Isherwood, C., *Journey to a War*, London: Faber and Faber, 1973.
Barth, A., *The Religions of India*, translated by Rev. J. Wood,
           London: Kegan Paul, Trench, Trubner & Co, 1932.
Bartlett, N., *Who Was That Man?* London: Serpent's Tail, 1988.
Bayley, J. *Housman's Poems*, Oxford: Clarendon Press, 1992.
Beauman, N., *Morgan: A Biography of E. M. Forster*, London: Hodder and Stoughton, 1993.
           A Very Great Profession, London: Virago Press, 1983.
Beer, J., *A Passage to India: Essays in Interpretation*. London: Macmillan Press, 1985.
Beer, J. B., *The Achievement of E. M. Forster*, London: Chatto and Windus, 1968.
Belshaw, P., *A Kind of Private Magic*, London: Andrew Deutsch, 1994.
Benson, A. C., *Edward Fitzgerald*, London: Macmillan and Co, 1925.
Benson, E. F., *As We Were: A Victorian Peep-show*, London: Longman, 1971.
Bergman, D., *Gaiety Transfigured*, Madison, Wisconsin and London:
           The University of Wisconsin Press, 1991.
Bhandarkar, R. G., *Vaisnavism, Saivism and Minor Religious Systems*,
           First Edition 1913. Reprint, New Delhi & Madras: Asian Educational Services, 1995.
Bharucha, R., 'Forster's Friends' *Raritan* 5, 4 (1986), 105-22.
Bloch, I., *The Sexual Life of Our Time*, London: William Heinemann, 1908.
Boswell J., *The Marriage of Likeness: Same Sex Unions in Pre-Modern Europe*,
           London: Fontana Press, 1996.
Bradbury, M. (editor), *A Passage to India,*London: Macmillan Casebook Series, 1986.
Bradford, Rev. E. E., *To Boys Unknown*, London: Gay Men's Press, 1988.
Brander, L., *E. M. Forster, A Critical Study*, London: Rupert Hart-Davies, 1968.
Bray, A., *Homosexuality in Renaissance England* (second edition), London: Gay Men's Press, 1988.
Braybrooke, N. (editor), *The Letters of J. R. Ackerley*, London: Duckworth, 1975.
Bristow, J., *Empire Boys: Adventures in a Man's World*, London: Harper Collins Academic, 1991.
           (editor) *Sexual Sameness: Textual Differences in Lesbian and Gay Writing*,
           London and New York: Routledge, 1992.
Brome, V., *Havelock Ellis: Philosopher of Sex*, London: Routledge and Kegan Paul, 1979.

Bullough, V. L., *Sexual Variance in Society and History*, New York: John Wiley & Sons, 1976.

Burton, Sir R., *Love, War and Fancy: The Customs and Manners of the East from Writings on The Arabian Nights* by Sir Richard Burton, edited by K. Walker. London: William Kimber & Co, 1964.

Carpenter, E., *From Adam's Peak to Elephanta: Sketches in Ceylon and India*, second edition London: Swan Sonnenschein & Co, 1910.

    Towards Democracy, London: George Allen & Unwin, 1915.

    Days With Walt Whitman, London: George Allen & Unwin, 1921.

    Anthology of Friendship (Ioläus), London: George Allen and Unwin, 1929.

    Selected Writings Volume One: Sex, London: Gay Men's Press, 1984.

Carpenter, H., *W. H. Auden: A biography*, London: George Allen & Unwin, 1981.

    Benjamin Britten: A Biography, London: Faber and Faber, 1992.

Cavaliero, G., *A Reading of E. M. Forster*, London: Macmillan Press, 1979.

Chaudhuri, N. C., *The Continent of Circe*, Bombay: Jaico, 1965.

Chitre, D., *Says Tuka: Selected Poetry of Tukaram*, New Delhi: Penguin, 1991.

Clarke, C. (editor), *The Rainbow and Women in Love*, London: Macmillan Casebook Series, 1969.

Cockshut, A. O. J., *Man and Woman: A Study of Love and the Novel 1740–1940*, London: Collins, 1977.

Colmer, J., *E. M. Forster: The Personal Voice*, London: Routledge and Kegan Paul, 1975.

Daley, H,. *This Small Cloud*, London: Weidenfeld and Nicholson, 1986.

Das, G. K. and Beer, J. (editors), *E. M. Forster: A Human Exploration*, London: Macmillan Press, 1979.

Davies, T. and Wood, N. (editors), *A Passage to India*, London: Open University Press, Theory in Practice series, 1994.

Dellamora, R., *Masculine Desire: The Sexual Politics of Victorian Aestheticism*, Chapel Hill: University of North Carolina Press, 1990.

Dick, K. (editor), *Writers at Work*, Harmondsworth: Penguin, 1972.

Dickinson, G. L., *The Greek View of Life*, seventh edition. London: Methuen and Co, 1909.

    Appearances; being notes of Travel, London & Toronto: J. M. Dent & Sons, 1914.

    Plato and his Dialogues, London: George Allen and Unwin, 1944.

    Letters from John Chinaman and other Essays, London: George Allen & Unwin, 1948.

    The Autobiography of G. Lowes Dickinson, edited by D. Proctor, London: Duckworth, 1973.

Dover, K. J., *Greek Homosexuality*, London: Duckworth, 1978.

Dowling, D., *Bloomsbury Aesthetics and the Novels of Forster and Woolf*, London: Macmillan Press, 1985.

Drabble, M., *The Oxford Companion to English Literature*, Oxford: Oxford University Press, 1993.

    Angus Wilson: A Biography, London: Secker & Warburg, 1995.

Dynes, W. R. (editor), *Encyclopedia of Homosexuality* (two volumes), Chicago and London: St James Press, 1990.

Eagleton, M., *Feminist Literary Theory; A Reader*, London: Basil Blackwell, 1986.

Edwardes, M., *Raj — The Story of British India*, London: Pan, 1967.

Ellis, H., Studies in the Psychology of Sex (two volumes), New York: Random House, undated.

Emerson, R. W., *The Conduct of Life and Society and Solitude*, London and New York: Macmillan and Co, 1888.

    Essays: First and Second Series, London: Dent and Co, 1906.

Epstein, J., 'One Cheer for E. M. Forster', *Quadrant* 29, 12 (218), (1985), 8-18.

Erkkila, B., *Whitman the Political Poet*, Oxford: Oxford University Press, 1989.

Fitzgerald, E., *Letters and Literary Remains of Edward Fitzgerald*, edited by William Aldis Wright (three volumes), London: Macmillan and Co, 1889.

Furbank, P. N., *E. M. Forster: A Life*

    Volume 1, 'The Growth of the Novelist' 1879–1914

    Volume 2, 'Polycrates' Ring' 1914–1970

published as one volume. London: Cardinal (Sphere Books), 1988.

Ganguly, A. P., *India: Mystic, Complex and Real — An Interpretation of E. M. Forster's A Passage to India*, Delhi: Motilal Banarsidass Publishers, 1990.

Gardner, E. A., *A Handbook of Greek Sculpture*, second edition, London: Macmillan and Co, 1920.

Gardner, P. (editor), *E. M. Forster: The Critical Heritage*, London: Routledge and Kegan Paul, 1984.

Gillie, C., *A Preface to Forster*, London: Longman, 1983.

Gishford, A. (editor), *Tribute to Benjamin Britten on his Fiftieth Birthday*, London: Faber and Faber, 1963.

Graves, R., *The Greek Myths* (two volumes), Harmondsworth: Penguin, 1977.

Graves, R. P., *A. E. Housman: The Scholar Poet*, London: Routledge and Kegan Paul, 1979.

Grey, A., *Quest For Justice: Towards Homosexual Emancipation*, London: Sinclair-Stevenson 1992.

Grosskurth, P., *Havelock Ellis*, London: Allen Lane, 1980.

Hammond, N. G. L., and Scullard, H. H., *The Oxford Classical Dictionary*, second edition, Oxford: Clarendon Press, 1970.

Herz, J. S., *The Short Narratives of E. M. Forster*, London: Macmillan Press, 1988.

Herz, J. S. and Martin, R. K., *E. M. Forster: Centenary Revaluations*, London: Macmillan Press, 1982.

Hoare, P., *Serious Pleasures: The Life of Stephen Tennant*, London: Hamish Mamilton, 1990.

Hodges, A., and Hutter, D., *With Downcast Gays*, London: Pomegranate Press, 1974.

Holroyd, M., *Lytton Strachey: A Biography*, Harmondsworth: Penguin, 1971.

Holt, L. E., 'E. M. Forster and Samuel Butler', *PMLA* 61 (1946), 804-19.

Housman, A. E., *Last Poems*, London: Grant Richards Ltd, 1922.

    The Collected Poems of A. E. Housman, London: Jonathan Cape, 1939.

Hyam, R., *Empire and Sexuality*, Manchester and New York: Manchester University Press, 1990.

Hyde, H. Montgomery, *Solitary in the Ranks*, London: Constable and Co, 1977.

Irigaray, L., 'When the Goods Get Together', in Marks, E. and de Courtivron, I, *New French Feminisms: An Anthology*, Amherst: University of Massachusetts Press, 1980.

Isherwood, C., *Ramakrishna and his Disciples*, London: Methuen & Co, 1965.

    Christopher and his Kind 1929–1939, London: Eyre Methuen, 1977.

    Diaries Volume One: 1939-1960, edited by Katherine Bucknell, London: Methuen, 1996.

Jaffrey, Z., *The Invisibles: A Tale of the Eunuchs of India*, London: Weidenfeld and Nicholson, 1997.

King, D., 'The Influence of Forster's Maurice on Lady Chatterley's Lover', *Contemporary Literature* 23, 1 (1982), 65-82.

King, F., *E. M. Forster and his World*, London: Thames and Hudson, 1978.

Knappert, J., *Indian Mythology*, New Delhi: HarperCollins, 1992.

von Krafft-Ebing, R., *Psychopathia Sexualis*, Philadelphia: F A Davis & Co, 1916.

Lago, M. and Furbank, P. N. (editors), *Selected Letters of E. M. Forster, Volume One 1879–1920*, London: Collins, 1983; *Volume Two 1921–1970*, London: Collins, 1985.

Lawrence, D. H., *Women in Love*, Harmondsworth: Penguin, 1960.

Lawrence, T. E., *Selected Letters of T. E. Lawrence*, edited by David Garnett, London: World Books, 1941.

    T. E. Lawrence: The Selected Letters, edited by Malcolm Brown, New York: Paragon House, 1992.

Lehmann, J., *Christopher Isherwood: A Personal Memoir*, New York: Henry Holt and Company, 1987.

Lodge, D., *Modern Criticism and Theory*, London: Longman, 1988.

Macaulay, R., *The Writings of E. M. Forster*, London: The Hogarth Press, 1970.

Mahood, M., *The Colonial Encounter*, London: Rex Collings, 1977.

Mangan, J. A. and Walvin, J. (editors), *Manliness and Morality*, Manchester and New York: Manchester University Press, 1987.

Martin, J. S., *E. M. Forster: The Endless Journey*, Cambridge: Cambridge University Press, 1976.

Martin, R. B., *With Friends Possessed: A Life of Edward Fitzgerald*,

London: Faber and Faber Ltd, 1985.

Martin, R. K. and Piggford, G., *Queer Forster*, Chicago: University of Chicago Press, 1997.

Masters, B., *The Life of E. F. Benson*, London: Chatto & Windus, 1991.

McConkey, J. R., *The Novels of E. M. Forster*,
Ithaca, New York State: Cornell University Press, 1957.

McDowall, F. P. W., *E. M. Forster*, Boston: Twayne Publishers, 1982.

Meyers, J., *Homosexuality and Literature 1890–1930*, London and Atlantic Highlands, New Jersey:
The Athlone Press, 1977.

Moi, T., *Sexual/Textual Politics*, London: Methuen, 1985.

Murray, P. and Murray, L., *A Dictionary of Art and Artists*, Harmondsworth: Penguin, 1972.

Murray, S. O. and Roscoe, W. (eds), *Islamic Homosexualities: Culture, History, and Literature*,
New York: New York University Press, 1997.

Nanda, S., 'Gender Roles in India', in *Naz Ki Pukaar* issue 12 (January 1996).

Oosterhuis, H. and Kennedy, H., *Homosexuality and Male Bonding in Pre-Nazi Germany*,
Binghampton, New York: Harrington Park Press, 1991.

Page, N., *E. M. Forster's Posthumous Fiction*,
Victoria, British Columbia: University of Victoria Press, 1977.

Parker, P., *Ackerley: A Life of J. R. Ackerley*, London: Constable, 1989.

Pater, W., *Greek Studies*, London: Macmillan and Co, 1928.

Pinchin, J. L., *Alexandria Still; Forster, Durrell and Cavafy*,
Princeton: Princeton University Press, 1977.

Plato, *The Dialogues of Plato*, translated by Benjamin Jowett (five volumes),
Oxford: Clarendon Press, 1875.

Plato, and Xenophon, *Socratic Discourses*, London: J. M. Dent & Sons, 1913.

Plomer, W., *Electric Delights*, London: Jonathan Cape, 1978.

Raby, P., *Samuel Butler: A Biography*, London: The Hogarth Press, 1991.

Rahman, Tariq, 'The Significance of Oriental Poetry in E. M. Forster's *A Passage to India*',
Durham University Journal 81, 1 (1988), 101-110.
'The Homosexual Aspect of Forster's *A Passage to India*', *Studies in English Literature*,
Vol. Eng. (1984), 37-54.
'A Study of the Under-plot in E. M. Forster's *Where Angels Fear To Tread*',
Studies in English Literature (1988), 51-69.
'The Use of the Double Plot in E. M. Forster's "Ralph and Tony" and Other Stories',
The Literary Endeavour 9, (1-4), (1987–88), 49-59.

Raymond, E., *Tell England*, London: Cassell & Co Ltd, 1928.
The Story of My Days: An Autobiography 1888-1922, London: Cassell and Co, 1968.

Rau, S. R., *A Passage to India*, Madras: Oxford University Press, 1983.

Reade, B., *Sexual Heretics: Male Homosexuality in English Literature from 1850 to 1900*, London:
Routledge and Kegan Paul, 1970.

Rist, A. (trans.), *The Poems of Theocritus*,
Chapel Hill: The University of North Carolina Press, 1978.

Rolfe, F. W. (Baron Corvo), *Stories Toto Told Me*, London: Collins, 1969.
Collected Poems, London: Cecil & Amelia Woolf, 1974.
The Venice Letters, London: Cecil & Amelia Woolf, 1974.

Rose, M., *E. M. Forster*, London: Evans Bros Ltd, 1970.

Rowse, A. L., *Homosexuals in History: A Study in Ambivalence in Society, Literature and the Arts*,
London: Weidenfeld and Nicolson, 1977.

Rutherford, A. (editor), *Twentieth Century Interpretations of A Passage to India*, Englewood Cliffs,
New Jersey: Prentice-Hall, 1970.

Sadie, S. (editor), *The New Grove Dictionary of Music and Musicians*, 20 vols,
London: Macmillan, 1980

Said, E., *Orientalism*, Harmondsworth: Penguin, 1991.

Schmitt, A. and Sofer, J. (eds), *Sexuality and Eroticism among Males in Muslim Societies*,
New York: Harrington Park Press, 1992.

Sedgwick, E. K., *Between Men: English Literature and Male Homosocial Desire*, New York:
    Columbia University Press, 1985.
Shelley, P. B., *Shelley Memorials*, edited by Lady Shelley, London: Smith, Elder & Co, 1859.
Shonfield, A. et al, 'Forster's Earlier Life — extracts from a Radio 3 Discussion' in
    The Listener, 16 July 1970.
Sri Ramakrishna, *The Gospel of Sri Ramakrishna*, translated into English with an Introduction by
    Swami Nikhilananda, New York: Ramakrishna-Vivekananda Center, 1973.
Stallybrass, O., *Aspects of E. M. Forster*, London: Edward Arnold, 1969.
Stape, J. H., *An E. M. Forster Chronology*, London: Macmillan Press, 1993.
Stone, W., *The Cave and the Mountain: A Study of E. M. Forster*, Stanford:
    Stanford University Press, 1966.
Symonds, J. A., *In the Key of Blue*, London: Elkin Matthews & John Lane, 1893.
    Sketches and Studies in Italy, London, Smith, Elder & Co, 1879.
    The Memoirs of John Addington Symonds, edited by P. Grosskurth,
    New York: Random House, 1984.
    Shelley, London: Macmillan & Co, 1895.
    *A Problem in Greek Ethics: Being an Inquiry into the Phenomenon of Sexual Inversion
    addressed especially to Medical Psychologists and Jurists*, London: Privately Printed, 1908.
Theogood, J., 'Worlds Apart: A Propos E. M. Forster's Maurice',
    Recovering Literature 12 (1984), 41-50.
Thoreau, H. D., *Walden and Civil Disobedience*, New York: W W Norton & Co Inc, 1966.
Trevelyan, R., *The Golden Oriole*, New York: Touchstone, 1988.
Trevelyan, R. C., *The Collected Works of R. C. Trevelyan, Volume 1 Poems, Volume 2 Plays*, London:
    Longmans Green & Co Ltd, 1939.
Trilling, L., *E. M. Forster*, London: The Hogarth Press, 1967.
Tsuzuki, C., *Edward Carpenter*, Cambridge: Cambridge University Press, 1980.
Varty, A., 'E M Forster, Arnold Böcklin, and Pan',
    Review of English Studies 39, 156 (1988), 513-8.
Vidal, G., *The City and the Pillar*, London: NEL Four Square Books, 1967.
    Palimpsest: A Memoir, London: Abacus, 1996.
Walker, B., *Hindu World: An Encyclopedic Survey of Hinduism*, two volumes,
    London: George Allen and Unwin, 1968.
Watt, D., 'Mohammed el Adl and *A Passage to India*',
    Journal of Modern Literature 10, 2 (1983), 311-326.
Weeks, J., *Coming Out: Homosexual Politics in Britain from the Nineteenth Century to the Present*,
    London: Quartet Books, 1977.
    'Inverts, Perverts, and Mary-Annes: Male Prostitution and the Regulation of
    Homosexuality in England in the Nineteenth and Early Twentieth Centuries'
    in Duberman, M. B., Vicinus, M. and Chauncey Jr, G. (editors), *Hidden From History*,
    Harmondsworth: Penguin, 1991.
Weiermair, P. *Wilhelm von Gloeden*, Cologne: Benedikt Taschen, 1994.
Whitman, W., *Prose Works 1892, Volume 1, Specimen Days*, edited by Floyd Stovall,
    New York: New York University Press, 1963.
Whitehead, H., *The Village Gods of South India*, Second Edition 1921;
    reprinted New Delhi & Madras: Asian Educational Services, 1988.
Wildeblood, P., *Against the Law*, London: Weidenfeld and Nicolson, 1955.

recent scholarly titles from The Gay Men's Press:

Joseph Geraci, editor
DARES TO SPEAK
Historical and Contemporary Perspectives on Boy-Love

What was Oscar Wilde imprisoned for a hundred years ago if not the love of boys? Today once more, the 'love that dares not speak its name' is despised and rejected, as if the sexual mores of classical Greece, medieval Japan or Islamic civilization could be adequately comprehended under a heading such as 'child abuse'. This pioneering anthology gathers contributions from a wide range of international authorities, broadly divided into cross-cultural and historical on the one hand, and contemporary controversy on the other. Contributors include Vern Bullough, Gilbert Herdt, Gisela Bleibtreu-Ehrenberg, Holliday Wakefield and Ralph Underwager, as well as pieces on the Uranian poets and John Henry Mackay, 'satanic ritual abuse', and legal changes in the Netherlands.

ISBN 0 85449 241 0
UK £14.95 US $19.95 AUS $29.95

André Gide
CORYDON

The year before his death, André Gide wrote: "*Corydon* remains in my opinion the most important of my books." Begun in 1907, this essay on homosexuality and its place in society, in the form of a Socratic dialogue, was designed to remove "the veil of lies, convention, and hypocrisy which still stifles and important and not contemptible part of humanity". Printed at first anonymously and for private circulation, a commercial edition under the name of its famous author eventually appeared in 1924. Gide's arguments are vividly recreated in this spendid translation by Pulitzer Prize-winning poet Richard Howard.

"Once past the shock that the same arguments are still having to be made, the reader will encounter in this book unexpected pleasures: civilized wit, sophistication, surprising insights" — John Rechy, *Los Angeles Times*

"Gide at his liveliest... Howard makes this translation sound as if Gide were speaking directly in English" — *Library Journal*

ISBN 0 85449 269 0
UK £7.95 ex-USA AUS $16.95

Louis Crompton
BYRON AND GREEK LOVE:
Homophobia in 19th-Century England

How important to Byron was the love of men — a love he found celebrated in classical literature? And how did his contemporaries regard such relations? Making use of previously unpublished letters from the poet and his circle, Louis Crompton traces Byron's many homoerotic involvements — from his idealistic schoolboy enthusiasms to the unhappy love affair he was embroiled in at the end of his life. Professor Crompton argues that Byron's homosexuality was a motive for his first journey to Greece and his later ostracism and exile from England, and an important source for the mood of proud alienation that colours his serious poetry. *Byron and Greek Love* is at once a fascinating biography and an incisive social commentary; its far-reaching implications for the social and cultural history of early 19th-century England have been widely acclaimed.

Louis Crompton has recently retired as Professor of English Literature at the University of Nebraska. His other publications include *Shaw the Dramatist,* and he co-founded the Gay Caucus for the Modern Languages.

"Admirably lucid... illuminating and important" — *Christopher Street*

"Rich, lively, and judicious" — Sir Kenneth Dover, *Byron Journal*

"A distinguished specimen of gay history" — *New York Review of Books*

ISBN 0 85449 263 1
UK £14.95 US $19.95 AUS $24.95

Heinz Heger
THE MEN WITH THE PINK TRIANGLE

A unique first-hand account of the life and death of homosexual prisoners in the Nazi concentration camps

"Heger tells his horrific tale of brutalisation, torture and the systematic destruction of human beings with a calm economy which I found as moving as the events he recounts" — Alison Hennegan, *Gay News*

"A moving example of the will to 'bear witness' on the part of people who survived the death camps" — Harold Poor, *Times Literary Supplement*

ISBN 0 85449 270 4
UK £7.95 ex-USA AUS $16.95

Hardback edition also available:
ISBN 0 85449 014 0 UK £7.95 ex-US ex-AUS

Send for our free catalogue to GMP Publishers Ltd,
BCM 6159, London WC1N 3XX, England

Gay Men's Press books can be ordered from any bookshop in the UK,
North America and Australia, and from
specialised bookshops elsewhere.

Our distributors whose addresses are given in the front pages of this
book can also supply individual customers by mail order. Send retail
price as given plus 10% for postage and packing.

*For payment by Mastercard/American Express/Visa, please give number,
expiry date and signature.*

————————————————————————————————

————————————————————————————————

Name and address in block letters please:

Name
————————————————————————————————

Address
————————————————————————————————

————————————————————————————————

————————————————————————————————